DISCARDED

D0787074

Resistance at Christiana

Resistance at Christiana

THE FUGITIVE SLAVE REBELLION, CHRISTIANA, PENNSYLVANIA, SEPTEMBER 11, 1851

A Documentary Account

by Jonathan Katz

THOMAS Y. CROWELL COMPANY
Established 1834   New York

COLLEGE OF THE SEQUOIAS
LIBRARY

The shortened forms of book titles in the illustration credits are the same as those in the Bibliographical Abbreviations, pages 311–313.

Copyright © 1974 by Jonathan Katz

All rights reserved. Except for use in a review, the reproduction or utilization of this work in any form or by any electronic, mechanical, or other means, now known or hereafter invented, including xerography, photocopying, and recording, and in any information storage and retrieval system is forbidden without the written permission of the publisher. Published simultaneously in Canada by Fitzhenry & Whiteside Limited, Toronto.

Designed by Ingrid Beckman

Manufactured in the United States of America

Library of Congress Cataloging in Publication Data

Katz, Jonathan.
  Resistance at Christiana; the fugitive slave rebellion, Christiana, Pennsylvania, September 11, 1851: a documentary account.

  Includes bibliographical references.
  1. Christiana, Pa.—Riot, 1851. I. Title.
E450.K28   974.8′15′03   73–21907
ISBN 0–690–00307–2

1 2 3 4 5 6 7 8 9 10

For the resistance;
for all the liberations.

Contents

III. FREEDOM-BOUND

I RESISTANCE

Prologue

EARLY ONE FOGGY MORNING in September, 1851, a posse of white men cautiously approached a two-story stone house near Christiana, a small town in the free State of Pennsylvania. Among this posse was a Maryland slave owner and a U.S. marshal, with warrants for several fugitive slaves. Suddenly the posse spied a black man running up the lane and into the house. His cry "Kidnappers! kidnappers!" broke the silence of the morning. The posse gave chase. The slave owner and the marshal entered the house. The rest of the posse, their guns loaded, stood guard outside.

Inside the house a young black man named William Parker stood defiantly at the top of the stairs. His leadership of a local black self-defense organization had prepared him for this moment. The slave owner demanded his fugitives. Parker denied the runaways were in the house. He warned the slave catchers to withdraw before blood was shed. Encouraged by Parker, the black men and women upstairs in the house began to load their guns. In the room below the slave owner and the marshal heard the ominous sound. These black people had decided to resist with force any attempt to return them to slavery.

This was the beginning of a historic conflict between black people and white. Its fatal outcome would arouse the nation. The

3

battle's effects, declared the Governor of Maryland, "would penetrate the soul of the South." The white press called it "The Christiana Riot." Frederick Douglass called it "the battle for liberty at Christiana." This was the armed black resistance which, ten years before the national conflagration, a tiny Pennsylvania newspaper prophetically headlined: "Civil War, First Blow Struck."

In 1850, the United States Congress had passed a harsh new law to ensure the return of fugitive slaves. The bloody battle at Christiana was the first nationally publicized, armed, and fatal resistance to the new law. Following the Christiana resistance thirty-six black and five white alleged participants were charged with treason against the United States, the largest number ever simultaneously indicted for this high crime. The charge occasioned a dramatic and historic treason trial. At the beginning of the twentieth century a Pennsylvania chronicler still recalled the Christiana resistance, along with John Brown's raid, as a major harbinger of the Civil War. Although not so bloody, the Christiana resistance ranks with the Nat Turner uprising as among the major episodes of black resistance in American history.

Today the Christiana resistance is barely remembered. When it does receive brief notice its details are usually misstated. The leading role of black people in the battle is often ignored. The activities of a local black self-defense organization are rarely mentioned. Ironically, in the aftermath of the 1851 violence a pacifistic white man was charged and tried for inciting the blacks to battle. Its actual black leader, the early militant William Parker, has remained almost unknown.

The Christiana resistance briefly awoke the nation to a sense of impending crisis. Then it was forgotten. The resistance at Christiana became a non-event, and William Parker a non-person of American history, a truly invisible man. This "battle for liberty" is but one of the many neglected episodes in the history of black resistance.

In this documented history no detail has been invented, nothing is fictionalized. As often as possible the Christiana resistance is described in the words of those who acted in it and observed it. Here these historymakers speak for themselves. Hopefully, the often evocative language of these long-dead witnesses will bring to life the era, issues, and characters opposing each other in this fatal encounter.

The battle for liberty at Christiana is in many ways a microcosm of the present conflict between black people and white. Thus this history of the Christiana resistance may help to illuminate the roots and nature of our current crisis.

1 Parker

HIS NAME WAS WILLIAM PARKER. He was a black man. He was a
fighter. He was born a slave on a plantation in Anne Arundel
County, the State of Maryland. As a child he lived in the slave
quarter of the plantation, in a long, 100 by 30 foot building that
housed the single people and other slave children who were
orphaned like himself or whose parents had been "sold away."
There were two fireplaces at either end of the building, "and small
rooms arranged along the sides." In winter, says Parker, in an
autobiographical narrative written in his mid-30s,[1] in the competition for the warmest rooms nearest these fireplaces, "the smaller
and weaker" slave children were

> subject to the whims and caprices of the larger and
> stronger. The largest children would always seize upon the
> warmest and best places, and say to us who were smaller,
> "Stand back, little chap, out of my way"; and we had to
> stand back or get a thrashing.

Young Parker had no one to complain to of his ill treatment. As
a result, he says, "my juvenile days enjoyed but little rest from my
domineering superiors in years and strength." Young Parker was
compelled to submit to the "abuse and indifference" of the bigger
boys

6

until I grew older, when by fighting first with one and then with another, I became "too many" for them, and could have a seat at the fire as well as the best. This experience of my boyhood has since been repeated in my manhood. My rights at the fireplace were won by my child-fists; my rights as a freeman were, under God, secured by my own right arm.[2]

Parker also describes himself as a fighter in a story he once told a white Pennsylvania neighbor, George Steele. Steele reports:

I knew Parker very well. He told me that when a slave his owner was a sporting man and attended fairs and horse races and big sales and took him along and would arrange prize fights between him and some other man's slave, and bet money on him (Parker) and that he always won.[3]

In his own narrative, and in the story he told George Steele, William Parker presents himself as having early become a fighter. In each story Parker reports his fighting other blacks; but he who first turned his fists against his own people would later turn against their common enemy.

Parker's story of prizefighting for his master at horse races is given credence by the fact that there were old tracks at Annapolis and elsewhere in Maryland. Parker's owners, the Brogdens of Maryland, did have a long-standing interest in horse breeding and racing. As recently as 1943, "the official publication of the Maryland Horse Breeders Association" reports a Major Stephen Brogden doing "a capital job" in judging an equestrian event. The Major, it is said,

comes from Anne Arundel County, where an ancestor, William Brogden, resided, and bred and raced thorough-breds. He was a prominent member of the old Maryland Jockey Club at Annapolis when George Washington attended its meetings. . . .

This early William Brogden, Parker's first owner, probably attended those same races at which Washington's diary notes the first President was a "consistent and persistent loser." [4]

Major William Brogden died when Parker was very young and

the slave knew of him only from stories told by fellow slaves or overheard from white people. From these stories Parker concludes that Major Brogden was "not remarkable," either for the "severity" or "indulgence" shown his slaves. Major Brogden was, says Parker, "one of the wealthy men" of the Anne Arundel region. Brogden, born in 1741, had "served with credit" in the American Revolution. It was this American revolutionary, the owner of seventy slaves, into whose possession William Parker was born, about 1822, two years before his owner's death.[5]

Like many others born into slavery, William Parker never knew his exact date of birth. From the comments of "neighbors" he could guess only his approximate age. One day, Parker would speak like numbers of other ex-slaves, with regret and resentment at this lack of knowledge:

> Slave holders are particular to keep the pedigree and age of favorite horses and dogs, but are quite indifferent about the age of their servants until they want to purchase. Then they are careful to select young persons, though not one in twenty can tell year, month, or day. Speaking of births,—it is the time of "corn-planting," "corn-husking," "Christmas," "New Year," "Easter," "the Fourth of July," or some similar indefinite date. My own time of birth was no more exact; so that to this day I am uncertain how old I am.[6]

Parker shared this uncertainty with another young Maryland slave acquaintance. This friend, Frederick Augustus Washington Bailey, later known as Frederick Douglass, recalls that not knowing his date of birth was

> a source of unhappiness to me even during childhood. The white children could tell their ages. I could not tell why I ought to be deprived of the same privilege.[7]

Growing up in Maryland Douglass learned

> that my master—and this is the case with masters generally—allowed no questions to be put to him, by which a slave might learn his age. Such questions are deemed evidence of impatience, and even impudent curiosity.[8]

To keep slaves ignorant was to keep them in their place. The security of the slave system depended on the enforced ignorance of its subjects. Slaves must learn nothing which might make them feel equal to their master. To deny young Parker the knowledge of his date of birth was to dispossess him of his history. It was to deny him a day by which he might annually mark his own private passage of time, his coming to manhood.

Parker's mother, Louisa Simms, died when he was very young. She had been a field hand, like most of the plantation's slaves. Parker does not speak of his father. His brothers, John and Charles, are rarely mentioned. To his grandmother Parker says he was "indebted for the very little kindness I received in my early childhood. . . ." But "this kindness could only be shown me at long intervals, and in a hurried way. . . ." Parker's grandmother was kept busy as cook at the "great house," where she evidently also lived. When she came to look after him, Parker recalls his grandmother "always brought me a morsel privately," and her presence temporarily protected him from annoyance by the older boys:

> When my grandmother would inquire of the others how her "little boy" was getting on, they would tell her that I was doing well, and kindly invite me to the fire to warm myself.

If Parker complained to his grandmother of ill treatment by the older boys "they would have beaten me, after she had gone to the 'great house' again." Since his grandmother had time to visit him "only once in twenty-four hours," Parker could not depend on her for protection. The boy felt safe with an "Uncle Sammy," and found enough comfort in the presence of the plantation's black community to be deeply disturbed when the slave sales from time to time disrupted it. But for the most part Parker was on his own.[9]

About 1830, six years after Major William Brogden's death, the slave owner's two sons, William and David, divided up their father's land and slaves. The eight-year-old William Parker, a brother, and an uncle became the property of David McCulloch Brogden, or "Master Mack," as Parker says the slaves called his new owner. They lived on the southeast part of the old plantation, which their new master renamed "Nearo." Parker recalls that

David Brogden was for some years a member of the Maryland
legislature, while the young William Brogden was a doctor.[10]

The Brogden brothers' position in Maryland society is indicated
by their membership in the old South River Club, to which their
father and later generations of their family belonged. When, about
1905, a Harry Brogden presided at the South River Club's annual
Independence Day dinner, the scene no doubt closely resembled
dinners attended some seventy-five years before, in the same
unpretentious clubhouse, by William Parker's master.

As the Club's secretary reports, the 1905 dinner was graced by
important members of Maryland society:

> There were in the crowd that gathered about the table
> inside the humble little cabin, merchants, bankers, brokers,
> members of the Stock Exchange, lawyers and farmers,
> many of these men of means and mark, but all imbued with
> an intense pride in the South River Club.

Harry Brogden carved "the *pièce de résistance*," a "fine young
well-roasted pig," and "spoke of the pleasure and pride in the club
taken by its members. . . ." Brogden received "a handsome silver
loving cup," which was filled with the "far-famed South River
punch" and passed around the table.[11] Similarly, one can imagine
William Parker's master, David McCulloch Brogden, drinking
amicably with members of the South River Club three-quarters of
a century earlier.

David Brogden, like his father, was, on Parker's report, rather
lenient with his slaves. But, says Parker, David's wife, Margaret,
was "hard to please." Once when her husband was away at
Annapolis, Margaret Brogden ordered overseer Robert Brown to
whip one of the house servants. The young serving woman
"refused to be whipped," and the overseer, angered by her
resistant spirit, "beat her so badly that she was nearly killed before
she gave up." When David Brogden returned home and discovered the slave's condition, he angrily dismissed the overseer who
had too zealously carried out his wife's orders, and mistreated his
property. A trusty slave named Bob Wallace who, Parker says,
"understood farming thoroughly" was installed as the new foreman. "Everything went on well for a while under Wallace, and the

slaves," says Parker, "were as contented as it is possible for slaves to be."

Neither David Brogden nor his brother, says Parker,

> would allow his hands to be beaten, or abused, as many slaveholders would, but every year they sold one or more of them,—sometimes as many as six at a time.[12]

It was the Brogdens' sale and separation of slaves from their families that first provoked Parker's desire to escape his helpless situation. In 1832 or 1833, when Parker was ten or eleven years old, he encountered his first slave sale. One morning all the slaves on the plantation were called to the "great house." "As we were about obeying the summons," says Parker, "a number of strange white men rode up to the mansion. They were negro-traders."

> It was a serious time while they remained. Men, women, and children, all were crying, and general confusion prevailed. For years they had associated together in their rude way,—the old counselling the young, recounting their experience, and sympathizing in their trials, and now, without a word of warning, and for no fault of their own, parents and children, husbands and wives, brothers and sisters, were separated to meet no more on earth. A slave sale of this sort is always as solemn as a funeral.

Taking alarm Parker ran away to the woods with another slave boy of about his own age, named Levi Storax. Levi and Parker climbed a pine tree and discussed their next move. Parker urged Levi to leave with him for the free states or Canada, "and not be sold like the rest." Levi was afraid. If they were not sold this time, said Levi, he would "go to Master William, and ask him" not to sell them. "What will you get by going to Master William?" Parker asked Levi. "If we see him, and ask him not to sell us, he will do as he pleases."

Parker again urged Levi to run away to the north. Levi objected: "See how many start for the Free States, and are brought back, and sold away down South." Levi also objected that Canada was too far away, the route forbidding and cold. A bleak image of Canada as "a vast and cheerless waste of ice and snow," plus fears of being recaptured and sold into the deep south, put a temporary damper on young Parker's plans for escape. As a punishment, says Parker, nothing was so much dreaded by the slave as being sold into one of the most southern slave states. Tales of the lengthy, difficult trip and "attrocities" committed on far south plantations made being sold "down the river" one of the slaves' worst fears.

Parker and Levi remained in the woods until the slave sale ended and the traders drove away. When darkness fell, Levi wanted to go back and see if his mother had been sold. Parker had no mother to lose, but he felt sad and alone:

> How desolate I was! No home, no protector, no mother, no attachments. As we turned our faces toward the Quarter,— where we might at any moment be sold to satisfy a debt or replenish a failing purse,—I felt myself to be what I really was, a poor, friendless slave-boy.

In the confusion the two boys had evidently not been missed. Levi's mother had not been sold, but Parker saw how sad Levi was that she could afford him no protection. This need for "protection" would later be a motivating force in Parker's life.

A good many slaves had been sold away, among them Levi's uncles, Anthony and Dennis, as well as Parker's Aunt Rachel, with her children, Jacob and Priscilla. Parker asked anxiously for "Uncle Sammy" and was reassured that he had not been sold.

Both the northern and southern apologists for slavery, says Parker,

> denied that the separation of families, except for punishment, was perpetrated by Southern masters; but my experience of slavery was, that separation by sale was part of the system. Not only was it resorted to by severe masters, but as in my own case, by those generally regarded as mild.

The slaves' "utter helplessness," even "under the most humane masters and overseers," in the more northern slave states, was a pronounced characteristic of life in bondage.[13] Slave sales were a major source of income for Maryland planters. From 1820 to 1860, including the years of Parker's childhood, the state was in the midst of an economic and agricultural revival. Maryland was a major source of slaves for the economy of the lower south; the economy of Maryland depended on the sale of these surplus slaves. Income from slave sales offset agricultural losses and made possible investments in technological improvements; surplus slaves were transformed into capital by Maryland planters. The slave sales whose emotional effects Parker describes were an integral part of Maryland's economic life.[14]

Before the next big slave sale a few years later, a number of Brogden slaves were sold privately. These slaves had not necessarily done anything to offend their owner. Levi Storax, says Parker,

> was a likely lad, and, to all appearances, fully in the confidence of his master. Prompt and obedient, he seemed to some of us to enjoy high favor at the "great house." One morning he was told to take a letter to Mr. Henry Hall, an acquaintance of the family; and it being a part of his usual employment to bring and carry such missives, off he started, in bland confidence, to learn at the end of his journey that he had parted with parents, friends, and all, to find Mr. Hall a new master. Thus in a moment, his dearest ties were severed.

Parker only learned why his friend did not come home, and the manner of his delivery to Mr. Hall, when he met Levi two months later at the Cross-Road Meeting House on West River. Parker reminded Levi he had warned him of being sold; now Levi had a new master worse than the old. Parker suspected that he too would be sold one day. But if his master tried to sell him, bragged Parker, "he will have to do it running." Parker's conversation with Levi ended there. It was "not in our power," he says, to meet again.

Levi's fate causes Parker to bitterly describe

> slavery as the sum of all villainies; for no resort is too despicable, no subterfuge too vile, for its supporters. Is a slave intractable, the most wicked punishment is not too severe; is he timid, obedient, attached to his birthplace and kindred, no lie is so base that it may not be used to entrap him into a change of place or of owners.

Levi, says Parker, was the victim of a peculiarly southern stratagem, an action that grew directly out "of an institution which holds the bodies and souls of men as of no more account, for all moral purposes, than the unreasoning brutes. . . ." [15]

After Levi was sold Parker became friendly with another young slave, Alexander Brown, with whom he quietly discussed the subject of liberty:

> Though not permitted to learn to read and write, and kept in profound ignorance of everything, save what belonged strictly to our plantation duties, we were not without crude perceptions of the dignity and independence belonging to freedom; and, often, when out of hearing of the white people, or certain ones among our fellow-servants, Alexander and I would talk the subject over in our simple way.

During the next months, while Parker and Brown talked quietly, three more slaves were sold from the Brogden plantation. One day "Master Mack" told the black foreman, Bob Wallace, to go to Annapolis. Wallace was to take with him "a very likely young house-servant named Ann" who was between sixteen and eighteen years old. When Parker heard that Wallace and Ann were leaving he "had a presentiment that the purpose was to sell the girl. . . ." But Wallace had no similar fear.

> Wallace and Ann started for the city on horseback, and journeyed along pleasantly until they reached the town and were near the market-place, when a man came up to them, took Ann off the horse without ceremony. . . .

Wallace, evidently thinking the man a kidnapper, attacked him, "and came well-nigh getting into difficulty." The man turned out to be Brogden's agent and took Ann away to a slave jail to await sale.

> When Wallace returned, he said to Master Mack, "Why did you not tell me that Ann was sold, and not have me fighting for her? They might have put me in jail." But his master did not appear to hear him.

The next to be sold was William Brogden's slave "Uncle Henry," who, going one Saturday night to see his wife in

Annapolis, was put into jail for sale. That was the last the Brogden slaves saw or heard of him. The mother of Parker's new friend, Alexander Brown, was sold next. Parker now urged Brown to consider plans "to run away and be free." "But," says Parker of Brown,

> so thoroughly had his humanity been crushed by the foul spirit of Slavery, so apathetic had he—though in the vigor of youth—become from long oppression, that he would not agree to my suggestion.

The moral virtue of a non-resistant spirit was a favorite theme of southern ministers, when they preached to slaves. Parker recalls:

> The preachers of a slave-trading gospel frequently told us, in their sermons, that we should be "good boys" and not break into master's henroost, nor steal his bacon. . . .[16]

There were "very few" slaves, says Parker's Maryland acquaintance Frederick Douglass, who were not affected by such preaching:

> Trained from their cradle up to think and feel their masters were superior, and invested with a sort of sacredness, there were few who could rise above the control which that sentiment exercised.[17]

Parker emphasizes the profound effect the slave-traders' gospel and the watchful eye of overseer or master could have on the minds of slaves:

> The mandates of Slavery are like leaden sounds, sinking with dead weight into the very soul, only to deaden and destroy.

While a slave, the rebel in Parker had long resisted this soul deadening. This rebellious part of him was often filled with indignation at the freedom of the neighborhood's white boys:

> There were many poor white lads of about my own age, belonging to families scattered around, who were as poor in personal effects as we were; and yet, though our

companions, (when we chose to tolerate them,) they did not have to be controlled by a master, to go and come at his command, to be sold for his debts, or whenever he wanted pocket-money.

While southern preachers told slaves it was a sin to steal from their masters, Parker did not recall hearing the same sermon preached to the poor whites, who, it was well-known, "encouraged the slaves to steal, trafficked in stolen goods, and stole themselves." Parker says:

> I felt I was the equal of these poor whites, and naturally I concluded that we were greatly wronged, and that all this talk about obedience, duty, humility, and honesty was, in the phrase of my companions, "all gammon." [18]

Another side of Parker was deeply affected by that preaching which condemned rebelliousness in slaves. Before he could attempt escape from slavery Parker had to justify it to himself. He "did not like to go without first having a difficulty" with his master:

> Much as I disliked my condition, I was ignorant enough to think that something besides the fact that I was a slave was necessary to exonerate me from blame in running away.

A fist fight provoked with his owner preceded and justified Parker's "stealing away."

After the sale of Alexander Brown's mother, and Brown's own refusal to run off, Parker had "determined to be free." Saying no more to the apathetic Brown, Parker spoke to his brother Charles, who agreed to go. The two slaves kept their thoughts to themselves.

Soon after, in the month of May, a neighboring planter, Jefferson Dorsey, had a butchering. One of Dorsey's men told Parker that "Master Mack" had said he might go and lend a hand—and off Parker went. But Parker's master had not given permission for his slave to leave home and angrily sent for him, "with the threat of a whipping." Hearing of this threat from several slave women, Parker boasted, "Master Mack is 'most done whipping me." Returning to his plantation, and seeing that

"Master Mack" 's face and actions "foretold a storm," Parker "stole away" again to Dorsey's. The next day Parker prevailed upon Samuel Dorsey to go home with him, evidently to speak to "Master Mack" on his behalf:

> Master Mack told me to go to my work, and he would forgive me; but the next time he would pay me for "the new and the old." To work I went; but I determined not to be paid for "the new and the old."

After "Master Mack" 's threat Parker began making final preparations to leave. Through a friend, the slave managed to procure a counterfeit travel pass for which he paid five dollars, all the money he had been able to save. Now Parker felt he needed one final provocation to send him on his way.

> A cross word, a blow, a good fright, anything would do, it mattered not whence nor how it came. I told my brother Charles . . . to be ready; for the time was at hand when we should leave Old Maryland forever. I was only waiting for the first crooked word from my master.[19]

One day in June, probably in 1839, Parker refused to go to the fields to work. How old he was at the time, Parker says "I do not know; but from what the neighbors told me, I must have been about seventeen." His master saw him

> and wanted to know why I did not go out. I answered, that it was raining, that I was tired, and did not want to work. He then picked up a stick used for an ox-gad, and said, if I did not go to work, he would whip me as sure as there was a God in heaven. Then he struck at me, but I caught the stick, and we grappled, and handled each other roughly for a time. . . .

Parker's adversary was "badly hurt," and called for assistance. Before aid arrived, Parker let go his hold on his master, "bade him good-bye, and ran for the woods." As Parker ran rapidly through the fields he was joined by his brother Charles.

Parker's account does not describe how the two slaves managed to escape from their immediate neighborhood. He says simply:

> after gaining the woods we lurked about and discussed our plans until after dark. Then we stole back to the Quarter,

made up our bundles, bade some of our friends farewell, and at about nine o'clock of the night set out for Baltimore.

For the first time the black fighter had turned his fists against his master; his long liberation battle had begun. Later, Parker summed up this turning point:

> I was now at the beginning of a new and important era in my life. Although upon the threshold of manhood, I had, until the relation with my master was sundered, only dim perceptions of the responsibilities of a more independent position. I longed to cast off the chains of servitude because they chafed my free spirit, and because I had a notion that my position was founded in injustice; but it has only been since a struggle of many years, . . . that I have realized fully the grandeur of my position as a free man.[20]

When he was seventeen a fight with a tyrannical "slave-breaker" also played a crucial role in the life of Parker's friend Frederick Douglass. Says Douglass:

> I was a changed being after that fight. I was nothing before—I was a man now. It recalled to life my crushed self-respect, and my self-confidence, and inspired me with a renewed determination to be a free man.[21]

The night of Parker's fight with his master he and his brother set out on their long journey north, and experienced a new sense of freedom:

> . . . I was now on the high-road to liberty. I had broken the bonds that held me so firmly; and now, instead of fears of recapture, that before had haunted my imagination whenever I thought of running away, I felt as light as a feather, and seemed to be helped onward by an irresistible force.

"How shall I describe," asks Parker, "my first experience of free life?"

> Nothing can be greater than the contrast it affords to a plantation experience, under the suspicious and vigilant eye of a mercenary overseer or a watchful master. Day and

night are not more unlike. . . . The impulse of freedom
lends wings to the feet, buoys up the spirit within, and the
fugitive catches glorious glimpses of light through rifts and
seams in the accumulated ignorance of years of oppression.
How briskly we travelled on that eventful night and the
next day!

Parker and his brother Charles headed north. The pass which
Parker had bought he destroyed. It only accounted for one, and
both slaves could not use it safely.

We reached Baltimore on the following evening, between
seven and eight o'clock. When we neared the city, the
patrols were out, and the difficulty was to pass them unseen
or unsuspected. I learned of a brickyard at the entrance to
the city; and thither we went at once, took brick-dust and
threw it upon our clothes, hats, and boots, and then walked
on.

Whenever the two brothers met a passerby they would brush some
brick dust off their clothes and mutter something about that day's
hard work.

By this ruse we reached quiet quarters without arrest or
suspicion.[22]

The two fugitives remained in Baltimore a week, possibly
hidden among that city's large free black community. When
Parker described his escape it was still imprudent to reveal the
details of his accommodations.

After a week's rest the two brothers continued northward. But
their bright "visions of future independence" were "suddenly
dimmed by one of those unpleasant incidents which annoy the
fugitive at every step of his onward journey."

Late one evening, near Loganville, Pennsylvania, they were
stopped and questioned by three whites. One of the whites, "a
very large man," pulled out an advertisement exactly describing
the two blacks as fugitive slaves.[23] Parker challenged the man to
take him, and picked up a stick. When the man reached for the
stick, Parker struck him a violent blow on the arm that seemed to
break it. The white man turned and ran, with Parker after him.

> As he ran, he would look back over his shoulder, see me
> coming, and then run faster and halloo with all his might.

The two other whites also took to their heels, illustrating, says
Parker, "the valor of the chivalry." Parker soon gave up the chase,
and he and his brother continued quickly on, leaving the aroused
neighborhood behind them as fast as possible.

About four o'clock on the same morning, Parker and his
brother reached York, where they stayed all day. Like many
unworldly fugitives unused to travel they mistakenly thought they
had journeyed a tremendous distance, and were safely out of
danger of recapture. Fortunately the two met a friend in York
who warned them to move on.[24]

That night Parker and his brother started toward Wrightsville
and the bridge crossing the Susquehanna River to Columbia.
Once across this river fugitives would be relatively safe. According
to William Whipper, a wealthy black lumber merchant and
underground railroad agent of Columbia, whose house was the
first on the far side of the bridge, the Susquehanna was known as
the "boundary of the slaveholding empire," beyond which southern slave catchers could not openly proceed without risk. When
fugitives

> had crossed this bridge they could look back over its broad
> silvery stream . . . , and say to the slave power: "Thus far
> shalt thou come, and no farther."

Columbia's active and determined black community, many of
whom were themselves fugitives, saw to it that slave catchers took
careful notice of this warning.[25]

Parker and his brother had not quite reached the Susquehanna
when they heard voices behind them in the darkness. The fugitives
moved quickly to one side of the road and out of sight. Two men
came along, "apparently in earnest conversation." Suddenly, says
Parker, the clear voice of one of the men revealed him to be none
other than "Master Mack's brother-in-law." The subject of
conversation was the two fugitives:

> He remarked to his companion that they must hurry and
> get to the bridge before we crossed. He knew that we had
> not gone over yet. We were then near enough to have killed

William Whipper. (Still; Wm. L. Katz Collection)

them, concealed as we were by the darkness; but we permitted them to pass unmolested. . . .

That same night the fugitives reached Wrightsville on the southwest side of the Susquehanna.

Fortunately Parker and his brother did not have to cross the bridge where their pursuers were probably in wait. The next morning, "before it was light," the two fugitives were carried across the Susquehanna in a boat, perhaps rowed by a black man named Robert Loney, who performed that service for many a runaway.[26] William Parker and his brother had safely crossed the river. They had crossed from slavery into a new life.

2 "An Organization for Mutual Protection"

WILLIAM PARKER RECALLS after his escape, comparing his new life in Pennsylvania to his old life under slavery:

> While a slave, I was, as it were, groping in the dark, no ray of light penetrating the intense gloom surrounding me. My scanty garments felt too tight for me, my very respiration seemed to be restrained by some supernatural power. Now, free as I supposed, I felt like a bird on a pleasant May morning. Instead of the darkness of slavery, my eyes were almost blinded by the light of freedom.
>
> Those were memorable days, and yet much of this was boyish fancy. After a few years of life in a Free State, the enthusiasm of the lad materially sobered down, and I found, by bitter experience, that to preserve my stolen liberty I must pay, unremittingly, an almost sleepless vigilance; yet to this day I have never looked back regretfully to Old Maryland, nor yearned for her flesh-pots.

During those first months of liberty, while still filled with a sense of his own new freedom, Parker did not forget those blacks still left in bondage:

> I thought of my fellow-servants left behind, bound in the chains of slavery,—and I was free! I thought, that, if I had

the power, they should soon be as free as I was; and I formed a resolution that I would assist in liberating everyone within my reach, at the risk of my own life, and that I would devise some plan for their entire liberation.[1]

Although freer than any of the slave states, the Pennsylvania into which William Parker had moved in the summer of 1839 was no utopia for black people. There was no slavery in Pennsylvania, but jobs open to blacks were generally the most menial and lowest paid. The jobs blacks had previously won were then being challenged by the competition of white immigrants pouring into America. Black Pennsylvania coal miners, canal and railroad workers lost their jobs to the newly arrived Irishmen who formed a cheap labor force. Job competition led to violent clashes between whites and blacks. Between 1832 and 1849 whites touched off five major anti-black riots in Philadelphia and rioted against blacks in Pittsburgh and Columbia, Pennsylvania.

In 1838 Pennsylvania's white electorate voted in a new state constitution actually excluding blacks from voting. Previously, Pennsylvania blacks had not been legally disenfranchised, although white hostility had effectively kept them from the vote. Pennsylvanians also discussed, though they did not adopt, the restriction of black immigration. Public education was provided all Pennsylvania children, but schools were segregated by law, as was Philadelphia's transportation, churches, and housing. In Philadelphia's black ghetto, alcohol, exposure, and malnutrition caused high death and crime rates. In 1836 a Pennsylvania Senate committee reported: "Already are our prisons and poor houses crowded with blacks." This was the Pennsylvania in which fugitive slave William Parker "set to work in earnest." [2]

William Parker's first job as a free laborer was in a place about five miles from Lancaster, where he worked for three months. His wages were three dollars a month, low pay even in those days. But to the newly freed slave this seemed "an immense sum."

> Fast work was no trouble to me; for when the work was done, the money was mine. That was a great consideration. I could go out on Saturdays and Sundays, and home when I pleased, without being whipped.

When his work was done his life was his own.

At the end of three months, in the early fall of 1839, Parker went to visit his brother, who was employed in Bart Township, Lancaster County, near Smyrna. Parker got a job nearby, with Dr. Obadiah Dingee, "a warm sympathizer" with the anti-slavery movement. The doctor received the anti-slavery newspapers which Parker, unable to read himself, probably heard read aloud. Parker worked for and lived with Dr. Dingee and his family for a year and one month. He recalls:

> I have never been better treated than by the Doctor; I liked him and the family, and they seemed to think well of me.[3]

Sometime during his early years in Pennsylvania, possibly in the winter of 1843, Parker had his first opportunity to hear the famous anti-slavery speakers William Lloyd Garrison and Frederick Douglass. If the year was 1843 Douglass had not yet published the autobiography revealing his slave name and origin. One may imagine William Parker's surprise when the speaker billed as Frederick Douglass turned out to be the Frederick Bailey whom Parker had known as a slave in Maryland.[4]

Parker never forgot the "glowing words" of Garrison, the uncompromising, white anti-slavery leader, but Douglass's speech especially moved him. Parker was unprepared, he says, for the progress Douglass had made; Douglass's "free spoken and manly" words against slavery impressed him greatly. Though Parker later heard many abolitionist speakers, no doctrine ever seemed "so pure, so unworldly" as Douglass's on that day.

> I listened with the intense satisfaction that only a refugee could feel, when hearing, embodied in earnest, well-chosen, and strong speech, his own crude ideas of freedom, and his own hearty censure of the man-stealer. I believed, I knew, every word he said was true. It was the whole truth,—nothing kept back,—no trifling with human rights, no trading in the blood of the slave extenuated, nothing against the slaveholder said in malice. I have never listened to words from the lips of mortal man which were more acceptable to me. . . .[5]

Such anti-slavery sentiments were by no means so "acceptable" to many of the white people in William Parker's new neighborhood. The Pennsylvania Germans and Scotch-Irish Presbyterian farmers of the area were unsympathetic if not overtly hostile to the blacks who had settled among them.[6]

A different group of neighborhood whites were members of the Society of Friends, or Quakers, of whom the Hicksite branch was especially opposed to slavery. Many Quakers played an active part in the local operations of the underground railroad, a main line of which ran through the neighborhood. Without contradicting their non-violent principles these Quaker underground "conductors" helped many a fugitive avoid recapture.[7]

Of the local black population, some had been born free, most were probably fugitive slaves. Attempts at recapturing these fugitives and random kidnappings of free blacks were common. According to Parker:

> The whites of that region were generally such negro-haters, that it was a matter of no moment to them where fugitives were carried.[8]

The southern boundary of lower Lancaster County touched the border of Maryland—and the slave system. Slave catchers would often appear in the middle of the night, and carry off their black victims by force.

Although the 1776 Declaration of Independence had proclaimed all men endowed with the right to liberty, the Constitution adopted eleven years later explicitly sanctioned the existence of American slavery. A constitutional clause declared: "No person held to service or labor" under the laws of one state, and escaping into another, shall be "discharged from such service or labor, but shall be delivered up on claim" of the original master. There was no mention of the word "slave." The Constitutional fathers, perhaps disliking that word's undemocratic sound, adopted the term "person held to service or labor." As a result a runaway slave soon came to be called "a fugitive from labor." Perhaps unconsciously, the euphemism suggested the image of a lazy black running away from work—rather than enslavement.

In 1793 the United States Congress passed its first fugitive slave act. This law empowered a slave owner to seize, without warrant, any fugitive who had escaped to another state. Taken before a magistrate, and satisfactory oral or written "proof" being offered that the person seized was the person sought, the magistrate could issue a certificate for the fugitive's return to slavery. A $500 fine could be imposed on anyone hindering a fugitive's arrest—or harboring, concealing, or rescuing a runaway.

The U.S. fugitive slave law inevitably resulted in the indiscriminate seizure of black people, freeborn as well as runaways. Eruptions of violence occurred in northern communities when slave owners or profit-seeking kidnappers were resisted. These clashes, especially in rural areas, where whites and blacks lived and worked closely together, caused Pennsylvania and other northern states to pass "personal liberty" laws. The Pennsylvania law of 1820 was specifically designed to discourage the kidnapping of *free* blacks. In 1826 and 1827, however, the Pennsylvania legislature, complying with the wishes of Maryland, modified this law to facilitate the capture of fugitives.[9]

In William Parker's area of Pennsylvania blacks and sympathetic whites did not recognize the legal distinction between authorized slave catchers and unauthorized abductors. The term "kidnappers" applied equally to legally authorized slave catchers seeking a specific runaway under the federal fugitive slave act, as well as to those unauthorized, illegal gangs who abducted blacks at random, without any pretense of their being fugitives.

One particular gang of whites was notorious in the area for their attacks on black people. This band, known as the Gap Gang, apparently got its name from its usual hangout—a tavern at a place called the Gap, on the north side of Mine Range, about three miles from Christiana. The Gap Gang was said to inform and guide slave owners and kidnappers and act as deputy constables or as illegal man-stealers. Two locally well-known and disreputable individuals, Perry Marsh and Bill Baer, were evidently members of this gang. Baer was sometimes said to be the gang's leader, although an Amos Clemson is also mentioned in this connection. Both Baer and Marsh lived near the Gap and the tavern where the gang apparently met.[10]

During Parker's first year and a half in the free State of Pennsylvania, while he was at Dr. Dingee's from the fall of 1839 to the fall of 1840, kidnappers were terrifying the black community. According to Parker:

> Kidnapping was so common, while I lived with the Doctor, that we were kept in constant fear. We would hear of slaveholders or kidnappers every two or three weeks; sometimes a party of white men would break into a house and take a man away, no one knew where; and again, a whole family would be carried off. There was no power to protect them, nor prevent it. So completely roused were my feelings, that I vowed to let no slaveholder take back a fugitive, if I could but get my eye on him.

Not long after his settling in Pennsylvania, while he was at Dr. Dingee's, Parker says,

> a number of us had formed an organization for mutual protection against slaveholders and kidnappers, and had resolved to prevent any of our brethren being taken back into slavery, at the risk of our own lives. . . . Whether the kidnappers were clothed with legal authority or not, I did not care to inquire, as I never had faith in nor respect for the Fugitive Slave Law.

Parker with five to seven other black men banded together to protect the community against kidnapping attempts.

> The insolent and overbearing conduct of the Southerners, when on such errands to Pennsylvania, forced me to my course of action. They did not hesitate to break open doors, and to enter without ceremony the houses of colored men; and when refused admission, or when a manly and determined spirit was shown, they would present pistols and knock down men and women indiscriminately.[11]

Although Parker says it took him "a struggle of many years" to overcome the psychic effects of slavery, to realize "the grandeur" of his "position as a free man," it was after only a few months of free life that he organized with other blacks for their "mutual protection." These self-defense activities were, no doubt, one important means by which Parker came to feel his self-worth and freedom.

This self-defense organization was formed, controlled, and composed of blacks, for the protection of blacks. There is no evidence of any whites participating in the organization's formation, much less taking part in its armed actions. Most of the neighborhood's anti-slavery whites were "non-resistant" abolitionists, or non-violent Quakers. Undoubtedly these white abolitionists knew of, and passively sanctioned, the armed self-defense activities of the blacks. A few whites perhaps even made themselves useful to the blacks, warning them of any rumors of slave catchers. There is evidence of one white man lending his loaded gun to a black for self-defense. There is no evidence of any white person taking up arms to join the black community in defense of those attacked. The whites' intention was generally to keep the peace, to prevent violent confrontations between blacks and whites. They advised blacks to flee, rather than fight.[12]

William Parker was a young man of about seventeen when he first became active in the "organization for mutual protection." During Parker's twelve years in Pennsylvania he assumed a leading role in the self-defense organization and in the local black community. By 1851, Parker, then about twenty-nine years old, was called "the preacher." [13] He seems to have possessed the physical bearing of a leader, although the four known descriptions of his appearance are meager and not too reliable. The 1850 U.S. Census for Sadsbury Township describes Parker as "mulatto." Another description calls him "a rather tall mulatto." Another characterizes him as a "dark mulatto, of medium height, wonderful muscle. . . ." The last describes him simply as "a slender man, rather tall." [14]

Parker's home became a center and meeting place for the black people of the neighborhood. Peter Woods, a sixteen-year-old black resident of the area in 1850, recalls: "The colored fellows met at Parker's nearly every Sunday." There was a stream nearby, and Woods says, "A good many got their washing done there." Woods reports that when four new black men came into the neighborhood, "We knew that these colored fellows were escaped slaves. . . ." Woods adds:

> We colored fellows were all sworn in to keep secret what we knew and when these fellows came there they were sworn in too.

Although young Woods was apparently not an active member of Parker's self-defense organization, he does seem to have been part of a larger group of black people centering around Parker. The resistant spirit of this group is indicated by young Woods's reaction when a strange white man one day asked him for help. The white man wanted to locate "three or four big colored men," to cut wheat for him, he said, intimating vaguely that such information would be rewarded. From the man's statements Woods thought him to be a slave hunter, and, says Woods with evident understatement, he did not give him "much satisfaction."

Peter Woods remembers Parker's home as the scene of merriment, as well as resistance. He recalls Parker's having an apple-butter boiling party, not long before the big battle of 1851. This party is also recalled by another local black, Samuel Hopkins, who adds that those present danced around the boiling kettle singing a song whose refrain was: "Take me back to Canada, where de' cullud people's free." [15]

In Pennsylvania William Parker met and married young, dark-skinned Eliza Ann Elizabeth Howard, a fugitive from Maryland, whose "experience of slavery," says Parker, "had been much more bitter than my own." Whatever the exact nature of this experience, it prepared Eliza to become a determined fighter when the slave hunters appeared. The Parkers' first child, a daughter, Mariah L., was born in 1846, when Eliza herself was just sixteen. A son, John T., arrived in 1848, and a second daughter, Catherine, was born in 1849. The 1850 Census reports that four-year-old Mariah Parker attended school within the year, and lists William Parker as a "farmer." He probably did some farming for himself, as well as "attending a threshing machine" for George Whitson and Joseph Scarlett. [16]

The Parkers led a rather nomadic existence during their first few years of marriage, occupying a number of rented rooms and houses, in various locations. Parker recalls that he and his new wife

commenced house-keeping, renting a room from Enoch Johnson for one month. We did not like our landlord, and when the time was up left, and rented a house of Isaac Walker for one year. After the year was out, we left

From left to right: William and Eliza Parker's daughter Cynthia Parker Chase; her husband, Prince Chase; their son, Lorne Chase. Cynthia Parker is said to have looked much like her mother. (Courtesy Mrs. Lorne Chase, Fletcher, Ontario)

Walker's and went to Smyrna, and there I rented a house from Samuel D. Moore for another year. After the year was out we left Smyrna also, and went to Joseph Moore's to live. We lived on his place about five years.[17]

Eliza Parker's younger sister, Hannah, followed her to freedom.

The Parkers' home. (Courtesy the late Walter Miller, Christiana)

In 1850, when she was seventeen, Hannah married a twenty-seven-year-old black man named Alexander Pinckney. In 1851 the Pinckneys and Parkers were living together near Christiana, with their several children, in the two-story, stone house rented from Quaker Levi Pownall, whose own home was just up the hill. Probably that same year the two families were joined by a young black man named Abraham Johnson who, on Parker's report, proved himself to be a determined resister, trusted associate, and longtime friend.[18]

Abraham Johnson's early history can be pieced together from several sources. Pennsylvania chronicler R. C. Smedley reports that:

> Abraham Johnson, a young slave, belonging to a Mr. Wheeler, of Cecil County, Md., hearing that he was to be sold next day, told his mother. Early in the night they, with

his sister and her child, fled to that well known colored man, on the Susquehanna, Robert Loney, who ferried fugitives across the river in the night at various places below Columbia, and gave them into care of William Wright, who distributed them to other agents. These came to Jeremiah Moore's.[19]

Sarah, the daughter of Quaker Jeremiah Moore, confirms that

The man Abraham . . . was a runaway slave who came to my father's . . . with his mother, sister and sister's child, when he was but eighteen years of age, and lived with us continuously for six years. He told us the name of his master, who died a short time before he ran away, and Abraham was to be sold. We found him to be a very nice, good, faithful young man, very particular and conscientious in every respect. Judge for thyself, when I tell thee, toward the last of his living with us, my parents went to Bucks county on a visit of several weeks; the kidnappers came to our place to take him, but failed in their attempt; we were afraid they would come again when we were alone, and tried to persuade Abram to go away to some of the neighbors. He said: "No, I promised Jerry I would take care of the stock and things until he came home," and he would and did run the risk. Few white men would have done it under similar circumstances. Father at last thought it best for him to go somewhere else; for we had neighbors who were continually watching to get rid of him and did come several times; but he was protected by my parents. He at last went to the neighborhood of Parker's. . . .[20]

It was Abraham Johnson, described by this Quaker woman as a "nice, good, faithful young man," who would declare, when slave catchers came to Parker's: "I will fight till I die."

The exploits of the area's black self-defense organization were widely spoken of in Lancaster County. Local historian Smedley reports that William Parker acquired "a reputation among both the colored people and the kidnapping fraternity for undaunted boldness and remarkable power." Parker, says Smedley, was the one "above all others" whom the kidnappers "wished to get rid of." [21]

Lindley Coates. (Smedley)

The area's white abolitionists also knew of the self-defense organization's activities under Parker's leadership. Although these non-violent whites no doubt disagreed with Parker's methods, they evidently respected his objectives and admired him as a human being.

One of these whites was Lindley Coates, a local abolitionist whose barn was burned—a consequence of his anti-slavery activities, it was suspected. Coates, described by John G. Whittier as "that tall, gaunt, swarthy man, erect, eagle-faced, upon whose somewhat martial figure the Quaker coat seemed a little out of place, . . ." was a non-resistant abolitionist, yet Coates remembered William Parker's being as

> bold as a lion, the kindest of men, and the most steadfast of friends.[22]

Thomas Whitson, a white man and a Quaker, was a resident of the Lancaster County area, and a boy at the time of William Parker's activity in Pennsylvania. More than forty-five years later, in 1896, Whitson eulogized the black leader, emphasizing Parker's role as the true hero of the so-called Christiana "riot." In this eulogy Parker becomes an almost superhuman figure, on whose single-handed activity ordinary black folk seem to be totally dependent for their protection. While this is unjust to Parker's black allies, Whitson's comments do convey the legendary quality of Parker's reputation, both during and after the time he lived in Pennsylvania.

Thomas Whitson recalls that William Parker

at once impressed himself not only upon his own race, but upon the whites with whom he came in contact as well, as a man of wonderful force of character. I remember seeing him but once, and that was as far back as memory goes; but his personality is distinctly impressed upon my mind.

Parker, says Whitson, was

possessed of resolution, courage and action. The neighborhood was rife with stories of his physical feats. He could walk leisurely up to an ordinary post fence, leap over it without touching it with his hands, work hard all day, and travel from ten to fifteen miles during the night to organize his people into a society for their protection. . . . He was by common consent recognized by his race in the neighborhood as their leader. They depended on him with abiding confidence to keep from being taken back to slavery. They regarded him as their leader, their protector, their Moses, and their lawgiver all at once. The white people of the neighborhood knew that he possessed these qualities, that he was the Toussaint L'Ouverture of his people; that he could have commanded an army had he been educated, and he challenged the universal respect of all of them who did not have occasion to fear him.

Thomas Whitson ends his 1896 eulogy with an admonition: "while we all stand reverently at the memories" of the heroes of the American Revolution,

of men from whose well-decked brows I would not take a single flower, let us not forget to make one small niche in our tablet of heroes for this Afro-American, William Parker.[23]

3 Kidnappers

SOON AFTER ITS FORMATION the black self-defense organization went into action against slave catchers. While for the history of most of these episodes there is only the testimony of William Parker, for several important incidents there is external, corroborating evidence. Lancaster newspapers and other contemporary sources also report a number of cases similar, if not identical, to those described by Parker. Allowing for his characteristic bravado, the accuracy of Parker's accounts may be accepted with a fair measure of assurance.[1]

A short time after the formation of the "organization for mutual protection," while he was living at Dr. Dingee's, Parker reports that

> I was working in the barn-yard, when a man came to the fence, and, looking at me intently, went away. The Doctor's son, observing him, said,—
>
> "Parker, that man, from his movements, must be a slaveholder or kidnapper. This is the second time he has been looking at you. If not a kidnapper, why does he look so steadily at you and not tell his errand?"

"This man must be a fool," said Parker, if he returns "I shall say something to him." When, sure enough, the man rode up again Parker went to the fence

> and looking him steadily in the eye, said,—
> "Am I your slave?"
> He made no reply, but turned his horse and rode off, at full speed, towards the valley. We did not see him again; but that same evening word was brought that kidnappers were in the valley, and if we were not careful, they would "hook" some of us. This caused great excitement among the colored people of the neighborhood.

Parker and the other members of the self-defense organization

> collected together that evening, and went down to the valley; but the kidnappers had gone. We watched for them several nights in succession, without result; for so alarmed were the tavern-keepers by our demonstration, that they refused to let them stop over night with them.[2]

The first "demonstration" of the black self-defense organization had served as a warning.

The rescue of an arrested fugitive was the group's next action. Parker reports:

> One day word was sent to me that slaveholders had taken William Dorsey, and had put him into Lancaster jail to await trial. Dorsey had a wife and three or four children; but what was it to the slaveholder, if the wife and children should starve? We consulted together, as to what course to take to deliver him; but no plan that was proposed could be worked. At last we separated, determining to get him away some way or other on the day of trial. His case caused great excitement. We attended the trial, and eagerly watched all the movements from an outside position, and had a man to tell us how proceedings were going on within. He finally came out and said that the case would go against Dorsey. We then formed in a column at the court-house door, and when the slaveholders and Dorsey came out, we walked close to them,—behind and around them,—trying to separate them from him. Before we had gone far towards

the jail, a slaveholder drew a pistol on Williams Hopkins, one of our party. Hopkins defied him to shoot; but he did not. Then the slaveholder drew the pistol on me, saying, he would blow my black brains out, if I did not go away. I doubled my fists to knock him down, but some person behind caught my hand; this started a fracas, and we got Dorsey loose; but he was so confused that he stood stock still, until they tied him again. A general fight followed. Bricks, stones, and sticks fell in showers. We fought across the road and back again, and I thought our brains would be knocked out; when the whites, who were too numerous for us, commenced making arrests. They got me fast several times, but I succeeded in getting away. One of our men was arrested, and afterwards stood trial; but they did not convict him. Dorsey was put into jail, but was afterwards bought and liberated by friends.

My friends now said that I had got myself into a bad difficulty, and that my arrest would follow. In this they were mistaken. I never was disturbed because of it, nor was the house at which I lodged ever searched, although the neighbors were repeatedly annoyed in that way.[3]

If slave catchers were afraid to enter Parker's home, they did not hesitate to break into the houses of his black friends. Parker says:

I was sitting one evening in a friend's house, conversing about these marauding parties, when I remarked to him that a stop should be put to such "didos" [tricks], and declared, that, the next time a slaveholder came to a house where I was, I would refuse to admit him. His wife replied, "It will make a fuss." I told her, "It is time a fuss was made." She insisted that it would cause trouble, and it was best to let them alone and have peace. Then I told her we must have trouble before we could have peace. "The first slaveholder that draws a pistol on me I shall knock down."

Just at that moment, says Parker, there was a rap at the door:

"Who's there?" I asked.

"It's me! Who do you think? Open the door!" was the response, in a gruff tone.

"What do you want?" I asked.

Without replying, the man opened the door and came in, followed by two others.

The first one said,—

"Have you any niggers here?"

"What have we to do with your niggers?" said I.

After bandying a few words, he drew his pistol upon me. Before he could bring the weapon to bear, I seized a pair of heavy tongs, and struck him a violent blow across the face and neck, which knocked him down. He lay for a few minutes senseless, but afterwards rose, and walked out of the house without a word, followed by his comrades, who also said nothing to us, but merely asked their leader, as they went out, if he was hurt.[4]

Although Parker's single-handed victory and the slave catchers' peaceful retreat seem somewhat unbelievable, similar white provocations and black resistances are reported in the local papers.

Parker and Pennsylvania historian R. C. Smedley both supply versions of the next major kidnapping attempt.[5] The incident began at the home of Moses Whitson, in Chester County, near Parker's. Whitson, a well-known Quaker and abolitionist, employed a black woman named Elizabeth who had arrived at Whitson's via the underground railroad.

Early one morning a slave owner and one or two others entered Whitson's kitchen, and seized Elizabeth, the slave owner claiming her as his property. Friend Whitson asked Elizabeth if any of them were her master. "No!" she said. The slave owner insisted Elizabeth was his property; Smedley sustains the claim; Parker simply reports Elizabeth's emphatic denial. Despite the black woman's protestations, the slave catchers forcibly bound her and took her away in a carriage. The non-violent Whitson watched helplessly.

Thinking themselves secure, the slave owner's party stopped at Mount Vernon tavern in Lancaster County to have their breakfast. But the alarm had been sounded that "kidnappers were at Whitson's"; Benjamin Whipper, a black man living at Whitson's, notified Parker and others of the abduction. When the slave hunters left the tavern with Elizabeth, Benjamin Whipper rode behind them at a distance, mounted on Moses Whitson's well-known white horse, thereby distinguishing their wagon from others. Near a place called Gap-Hill, Parker and six or seven others (Smedley says "four or five") sprang from their hiding place by the roadside.

Parker says that, after freeing Elizabeth and exchanging gunfire, "we beat the kidnappers and let them go." Smedley says:

> The slaveholder drew a pistol, but before he could fire, one of the colored men struck him upon the arm, breaking it. The other man fired, but without effect.

The blacks, says Smedley, then "pummelled" the slave catchers "severely" and let them go.

According to Parker a conversation occurred after this battle, between the kidnappers and "two respectable citizens of the town" who had observed it. One of these "respectable citizens," Squire Henderson, asked the slaveholder, "What's the matter?" [6]

> *Slaveholder.* You may ask, what's the matter! Is this the way you allow your niggers to do?
>
> *Squire.* Why did you not shoot them?
>
> *Slaveholder.* We did shoot at them, but it did not take effect.
>
> *Squire.* There's no use shooting at our niggers, for their heads are like iron pots; the balls will glance off. What were you doing?
>
> *Slaveholder.* Taking our property, when the niggers jumped on us and nearly killed some of the men.
>
> *Squire.* Men coming after such property ought to be killed.

No doubt taken aback, the startled slaveholder asked, "Do you know where we can find a doctor?" "Yes," answered the Squire, "there are plenty of doctors South."

Parker says that the enraged and badly wounded slave catchers traveled on until they reached McKenzie's tavern, where their wounds were attended to inexpertly. Parker claims that

> Dr. Lemmon,[7] a physician on the road to Lancaster, refused to attend the slaveholders; so that by the time they

got to the city, from being so long without surgical aid,
their limbs were past setting, and two of them died, . . .
while the other survived but a short time after reaching
Maryland.

Smedley's account does not mention any fatalities. According to
Parker, "Only one of our men was hurt, and he had only a slight
injury in the hand." Parker reports that the Maryland authorities
offered a large reward "for the perpetrators of the flogging, but
without effect."

McKenzie, at whose tavern the slaveholders received aid, is said
by Parker to have been so strongly "in sympathy with these
demons, that he declared he would never employ another nigger,
and actually discharged a faithful colored woman who had lived a
long time in his employ." McKenzie further boasted "that he
would entertain all slaveholders who came along, and help them
recapture their slaves." But, says Parker, "We were equally
determined he should not, if we could prevent it. The following af-
fliction," says Parker, "was eventually the means, under Providence," by which McKenzie "was led to adopt other views, and
became a practical Abolitionist": One night soon after the
previous confrontation, when McKenzie's barn caught fire, a band
of five black men stood off in the darkness and watched "with
evident satisfaction" the "curling flames" ascend "from girder to
roof, and lap and lash their angry tongues in wild license, until
every vestige of the building was consumed." After that "mysteri-
ous occurrence," says Parker, "the poor fugitive had no better
friend than the publican McKenzie." [8] The country was in a state
of warfare, lives were at stake, and each side used whatever
weapons seemed effective. Parker does not comment on the
morality of barn burning.

While Parker and his wife were living on Joseph Moore's place[9]
several kidnappers abducted a black man and started for Maryland. Parker reports:

Seven of us set out in pursuit, and, soon getting on their
track, followed them to a tavern on the Westchester road,
in Chester County. Learning that they were to remain for
the night, I went to the door and asked for admittance.

The tavern keeper, looking out into the dark night, wanted to know if Parker's group was white or colored.

> I told him colored. He then told us to be gone, or he would blow out our brains. We walked aside a little distance, and consulted about what we should do. Our men seemed to dread the undertaking. . . .

Parker told his men they could overcome those in the tavern, and that he was going in. Only one of Parker's men agreed to accompany him, saying "he would follow at the risk of his life."

> The other five said we should all get killed,—that we were men with families,—that our wives and children needed our assistance,—and that they did not think we would be doing our families justice by risking our lives for one man.

Leaving these five behind, Parker and his single comrade returned to the tavern, and after knocking once more, were again told by the tavern keeper to depart. When the tavern keeper put his head out the window, "and threatened again to shoot us," Parker's comrade "raised his gun and would have shot him down," but Parker had caught his arm and persuaded him not to fire. Parker says he then went to the yard, found a piece of wood for a battering ram, and after a short time forced open the door:

> As soon as the door flew open, a kidnapper shot at us, and the ball lodged in my ankle, bringing me to the ground. But I soon rose, and my comrade then firing on them, they took to their heels. As they ran away, I heard one say, "We have killed one of them."

Parker and his one companion rushed into the tavern, unbound the black prisoner, and started out the door. They "had hardly crossed the door-sill before people from the neighboring houses began to fire on us." All seemed lost, until from out of the darkness came the other five members of Parker's band:

> Firing on both sides was kept up for ten or fifteen minutes, when the whites called for quarter, and offered to withdraw, if we would stop firing. On this assurance we started off with the man, and reached home safely.

The next day my ankle was very painful. With a knife I extracted the ball, but kept the wound secret; as long before we had learned that for our own security it was best not to let such things be generally known.[10]

One Sunday night in September, 1850, Parker was notified that kidnappers had taken Henry Williams from the home of another black man, Allen Williams; his band set out after the abductors, but did not catch them.[11] Parker was delegated to discover who had betrayed the kidnapped black man to the slave catchers. After some quiet sleuthing Parker learned that the traitor was none other than Allen Williams, the black man in whose house the kidnapping had taken place.

The members of the self-defense organization met at Parker's,

talked the matter over, and, after most solemnly weighing all the facts and evidence, we resolved that he should die. . . .

Parker explains this recourse to "lynch law," as he calls it, by the circumstances of the case. He admits that such lynch law "is of so diabolical a character as to be without justification, except when enforced by men of pure motives, and then only in extreme cases. . . ." This, he maintains, was such a case. Legal action against the traitor would expose other blacks to arrest as fugitive slaves. The traitor had it in his power to betray others; lives were endangered. Circumstances all combined "to make an appeal to the Lynch Code . . . excusable, if not altogether justifiable":

Ourselves, our wives, our little ones, were insecure, and all we had was liable to seizure. We felt that something must be done. . . .

Parker's band went to Allen Williams's house the same night they reached their verdict. They beat Williams until someone approaching caused the band to flee. Parker says their early departure saved the informer's life, but Williams's survival suggests a lack of determination to kill him.[12]

According to Parker, there lived near Christiana another black man who, under the guise of friendship for newly arrived fugitives, would discover the names and addresses of their masters, and betray their whereabouts. Through the traitor's activity many blacks, "mostly young people, had disappeared mysteriously. . . ." When the traitor's connection with these disappearances was at last "clearly traced," Parker and "six of our most reliable men" resolved to shoot the betrayer. One night after swearing in his men "in the usual form," Parker says he and the others armed themselves and went to the traitor's house. Setting it on fire they waited to shoot the informer when he ran out the back door. But "just before the roof fell in" the traitor rushed out the front door to his neighbors, and escaped. Parker says that the betrayer ran "not only as if his life was in danger, but as if the spirit of his evil deeds was after him." This event apparently ended the traitor's activities in the area.[13]

The last kidnapping in which the black self-defense organization intervened took place on January 13, 1851, and is fully documented.[14] John Williams, a black in his mid-thirties, lived with the family of a white man, William Marsh Chamberlain, working as a laborer on their farm. Smedley indicates that Williams was a fugitive, one of several "slaves belonging to a widow in Elkton, Md." The widow had remarried and her new husband "at once instituted search for the absconded property," advertising for the fugitives in the newspapers. William Baer, "who was not known to reject emoluments offered for returning slaves," saw that the description of one of the fugitives fitted the black man who lived and worked at Chamberlain's. Baer corresponded with the slave owner, who offered $200 for the fugitive's return. Baer and others, says Smedley, went to Chamberlain's "one evening after dark . . . ." [15]

One evening at about eight o'clock, eyewitness Henry Rhay reports:

> I overtook a company at the end of Marsh Chamberlain's lane; . . . one came up to me and said, "Say nothing;" he had something in his hand. I took it to be a pistol.

The man was Perry Marsh. Rhay told Perry Marsh that

> I would say what I pleased, and that was, that they were after no good. I was about to leave, and one of the men in the company said they were going to Marsh Chamberlain's, to take a black man.

Rhay noticed that another in the company was William Baer.[16]

Thomas Pennington, Mrs. Chamberlain's father, recalls the sad events on the evening of the kidnapping:

> It was in the month of January. . . . In the evening a little after night my son and two of my grandsons were out of doors; they came into my house and told my son-in-law there were two men outside. . . . These men told the boys . . . they had heard my son-in-law had chickens to sell. He went out and talked some ten minutes, I suppose, and told them he had not any. They came up to the porch and they talked there. I was inside. . . . one looked into the window, and the black man was sitting behind the stove. They couldn't help seeing him; they then went away.[17]

About half an hour later, Pennington's son-in-law had gone out, and he was "sitting at the table reading." John Williams "was sitting behind the stove with his boots and hat off." There was a knock at the door; Pennington called "come in." Two men entered together, quickly moved past Pennington to the black man,

> and presented a pistol to his head and told him they would blow his brains out if he made any resistance. I didn't speak to them at all after they entered the door.

"A struggle ensued" between the black man and the kidnappers, says Pennington. Then more kidnappers entered, and John Williams continued to struggle against all of the intruders:

> I suppose the black man resisted; they were between him and me, and I could not see what was going on.

When the "five or six" additional gang members entered, Pennington moved toward the door, and suddenly found himself face to face with Perry Marsh:

> he had a stick in his hand . . . and I had seen something sticking out partly from the cuff of the coat and partly inside. I judge it was a slung shot. He passed right by me, he struck the lamp and it fell on the floor and went out; and after that it was dark, and I . . . could not tell much what passed between the parties.

In the room above, Pennington's daughter, Rachel Chamberlain, observed the struggle between the kidnappers and the black man through a stovepipe hole in the floor. Then, says Pennington,

> my daughter . . . she came down and begged me to come up stairs, she thought I would get hurt, [and] appeared to be frantic with fright. I accordingly went up stairs, and remained there till these persons left the house. They were dragging the man out to the porch when we went up stairs. They bound him and dragged him off. . . . After they went away, as we supposed, I went down and got a little light, a candle, and examined the floor. . . . I found large quantities of blood along on the porch floor, and next morning when I got up, the first thing I done I tracked them by the blood. It was along the road they dragged him, along to the woods; . . . it appeared there had been a horse and carriage standing. . . .

Pennington noticed that during John Williams's struggle with his abductors "they had broken a chair into four or five pieces." [18]

On the evening of this abduction, William Parker recalls he was sitting at home,

> talking with Pinckney and Samuel Thompson about how I was getting on with my work, when I thought I heard some one call my name. I went out, but all was quiet. When I went in, Pinckney and Thompson laughed at me, and said I had become so "scary" that I could not stay in the house. But I was not satisfied. I was sure some one had called me. I said so, and that I would go to Marsh Chamberlain's to see if anything was wrong. They concluded to go also, and we started.
>
> Arriving near the house, I told Pinckney and Thompson to stop outside, and I would go in, and if anything was wrong, would call them. When I reached the house, I saw a chair broken in pieces, and knew that something had happened. I said,—
> "Hallo, Marsh!"
> "Who is that?" said he.
> And his wife said,—

"Parker, is that you?"

"Yes," I said.

"Oh, Parker, come here," she called.

I called Pinckney and Thompson, and we went in. Marsh met us, and said that kidnappers had been there, had taken John Williams, and gone with him towards Buck Hill. They had been gone about fifteen minutes. Off we started on a rapid run to save him. We ran to a stable, got out two horses, and Pinckney and I rode on. Thompson soon got the rest of our party together and followed. We were going at a pretty good gait, when Pinckney's horse stumbled and fell, fastening his rider's leg; but I did not halt. Pinckney got his horse up and caught up with me.

"You would not care," said he, "if a man were to get killed! You would not help him!"

"Not in a case as this," I replied. We rode on to the Maryland line, but could not overtake them. We were obliged to return, as it was near day-break. The next day a friend of ours went to Maryland to see what had been done with Williams. He went to Dr. Savington's, and the Doctor told him that the fugitive could not live,—the kidnappers had broken his skull, and otherwise beaten him very badly; his ankle, too, was out of place. In consequence of his maimed condition, his mistress refused to pay the men anything for bringing him home. That was the last we ever heard of poor John Williams. . . .

Smedley adds that, though the slave owner who had instigated the abduction "refused to pay the stipulated reward" to John Williams's captors, the master succeeded, "in selling the negro, and [William] Baer received his portion of the price. . . ." [19]

The possibility of taking legal action against John Williams's abductors was investigated by six white Pennsylvania abolitionists. Smedley reports that

Moses Whitson, Samuel Whitson, Samuel Brinton, John Cain and Dr. Augustus W. Cain, held a private meeting at the house of Lindley Coates to consider the propriety of taking some action in reference to the case. They believed that the manner in which the man had been taken would be clearly defined by law as kidnapping. Samuel Whitson and Dr. Cain were appointed a committee to visit Elkton [Maryland], ascertain the particulars of the case, and if sufficient evidence could be adduced to commit Baer, they would commence prosecution against him. On consulting Lawyer Earle of that place, he told them nothing could be done as the slave had been delivered to his legal master, although he admitted the man was not arrested precisely according to the law.

Threats were now made that the barns of Samuel Whitson, Lindley Coates, and Dr. Cain would be burned. The two former fell a sacrifice to the flames, but whether in consequence of the threat or not was never ascertained. Dr. Cain kept a guard around his barn for two months and it escaped.[20]

Such was the state of things near Christiana, Sadsbury Township, Lancaster County, the Commonwealth of Pennsylvania, in the United States of America, some eight months before the fatal attack on William Parker's in September, 1851.

4 1851

AMERICANS AT MID-CENTURY were moving west and with the most ruthless brutality, forcibly appropriating a continent from its resistant red-skinned natives. While Americans, recalling the heroes and battles of their own independence struggle, lauded leaders of national independence movements in other lands, America was reaching westward and southward.

In 1847, U.S. troops were at war in Mexico; in 1848 Mexico was forced to cede New Mexico and California. In 1850, the United States and Great Britain agreed that neither would ever obtain "exclusive control" over any canal across Nicaragua, nor "exercise any dominion over any part of Central America." In 1851, with southern support, a Cuban refugee, Narciso López, leading a company of Americans recruited in Louisiana, invaded Cuba for the purpose of making that island a new slave state. López was captured and shot, his men were killed or imprisoned, and the Cuban invasion of 1851 was a total fiasco. This did not prevent the newly elected U.S. President, Franklin Pierce, in his inaugural address of 1853, from urging the annexation of Cuba. In 1853 Commodore Matthew Perry arrived in Yedo Bay, Japan, marking the first American commercial-military move in Asia.

In 1848 the American public, imbued with the spirit of their own revolution of only seventy-two years before, heartily approved the revolutionary uprisings which swept over France, Germany, Hungary, and Italy. The leaders of these movements for national unity and self-determination were honored men in America, both north and south. Although Americans generally did not relate the battles of these white revolutionaries to the liberation struggles of American blacks, the names of O'Connell, the Irish nationalist; Mazzini and Garibaldi, the Italian revolutionaries; and Kosuth, the Hungarian would be among those commonly invoked by the defenders of the black rebels of Christiana.

Although the European revolutions of 1848 were eventually put down, and reaction triumphed, they inspired a lasting legacy of hope among liberal Americans. Walt Whitman expressed this optimism when he wrote, in 1850, of Europe in 1848, and by allusion, of his own country:

> God, 'twas delicious!
> That brief, tight, glorious grip
> Upon the throats of kings.

But, said Whitman, the peoples' mercy "brewed bitter destruction,"

> And frightened rulers come back:
> Each comes in state, with his train,
> Hangman, priest, and tax-gatherer,
> Soldier, lawyer, and sycophant;
> An appalling procession of locusts,
> And the king struts grandly again.

Despite the triumph of tyranny, Whitman assured his readers that the spirit of liberty would eventually triumph:

> Not a grave of those slaughtered ones,
> But is growing its seed of freedom,
> In its turn to bear seed,
> Which the winds shall carry afar and resow,
> And the rain nourish.[1]

Southern slaves had long been running off with themselves. In 1832 a bondswoman named Margaret Morgan fled from her Maryland mistress to freedom in Pennsylvania. In 1837 slave catchers led by Edward Prigg carried the black woman and her children back to Maryland. One of these children, born in Pennsylvania, was, it was claimed in that state, a free person. Prigg and associates were accused of kidnapping and found guilty in a county court, and later by the supreme court of Pennsylvania. Prigg appealed to the U.S. Supreme Court which, in 1842, ruled that Pennsylvania laws obstructing the return of fugitive slaves were unconstitutional; Prigg's indictment was voided. The court ruled, however, that state officials were not responsible for executing the U.S. fugitive law, which thereafter became sole province of federal officers. By taking enforcement of the federal law out of the hands of state officials the Court's decision in the Prigg case had the effect of facilitating the escape of fugitives.[2]

Northern black communities took an active part in protecting those fugitives who came into their midst. The *Carlisle* [Pennsylvania] *Herald* of June 3, 1847, reports:

> Our town was thrown into great commotion and excitement yesterday afternoon, by an attempt on the part of a large portion of our colored population to rescue several slaves who had been arrested as fugitives. The slaves (one man, a woman and little girl) were . . . taken before Judge Hepburn, . . . which resulted in their being fully identified as the property of Col. Hollingsworth and Mr. Kennedy, of Hagerstown, Md. They were therefore remanded to their owners.
>
> During the hearing a large crowd of infuriated negro men and women gathered in and about the Court House, who evidenced by their violent conduct a disposition to rescue the fugitives by force. An attempt was made first in the court room, but quickly frustrated by the constables.
>
> A second attempt was made as the slaves were brought down from the court room to the carriage, which resulted in a serious riot.—The attack was commenced at the door of the carriage, where, before the slaves were got into the vehicle, a general rush was made on the slave owners and constables by the negro men and women, and a frightful melee ensued in the street in which for some minutes paving stones were hurled in showers, and clubs and canes

used with terrible energy. The result was that the woman and girl escaped, while the man was secured and taken back to Maryland. We regret to say that Mr. Kennedy, one of the owners, was very severely hurt, having been felled to the earth under a succession of blows from stones and clubs which completely disabled him.

. . . Much excitement prevails in our community in relation to this unfortunate affair, and the Sheriff and Constables have arrested a score or more of negroes, who were identified as leaders in the riot, who are now confined to jail to await their trial.—Our citizens generally made no interference. The evidence that the slaves were fugitives was clear, and the mass of our citizens therefore regarded them as the rightful property of their owners.

The Carlisle paper subsequently announced the death of slave owner James H. Kennedy from injuries received in the "riot." [3] This "murder" of a Maryland slave owner would be recalled when the Christiana "riot" occurred at William Parker's four years later.

By 1850, the difficulty of seizing and recovering runaways had become so great that southern slave owners were demanding a more effective federal fugitive slave act. The southern slave-labor economy was in open conflict with the developing free-labor capitalism in the north. The politicians of the slave system felt their former power over the United States Congress slipping from their grasp. The slavocracy feared their power in Congress would be more and more diminished if the Western territories entered the Union as non-slave states.

With secessionists already pushing for disunion, the more moderate faction of southerners sought a national legislative act to assure slave owners of their continued power. The result was the 1850 Congressional compromise between northern and southern interests. This set of laws provided, among other things, that California would enter the Union as a free state, the existence of slavery in the new territories would later be decided by their citizens, the slave trade would be discontinued in the nation's capital, and the runaway property of southern slave owners would be protected by a more effective federal fugitive slave law.

The new U.S. fugitive slave law of 1850 provided for the

COLLEGE OF THE SEQUOIAS
LIBRARY

appointment of special federal commissioners to facilitate the reclaiming of runaways. These commissioners could appoint marshals to arrest fugitives, and these marshals could, in turn, "call to their aid" any bystanders at the scene of an arrest, who were "commanded" to "assist in the prompt and efficient execution of this law. . . ."

Slave owners could "pursue and reclaim" fugitives with or without a warrant; the commissioner would judge the case without a jury. In addition:

> In no trial or hearing under this act shall the testimony of such alleged fugitive be admitted in evidence.

"Satisfactory" written or oral "proof" being offered that the person arrested was the sought-for fugitive, the commissioner would issue a certificate. The slave owner was authorized to use all "reasonable force" necessary to take a fugitive back to the place of his or her escape. If a slave owner feared "that such fugitive will be rescued by force" it was the duty of the officer involved to employ any number of persons necessary "to overcome such force," and deliver the fugitive back to the fugitive's owner.

Any marshal who failed to properly execute the fugitive law was to be fined $1000; the marshal was also liable for the full value of any fugitive escaping from his custody. A fine not larger than $1000, and imprisonment for not longer than six months, was the penalty for knowingly obstructing a fugitive's arrest, for assisting a fugitive's escape—or for harboring or concealing a fugitive. Anyone guilty of the above offenses was also required to pay $1000 for each escaping fugitive.

And last but not least, an officer was "entitled to a fee of five dollars each" for every person he arrested; a commissioner was "entitled to a fee of ten dollars" if he delivered a fugitive to a slave owner, but only five dollars if he freed the black claimed. Despite this built-in bribery the new fugitive slave law was approved by Congress on September 18, 1850, exactly one year, minus seven days, before the Christiana resistance of September 11, 1851.[4]

While the debate over the fugitive law was still in progress, the already evident capitulation of northern to southern politicians angered the young Walt Whitman, and led to a series of topical verses, the first in his own personal style published in the New

York newspapers. Whitman's poem "Blood-Money" was probably inspired by Daniel Webster's famous speech of March 7, 1850, in which the formerly anti-slavery senator supported the proposed new fugitive slave law. The poem compares those who sold out Jesus to more contemporary betrayers;

> Of olden time, when it came to pass
> That the beautiful god, Jesus, should finish
>   his work on earth,
> Then went Judas, and sold the divine youth,
> And took pay for his body.
>
> Curs'd was the deed, even before the sweat
>   of the clutching hand grew dry;
> And darkness frown'd upon the seller
>   of the like of God. . . .

Since that day, said Whitman, many a purse had closed upon its fee. Again came a man who asked: "What will ye give me and I will deliver this man unto you?" And still, said Whitman bitterly, "They make the covenant, and pay the pieces of silver. . . . And still Iscariot plies his trade."

Whitman's poem "The House of Friends" also condemned those northern politicians, supposedly the friends of freedom, who were compromising with the defenders of slavery. He cursed these politicians as

> Doughfaces, Crawlers, Lice of Humanity—
> Terrific screamers of Freedom
> Who roar and bawl, and get hot i' the face . . .
> Muck-worms creeping flat to the ground
> A dollar dearer to them than Christ's blessing. . . .

The thirty-one-year-old Whitman called upon his peers to revolt against the gray-headed compromisers:

> Arise, young North
> Our elder blood flows in the veins of cowards.

And last the poet warned of the betrayal of liberty that came snakelike from within the "House of Friends":

> Fear most the still and forked fang
> That starts from the grass at your feet.[5]

Robert Purvis. (Smedley)

In October, 1850, a few weeks after the passage of the new fugitive slave law, an abolitionist meeting took place in Georgetown, in Bart Township, four miles from William Parker's. The meeting unanimously resolved not to assist in the recapture of fugitives, and declared, in reference to the new fugitive act: "we will obey no such law." Another unanimous resolution stated: "we will harbor, feed, and aid the escape of fugitive slaves in opposition to the law." [6]

The annual convention of the Pennsylvania Anti-slavery Society took place that same October, in nearby West Chester, at the Horticultural Hall. A correspondent for the Philadelphia *Evening Bulletin* reports:

> I understand that certain Southern slave owners, principally of Baltimore, have sent hither their agents, and this will account for the thin sprinkling of negroes at hand.

With Robert Purvis, a wealthy, free black as chairman, the Pennsylvanians listened (as the Philadelphia paper reports) to "some of the most eminent New England fanatics."

Parker Pillsbury, of Massachusetts,

> commenced by saying that the Revolution of 1776, and its heroes, were all failures. He hoped the abolition revolution would not prove equally abortive. . . . George Washington, he continued, was as infamous and vile for signing the [fugitive] act of 1793, as Millard Fillmore is for signing the

William Lloyd Garrison. (Still; Wm. L. Katz Collection)

act of 1850. . . . Were it not for the grave stones on Bunker
Hill, . . . who would ever know that there had been a war
for liberty or human rights in this country?" [7]

Abolitionists of 1851 were sharply divided on the morality and
tactics of different forms of anti-slavery activity. One large group
of abolitionists formed the American and Foreign Anti-Slavery
Society. This group had decided that legal and political anti-slavery activities could be carried on within the system established by
the United States Constitution. In 1840 they formed the Liberty
Party and ran a candidate for President on an anti-slavery
platform. Other men of varying degrees of anti-slavery opinion, in
both the Democratic and Whig parties, were elected to office.

William Lloyd Garrison, editor of the Boston-based *Liberator*,
and founder of the New England Anti-Slavery Society, led
another group of abolitionists passionately advocating the immediate and total end of slavery. The Garrisonians' anti-slavery
principles condemned any union with the slave system. Their
radical, anti-gradualist, uncompromising demands caused the
Garrisonians to be widely considered the militant fanatics of the
anti-slavery movement. This despite the fact that the main tactic
advocated by the Garrisonians was a non-violent appeal to
conscience. Denouncing the United States Constitution as a
pro-slavery document, the morally uncompromising Garrisonians
refused to participate in electoral politics, even that aimed at the
abolition of slavery.

Although on principle opposed to violent resistance, the Garrisonians did not condemn it when it occurred, but focused their

criticism on the immoral, oppressive slave system which had caused it. And, like the pacifistic Quakers, the Garrisonians, on the basis of their "higher law," could justify the most militant, non-violent resistance to the U.S. fugitive slave law.

Another group of abolitionists more militant than the Garrisonians in terms of tactics, if not basic aims, favored a violent attack on the slave system, and advocated armed resistance to the fugitive slave law. Among these radical abolitionists were a number of black leaders, and some whites, including a Massachusetts wool merchant named John Brown.

In December, 1847, John Brown met for the first time with the prominent black leader Frederick Douglass at Brown's Springfield, Massachusetts, home. After a hearty supper, Brown and Douglass sat from eight o'clock at night until three in the morning discussing Brown's plan for guerrilla warfare against the slave system. Douglass says that John Brown

> denounced slavery in look and language fierce and bitter; thought that slaveholders had forfeited their right to live; that the slaves had the right to gain their liberty in any way they could; did not believe that moral suasion would ever liberate the slave, or that political action would abolish the system. He said that he had long had a plan which could accomplish this end, and he had invited me to his house to lay that plan before me. He said he had been for some time looking for colored men to whom he could safely reveal his secret, and at times he had almost despaired of finding such men; but that now he was encouraged, for he saw heads of such rising up in all directions. . . . He was not averse to the shedding of blood, and thought the practice of carrying arms would be a good one for the colored people to adopt, as it would give them a sense of their manhood. No people, he said, could have self-respect, or be respected, who would not fight for their freedom.

Brown's plan, as outlined to Douglass, contemplated "the creating of an armed force which should act in the very heart of the South." The plan was "to take at first about twenty-five picked men" into the Allegheny Mountains, who, from this base, would eventually run off slaves in large numbers. These actions, thought

Brown, would be a start at weakening the power of the slave system.

"Slavery was a state of war," said Brown, "and the slave had a right to anything necessary to his freedom." When Douglass, who was still under the influence of the Garrisonians, suggested "that we might convert the slaveholders," Brown

> became much excited, and said that could never be. He knew their proud hearts and that they would never be

John Brown. (Wm. L. Katz Collection)

induced to give up their slaves, until they felt a big stick about their heads.[8]

Two months after the passage of the second fugitive law, on November 28, 1850, John Brown wrote to his wife that he was encouraging his black friends "to 'trust in God and keep their powder dry.'" Nine months before the Christiana resistance, on January 15, 1851, in Springfield, Massachusetts, John Brown organized an armed black self-defense group called the League of the Gileadites. Brown took the group's name from the Biblical command, "Whosoever is fearful or afraid, let him return and depart early from Mount Gilead." The "Agreement and Rules" of this League, written by Brown, was signed by forty-four predominantly black men and women of Springfield. Brown's words of advice include several sharp warnings against black submissiveness, intended no doubt to provoke his readers to an angry, active response. Brown's rules for the Gileadites also constituted a practical manual of black resistance.

The "Agreement and Rules" is headed "Union Is Strength." It opens:

> Nothing so charms the American people as personal bravery. The trial for life of one bold and to some extent successful man, for defending his rights in good earnest, would arouse more sympathy throughout the nation than the accumulated wrongs and sufferings of more than three millions of our submissive colored population. We need not mention the Greeks struggling against the oppressive Turks, the Poles against Russia, nor the Hungarians against Austria and Russia combined, to prove this. *No jury can be found in the Northern States that would convict a man for defending his rights to the last extremity.* This is well understood by Southern Congressmen, who insisted that the right of trial by jury should not be granted to the fugitive. Colored people have more fast friends amongst the whites than they suppose, and would have ten times the number they now have were they but half as much in earnest to secure their dearest rights as they are to ape the follies and extravagances of their white neighbors, and to indulge in idle show, in ease, and in luxury.

Martin R. Delany. (W. J. Simmons, *Men of Mark*; Wm. L. Katz Collection)

Still provocative, Brown reminded the black Gileadites of the white money and martyrs given up to the anti-slavery cause. Brown then formulated practical plans for the armed, organized rescue of an arrested fugitive. Brown's general advice to these black resisters was:

> Be firm, determined and cool; but let it be understood that you are not to be driven to desperation without making it an awful job to others as well as to you. . . . Hold on to your weapons, and never be persuaded to leave them, part with them or have them far away from you. *Stand by one another, and by your friends, while a drop of blood remains; and be hanged, if you must, but tell no tales out of school. Make no confession.*

Brown assured the black Gileadites that some white friends would come to their aid voluntarily, while other whites who had pledged their support would waver when a showdown occurred.[9]

The passage of the 1850 fugitive slave law provoked a spirited response from black leaders. Editor, orator, and physician Martin R. Delany declared his house was his castle:

> If any man approaches that house in search of a slave, . . . if he crosses the threshold of my door, and I do not lay him a lifeless corpse at my feet, I hope the grave may refuse my body a resting place. . . .

Henry Highland Garnet. (W. J. Simmons, *Men of Mark*)

The Reverend J. W. Loguen, a fugitive slave, and leader in Syracuse, New York, exclaimed:

> I don't respect this law—I don't fear it—I won't obey it. It outlaws me, and I outlaw it, . . . if force is used to re-enslave me, I shall make preparations to meet the crisis as becomes a man.[10]

In the north black resistance took many forms.[11] All-black "vigilance committees" were organized in Boston, Cleveland, and Detroit, to obstruct the capture of fugitives and prevent their being returned to slavery. In Detroit, George De Baptiste and William Lambert led a secret and successful black underground railroad operation that made use of an intricate series of rituals, hand grips, and passwords. Blacks also played leading, active roles in the integrated vigilance committees of Albany, Syracuse, and New York City.

From 1838 to 1844 the Philadelphia Vigilance Committee, though interracial in form, was actually run by blacks. After 1844 a black Philadelphian, William Still, became the chairman of the group's Acting Committee. In 1851, this Philadelphia Vigilance Committee would play an important role in the prelude to the Christiana resistance.

Individual black people fed and sheltered fugitive slaves in their homes, and some became regular stations on the underground railroad. Northern black underground conductors carried fugitives in horse-drawn covered wagons from one station to another. In Boston, during the 1850s, a black lawyer, Robert Morris, helped defend arrested fugitives. Black clergymen sought funds for the aid of fugitives, and sheltered them in the basements of churches. Black intellectuals, orators, and writers, like Henry Highland Garnet and Frederick Douglass, urged and justified resistance to the fugitive slave law, and acted to defy it.

Some of the most daring black underground conductors, like Harriet Tubman, Leonard Grimes, and Josiah Henson, after having themselves escaped, ventured back many times into the slave states—to lead friends, relatives, and other eager blacks to freedom. Other blacks scrimped and saved to pay the expenses of a conductor to go south and lead their dear ones out of slavery. Some black underground agents living in the south operated right under the suspicious eyes of slave owners. These southern black agents put slaves in contact with boats going north and the friendly sailors who hid fugitives in dark holds. Other southern blacks secretly preached about the North Star, Canada, and freedom, using the spirituals as underground railroad signals. Some free southern blacks lent their papers to fugitives, and other southern blacks gave fugitives food, shelter, and directions on the long journey north.

After the passage of the 1850 fugitive slave law numerous examples of black resistance were reported in the newspapers.

Harriet Tubman. (Wm. L. Katz Collection)

In Columbia, Pennsylvania, in January, 1851, when slave catchers came to arrest fugitive Stephen Bennett, the fugitive's brother-in-law, a man named Cole, reportedly "discharged a pistol" at the pursuers. An unsympathetic correspondent from Columbia reports that when Bennett was taken to a lawyer's office in town

> A large concourse of people soon filled the street in front of the office, and in thirty minutes "Tow Hill" came down en masse, some of whom threatened a rescue. The women exhibited a more intractable spirit than the men, attributable no doubt to their ignorance of the law.

When the fugitive was taken out of the office on his way to Philadelphia

> the most intense feeling prevailed. . . . A fierce shout was given as a signal for rescue; but the leader, a desperate negro by the name of Cole, who swore he would shoot the police officers as he would squirrels, was felled to the earth just in time to save his life, for if he advanced two paces more, a dozen bullets would have riddled him. . . . He will be watched here, and probably will find "Tow Hill" too hot for his savage retreat. . . .[12]

When fugitive Bennett, a large, able-bodied man of thirty-five, with a wife and child, was brought before Commissioner Ingraham in Philadelphia, a committee of the Pennsylvania Anti-slavery Society "and several colored men were in attendance, superintending the case." When Ingraham remanded the slave to his master $700 was collected in Columbia to buy Bennett's freedom.[13]

On the morning of February 15, 1851, Boston attorney Richard H. Dana witnessed the proceedings against a fugitive, Fred Wilkins (or "Shadrach"), in the Court House, opposite his office. Dana returned to his office, and was planning the next legal step in Wilkins's defense when, according to Dana's diary,

> we heard a shout from the Court House, continued into a yell of triumph, & in an instant after, down the steps came two huge negroes, bearing the prisoner between them, with

> his clothes half torn off, & so stupefied by the sudden rescue and the violence of his dragging off, that he sat almost down, & I thought had fainted; but the men seized him, & being powerful fellows, hurried him through the Square into Court St., where he found the use of his feet, & they went off toward Cambridge, like a black squall, the crowd driving along with them & cheering as they went. It was all done in an instant, too quick to be believed, & so successful was it that not only was no negro arrested, but no attempt was made at pursuit.

Dana reports that no officers were injured in this black-led rescue, but that "the sword of Justice," which the fugitive slave commissioner" had displayed on his desk, was carried off by an old negro." [14]

While slave owners loudly proclaimed their chattel were content, black resistance to the fugitive slave law provided eloquent proof of an oppressed people's desire to be free.

In September, 1851, the very month that the Christiana resistance exploded in Pennsylvania, an article by Dr. Samuel Cartwright was appearing in *DeBow's Review*, a periodical published in Louisiana. *DeBow's* devoted its pages to the interests and enlightenment of American slave owners. Dr. Cartwright's article was devoted to the "Diseases and Peculiarities of the Negro Race." The doctor had discovered two diseases "peculiar to negroes." To one illness he gave the Latin name "Dysaethsia Aethiopica . . . called by Overseers, 'Rascality.'" This was the complaint that caused slaves

> to do much mischief which appears as if intentional, but is mostly owing to stupidness of mind and insensibility of nerves induced by the disease. Thus they break, waste, and destroy everything they handle,—abuse horses and cattle, —tear, burn, or rend their own clothing, and, paying no attention to the rights of property, steal others, to replace what they have destroyed. . . . They slight their work,—cut up corn, cane, cotton, or tobacco when hoeing, as if for pure mischief. They raise disturbances with their overseers and fellow-servants, and seem insensible to pain when subjected to punishment. . . .

The second disease discovered by Dr. Cartwright he named "Drapetomania, Or The Disease Causing Negroes to Run Away." The doctor derived his medical term from one Greek word meaning *runaway slave,* and another word meaning *mad* or *crazy.* The disease was "unknown to our medical authorities," said Dr. Cartwright,

> although its diagnostic symptom, the absconding from service, is well known to our planters and overseers. . . . The cause in most of the cases, that induces the negro to run away from service, is as much a disease of the mind as any other species of mental alienation, and much more curable as a general rule. With the advantages of proper medical advice, strictly followed, this troublesome practice that many negroes have of running away, can be almost entirely prevented, although the slaves be located on the borders of a free state; within a stone's throw of the abolitionists. . . .
>
> Before the negroes run away, unless they are frightened or panic-struck, they become sulky and dissatisfied. The cause of this sulkiness and dissatisfaction should be inquired into and removed, or they are apt to run away or fall into negro consumption. When sulky and dissatisfied with cause, the experience of . . . [overseers and slave owners] was decidedly in favor of whipping them out of it, as a preventive measure against absconding, or further bad conduct. It was called whipping the devil out of them.[15]

Although a later age may find it hard to believe Dr. Cartwright's diagnoses were not intended as satire, it does appear that the doctor was perfectly serious. Dr. Cartwright was a highly respected medical man, and a professor at the University of Louisiana, whose articles were widely published in the south. The doctor's attribution of slave resistance to "disease" reveals, in a startling way, the tremendous gulf between the races.

On June 5, 1851, a serialized novel by a Massachusetts woman began to appear in the *National Era,* a successful anti-slavery newspaper published in the nation's capital. The author's name was Harriet Beecher Stowe, and the novel was *Uncle Tom's Cabin.* It is a note of some irony that the book which created the prototype of the submissive, unresisting "Uncle Tom" appeared just three months before the battle at Christiana—a classic example of American black resistance. Like Mrs. Stowe's novel, the Christiana resistance even included among its participants a black heroine named Eliza, William Parker's wife. The black resisters at Christiana also reportedly sang a rousing slave hymn quoted in chapter four of Mrs. Stowe's book, the chorus of which was:

> Die on the field of battle,
> Die on the field of battle,
> Glory in my soul.[16]

5 Fugitives

ON CHRISTMAS DAY, 1849, a Maryland Quaker, before a justice of the peace, charged a free black man with the theft of some wheat. The Quaker, Elias Mathews,

> solemnly, seriously and truly declared and affirmed, that on the 2nd day of November last, a certain colored man named Abraham Johnston, brought to his grist mill, in Baltimore county, a lot of wheat (five bushels). . . .[1]

Johnston's bringing wheat to sell had made Mathews suspicious. The free black man had no land on which to raise wheat, and no money to buy it. Mathews asked Johnston where he got the wheat, and the black man, evidently trusting in the Quaker's sympathy, told him he had received it from several slaves of Edward Gorsuch. Johnston said "the person who had been in the habit of receiving from them had closed up. . . ." The Quaker immediately informed slave owner Edward Gorsuch who, upon going to see the wheat, claimed it as his. As a retailer of flour Gorsuch kept careful account of the wheat stored and withdrawn from his granary.

According to Gorsuch, "I said nothing to my colored boys" about the grain theft, but had a state warrant issued for the free black, Abraham Johnston.[2] The news of the warrant spread quickly and the black man went into hiding. The execution of the warrant was first entrusted to Constable Bond, but Bond being unsuccessful in his search, the job of finding and arresting the free black man was transferred to "Bill" Foster, "something of a local terror to wrongdoers." The black man was never caught.

It was November, and the Gorsuch farm was busy. The blacks

> were cutting and topping the corn, hauling in the un-shucked ears with ox-carts to the barn floor where, by the aid of lanterns, the whole household, mechanics and slaves engaged nightly in husking bee merriment.

But some of Gorsuch's slaves were not so merry. Rumors had spread that four of them had been implicated, with Johnston, in the grain theft. Although they had not yet been directly accused of any crime, Gorsuch's four "boys," George and Joshua Hammond, Nelson Ford, and Noah Buley, were restless and talked together quietly. One of the four asked two white carpenters working on the farm "if the Boss is going to husk corn tonight?" Another of the four announced he was going to set a rabbit trap, for it was "going to be a very dark night." The night *was* dark. After everyone was asleep the four slaves crawled quietly out the skylight of one of Gorsuch's back buildings, made their way down a handily placed ladder, and up the York turnpike.[3]

Gorsuch's four fugitives were evidently joined by Abraham Johnston. Gorsuch says that Johnston, hearing of the warrant out for his arrest, had

> secreted himself for a few days, till my boys found out what was going on, and he and four of my colored boys put out to Pennsylvania.

Gorsuch's carpenter remembered being aroused early one morning by the slave owner's son Dickinson, calling from downstairs, that "the boys are all gone." Perhaps the escape had been precipitated by the slaves' being caught stealing. But perhaps they had been stealing to get money for their escape. In any case, Gorsuch's four "boys" had decided to start the new year, and the second half of the century, as free men.[4]

Edward Gorsuch had been born on April 17, 1795, nineteen years after the American Revolution. He had inherited a number

"Retreat Farm," Home of the Gorsuches, between Monkton and Glencoe, Baltimore Co., Md. (Hensel, *Christiana*)

of slaves and several hundred acres of land; Gorsuch's home stood on property owned by his family for two hundred years. The Gorsuches were an old and prominent Maryland family. Charles Gorsuch, an Englishman by birth, and "a refugee from Cromwell's civil war," had settled in Virginia in 1652. Later, the Gorsuch family moved to Maryland, and Charles purchased 7,500 acres—land on which the town of Baltimore would one day be built. In 1851, Edward Gorsuch's homestead, "Retreat Farm," was situated about twenty miles from that city. Edward Gorsuch had five children, two daughters and three sons. His eldest son, John S., was a Methodist clergyman in the nation's capital.[5]

Edward Gorsuch was a "good" slave owner. As an active member of the Whig Party Gorsuch represented the more moderate members of his class. As an active member of the Methodist Episcopal Church Gorsuch believed that all white men were created equal. As a "class leader" in his church Gorsuch played an almost ministerial role. "Class meeting," as described by James Weldon Johnson, is

> the Methodist substitute for the Catholic confession. Each member of the class rises in turn and tells his class-leader what his spiritual experiences have been during the week past; whether there has been a falling from or a growth

toward grace. The leader then gives words of comfort and counsel to each as his case may require—a very self-satisfying function.[6]

Edward Gorsuch's great-granddaughter, interviewed recently in Maryland at the age of eighty-three—an alert, spry-sounding southern belle with a thick drawl—tells Gorsuch's story as it had come down to her. Neither the Civil War, nor any more recent occurrence seems to have affected her thinking in the slightest; her words would seem to accurately convey the family's feelings and attitudes even as they existed in Edward Gorsuch's own day.

The slave owner "was well thought of around here," she says:

> I imagine he was a benevolent lookin' old soul, from what I've understood; he had a beard on his face, he was tall, and being an English descendant, he was like the English people, he liked land and wanted it, and wanted it well taken care of. He would never allow anybody to call the soil "dirt"; that must be called "earth."

She had been told that Gorsuch "was a religious man," as was his son Dickinson. Edward Gorsuch was called a "church leader." Great-grandfather Gorsuch was said to go to one church in the morning, another in the afternoon, and another at night: "If you didn't go to church there wasn't very much to do." The religious life of Gorsuch's slaves was not ignored: "They taught them 'The Lord's Prayer' and the Commandments," says his great-granddaughter.

"The slaves were valuable," she says,

> my gracious, three hundred dollars wasn't anything in those days for a good man—because they were trained; the Southern people needed them, they couldn't go on without them. They treated them right, now I will tell you that! Say you had a valuable horse, you wouldn't treat it badly. They were owned by the masters, not as an animal, but as human beings, and they were treated right.

Edward Gorsuch is said to have given some of his slaves their freedom when they had served him twenty-eight years:

> After they were given their freedom they were paid wages. They still stayed on with the master, they still had their

cabin, just the same as in the slave days. They could go if they wanted to, but they didn't want to because it was home.[7]

The Governor of Maryland eulogized Edward Gorsuch as "a highly respectable citizen." Gorsuch was a liberal slave owner. Records are said to indicate his planning to emancipate at least six slaves. Uncle John Gorsuch had willed that Jarret Wallace and certain other slaves be emancipated upon reaching a stipulated age, and in 1849 Wallace was actually freed by Edward Gorsuch. The Gorsuch family reports:

> Jarret Wallace had during the period of his bondage so served his master and was so appreciated by him that after he became free Mr. Gorsuch retained him in his employ as his "market man" to sell his products in Baltimore.

In November, 1849, the month of his four slaves' escape, Gorsuch was building a new tenant house for his former slave Jarret Wallace.[8]

The four Gorsuch slaves implicated in the grain theft had also been scheduled for emancipation, which made it especially difficult for the slave owner's family to understand their theft— and their nerve in running away. According to the Reverend John S. Gorsuch, the slave owner's eldest son: "These negroes were to be free at the age of twenty-eight, and this fact they knew." After their escape it is said that news of the four fugitives reached the Gorsuch family:

> During the winter it was reported that these men were suffering for food. A colored man was sent to find them, and assure them that if they would come home and behave themselves nothing would be said to them about their theft. They were found, but did not return.[9]

Pennsylvania historian W. U. Hensel, who interviewed surviving family members in about 1911, reports:

> Mr. Gorsuch had such confidence in his benevolence as their master that he always believed if he could meet or communicate directly with them he could get them back.

Gorsuch's great-granddaughter emphasizes that Gorsuch thought his slaves "wanted to come home." [10] That the four fugitives might not regard the Gorsuch residence as "home," or their enslavement as benevolent, that they might not wish to return, did not apparently occur to the Gorsuch family.

The four fugitives had made their own home for themselves in Lancaster County, Pennsylvania, near William Parker's. Peter Woods, a black resident of Christiana, in his mid-teens at the time, recalls that Gorsuch's fugitives "were in our neighborhood a couple of years . . .":

> They lived here among us adjoining me. One lived with Joseph Pownall. His name was John Beard. He was a little brown-skinned fellow—a pleasant chap.

The 1850 Census lists "John Beard," a laborer, as living with the Joseph Pownall family, and gives his age as twenty-three. Woods told a neighbor that "John Beard" was the alias of Gorsuch's slave Nelson Ford. Fugitives commonly took new names to avoid discovery. It was this Nelson Ford, a teamster, whom the Gorsuch family claimed had always been spared heavy work by his master. Ford, it was said, always got help when he needed it because he was such a "delicate young fellow."

Peter Woods says that another of Gorsuch's fugitives, "Alexander Scott," "a tall yellow colored fellow with straight hair, told how they four happened to run away." Woods recalls vaguely that Scott said he brought Gorsuch's fugitives with him

> in a wagon to Baltimore, or he said he had come with a big load of grain for his master. He put them on the cars at Baltimore, then sent his master's team back and took the next train too, and that way they came up among the Quakers in this country which they knew was a good point on the underground railway.[11]

Meanwhile, back in Maryland, Edward Gorsuch had written to his governor. On November 29, 1849, soon after the discovery of the grain theft, and the disappearance of Abraham Johnston with his four slaves, Gorsuch asked the Governor of Maryland to ask the Governor of Pennsylvania to arrange for Johnston's extradi-

tion. The Governor of Maryland, on December 31, 1849, oblig-
ingly requested that the free black fugitive

>be apprehended and delivered to Dickinson Gorsuch who
>is hereby authorized to receive and convey him to the State
>of Maryland, there to be dealt with according to the law.

The Governor of Pennsylvania, a Whig with some anti-slavery
sentiment, did not act on the extradition request.[12]
A few weeks later on January 11, 1850, the persistent Edward
Gorsuch again wrote to his governor, asking him to ask the
Pennsylvania governor to arrest and extradite the four fugitives
implicated in the grain theft. Gorsuch, evidently somewhat
misinformed, said he had "good reason to believe" that the four
slaves were living in Chester, or Berks County, Pennsylvania, and
requested that his son Dickinson be appointed to go for the
fugitives. The Governor of Pennsylvania again apparently failed
to act.[13]
Almost two years after his four slaves' escape a letter was sent
to Edward Gorsuch by a Pennsylvania informer. Postmarked
Penningtonville, Pennsylvania, August 29, 1851, the letter reads
exactly as follows:

Lancaster, Co. 28 August 1851.
Respected friend, I have the required
Information of four men that is within
Two miles of each other. now the best
Way is for you to come as A hunter
Disguised about two days ahead of your son and let him
come
By way of Philadelphia and get the deputy marshal John
Nagle I think is his name. tell him the situation
And he can get force of the right kind it will take
About twelve so that they can divide and take them
All within half an hour. now if you can come on the 2nd or
3rd of September come on & I will
Meet you at the gap when you get their
Inquire for Benjamin Clay's tavern let
Your son and the marshal get out
Kinyer's hotel now if you cannot come

At the time spoken of write very soon
And let me know when you can
I wish you to come as soon as you possibly can
                              Very respectfully thy friend
                              William M.P.

On the bottom, in pencil, the letter was signed "Wm. M. Padgett." [14]

Sources differ on the identity of this Padgett. According to local historian W. U. Hensel, Padgett was a farmhand living with a family located between Gap and Christiana. The family had previously lived in Baltimore County, Maryland. According to George Steele, a resident of Christiana at the time, Padgett was a member of

> a gang of horse thieves and counterfeiters who had their headquarters at Clemson's Tavern near Mount Vernon. They had started the business of slave capturing.

Steele says that Padgett,

> was nominally a mender of clocks and tramped over the country and cultivated intimacy with runaway slaves and found out where they came from and the names of their owners and would write to the slave owners and guide them when they came to arrest their slaves, and get a reward.[15]

Whoever he was, William Padgett's letter to Gorsuch was reprinted in the anti-slavery press following the Christiana resistance.

This unflattering publicity is said to have brought Gorsuch's informer to Philadelphia to reprimand editor J. Miller McKim for publishing his name and deed in the *Anti-Slavery Standard*. McKim is said to have abruptly ended the interview by asking:

> Then I understand, sir, you have come here to discipline me for publishing your name in that capacity, and not to deny the charge?" [16]

Pennsylvanian R. C. Smedley, a third source on the informer's identity, says that the letter was written by one who had presented himself to the blacks as "their faithful friend":

J. Miller McKim. (Still; Wm. L. Katz Collection)

After the fear of the colored people had somewhat abated, their feeling of indignation toward him for this treacherous act became so intense, that, apprehending revenge from them, he disappeared from that section, and has not been known to return there since.[17]

Upon receiving Padgett's letter, the persistent slave owner, Edward Gorsuch, prepared to go to Pennsylvania. Gorsuch's son Dickinson, reports Smedley, argued with his father against the undertaking, "But the old man was 'determined to have his property,' and would not be counselled." [18] Edward Gorsuch's repeatedly proclaimed attachment to "his property" is mentioned by almost every participant in the events that followed.

In Maryland, Edward Gorsuch quickly gathered together a slave hunting party of six: himself; his son Dickinson; his nephew, Dr. Thomas Pearce; his cousin, Joshua M. Gorsuch; his two neighbors, Nathan Nelson and Nicholas Hutchings. Dr. Pearce, it is reported, was also seeking a fugitive of his own, who had escaped the same night as Gorsuch's. On September 8, Edward Gorsuch took an express train to Philadelphia, as informer Padgett had suggested, coming to that city ahead of the rest of his party.[19]

In Philadelphia, Gorsuch went to see fugitive slave commissioner Edward D. Ingraham, and on September 9 obtained four fugitive slave warrants. Ingraham was one of the few men in Pennsylvania who had accepted a special commission under the new fugitive slave law. Ingraham was notorious. Not many

Dickinson Gorsuch. (Lancaster County Historical Society)

months previously, in December, 1850, the Commissioner had heard the case of a black man arrested in Philadelphia by slave catchers; the black had reportedly "resisted the attempt, when a pistol was placed at his head." The prisoner claimed his name was Adam Gibson. A witness, who admitted he had previously been arrested for kidnapping, identified the black man as Emory Rice, a fugitive slave of William Knight, of Cecil County, Maryland. Two black witnesses "swore positively that they had known the man arrested from childhood, and that his name was Adam Gibson." Ingraham quickly handed the prisoner over to the slave catchers, and he was taken to Maryland. There slave owner William Knight declared that Gibson was not his slave. The black man was allowed to return to Philadelphia, and eventually brought suit against his abductors.[20]

On September 9 Commissioner Ingraham directed Henry H. Kline to head Edward Gorsuch's posse as deputy marshal. Kline was a slightly deaf, but formidably bearded and mustachioed officer, also notorious in the Philadelphia black community as a slave-catching constable. Two other officers, John Agan and Thompson Tully, engaged to join the posse, Edward Gorsuch paying them something in advance for their services.[21]

Marshal Kline and Gorsuch did not know their activities were being watched by the special secret vigilance committee of black Philadelphia abolitionists, led by William Still, an active agent of the Pennsylvania underground railroad. Still reports that, fortunately for Gorsuch's fugitives,

> the plans of the slave hunters and officials leaked out while arrangements were making in Philadelphia for the capture,

William Still. (Still; Wm. L. Katz Collection)

and information being sent to the Anti-slavery office, a messenger was at once dispatched to Christiana to put all persons supposed to be in danger on their guard.

Among those thus notified, were brave hearts, who did not believe in running away from slave-catchers. They resolved to stand up for the right of self-defense. They loved liberty and hated slavery, and when the slave-catchers arrived, they were prepared for them.

The messenger sent to Christiana was a "portly," light-skinned Philadelphian named Samuel Williams, whose tavern in the city's black community was named "The Bolivar House" after the South American creole revolutionary.[22]

Early on the morning of Wednesday, September 10, Samuel Williams took the train toward Christiana—and rode in the same coach as several members of the Gorsuch posse! Williams was recognized by John Agan, one of Gorsuch's hired officers. Williams's surprising lack of caution was apparently calculated; the black man no doubt wished to let the posse know their plans were detected, and the fugitives alerted, hoping by this tactic to discourage their slave-catching attempt. Most slave hunters counted on surprise for success and safety.

On the afternoon of the previous day, Tuesday, September 9, Marshal Kline had arrived alone in the Lancaster County area to make preliminary arrangements. There Kline hired a horse and wagon to take him to his Penningtonville rendezvous with the other posse members. But as he raced across the countryside, Kline began to experience a series of farcical misadventures more appropriate to a Keystone Cop than to a U.S. marshal. First Kline's wagon broke down, delaying him; it was therefore after twelve on the night of Wednesday, September 10 when he finally reached the Penningtonville tavern, to find his posse had already left.

To Kline's surprise, who should be standing outside the tavern but the black Philadelphian Samuel Williams, wearing a "white roundabout" and a "straw hat." Kline recognized Williams, and Williams recognized Kline. Marshal Kline says he attempted to confuse Williams about his real purpose in the area:

> I went into the tavern and talked about horse thieves. The colored man came in and talked about horse thieves, and I turned around and said, "Hello, Sam, what are you doing here?" . . . He said, "Your horse thieves were here and gone. You might as well go home."

By "horse thieves" Williams no doubt referred to Marshal Kline's own posse. When the Marshal pretended not to understand, Williams said, "Oh, I know what you are about."

Still claiming to be looking for "horse thieves," Kline started by wagon for the Gap. Looking back the marshal saw Williams following him. At a Gap tavern Kline stopped and, concluding that Williams would follow, also asked this tavern keeper if he had seen any horse thieves:

> He said no; but he had seen a couple of men, very suspicious looking, and they had gone to Philadelphia.[23]

This "suspicious looking" pair were probably Marshal Kline's own fellow officers, Agan and Tully, who had apparently announced their intention of returning home.

Samuel Williams did not follow Kline to the Gap, but went on to Christiana, where he left a note of warning with a local black man.[24] Marshal Kline remained an hour and a half at the Gap, then drove to Parkesburg where he finally found his officers, Agan and Tully, "in the bar-room asleep." The two were indeed on their way back to Philadelphia. Having seen Samuel Williams on the morning train, and realizing the posse had been discovered, Agan and Tully were apparently anxious to depart the scene of possible danger.

Leaving his two nervous officers, Kline at last met Edward Gorsuch in Sadsbury. Gorsuch was evidently angry with "the delinquent Marshal." It was already nine o'clock on Wednesday morning, too late to attempt the slave catching. The original plan had been to arrest the fugitives early Wednesday morning before daylight, "but this was frustrated by the non-appearance of the deputy marshal, who had the authority and papers." When Marshal Kline finally met Gorsuch he lied to the slave owner, blaming his delay on having "been followed by a negro, whom he knew to be a spy," and whom he had tried to elude by rapid driving, thus breaking his wagon. Kline's wagon had broken down *before* he met Samuel Williams.[25]

Edward Gorsuch went off alone to find officers Agan and Tully and try to persuade them to remain with the posse. He found them, gave them "more money," and they said they would return from Philadelphia late that night, perhaps promising to bring reinforcements.[26] At eleven o'clock that night the posse went to meet Agan and Tully, but when the train from Philadelphia arrived, the two officers were not on it, and never returned. The seven-man posse went on to the Gap, where they arrived at about 1:30 in the morning.

A few hours later, at about four o'clock on the morning of Thursday, September 11, the posse started toward Christiana. "It was a heavy, foggy morning." The party made its way down a railroad track. Between the Gap and Christiana they met a guide, "disguised," says Marshal Kline, by a straw hat with a handkerchief tied around it. This bonneted guide, a white man, was probably William Padgett.[27] The guide led the posse on, and finally pointed to a house. Here one of Gorsuch's fugitives was supposed to be living. Gorsuch wanted the marshal to split the slave-catching party, leaving a few posse members to go after this one slave, the rest going after two fugitives further on. The marshal did not want to split the posse; he told Gorsuch it would "take all the force we had" to take the other two slaves. Gorsuch relented—this one slave had a wife back in Maryland, and, thought Gorsuch, would probably "come home without any trouble." [28]

The posse continued on. They crossed a cornfield. About fifteen minutes before reaching their destination, they were startled to hear a horn or bugle sound, a short distance away. Gorsuch's neighbor Nathan Nelson "thought it was an early hour for breakfast." The sound seemed to come from the direction of the railroad, and was probably only a signal to awake the Irish railroad laborers laying a new track.[29] But the nervous posse was nearing its destination.

About two miles from Christiana they came to a long, narrow

The Parkers' Home. (Courtesy LaVerne D. Rettew, Christiana)

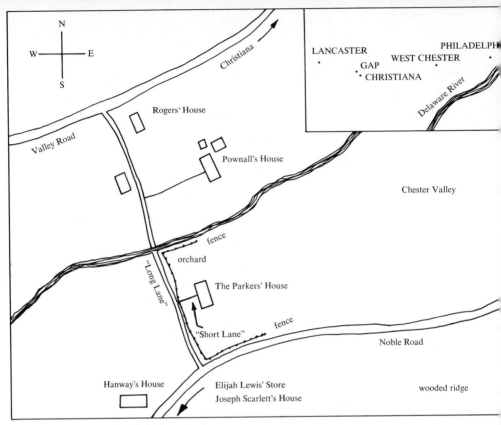

Site of the Christiana Resistance.

lane that crossed a shallow valley. They walked quietly down the lane, then stopped briefly for refreshments. According to the marshal:

> One of the party had a carpet bag, and we took out some cheese and crackers which we eat, and we fixed our amunitions and started.

As they passed a creek, Dr. Pearce stopped and was going to get a drink. The marshal told Pearce, "It won't do to stop, for it is daylight." The guide pointed to a short lane, leading up to a stone house. Here, he said, two of Gorsuch's slaves could be found. It was the home of William Parker. The guide left the posse. Suddenly, a black man walked out of the lane leading to the house. Spying the posse, he raced back to the house, chased by the whites. Running up the lane, Marshal Kline fell over a fence; his "revolvers fell one way and I the other." The marshal picked himself up, ran to the house, and followed Edward Gorsuch inside.[30]

6 Prelude

A SHORT TIME after the kidnapping at Chamberlain's in January, 1851, William Parker says,

> it was whispered about that the slaveholders intended to make an attack on my house; but, as I had often been threatened, I gave the report little attention. About the same time, however, two letters were found thrown carelessly about, as if to attract notice. These letters stated that kidnappers would be at my house on a certain night, and warned me to be on my guard. Still I did not let the matter trouble me. But it was not idle rumor. The bloodhounds were on my track.

On Wednesday, September 10, the day before the Gorsuch posse appeared at William Parker's, the neighborhood had been informed of the impending attack. According to Parker, the warning brought by Philadelphian Samuel Williams "spread through the vicinity like a fire in the prairies." [1]

That afternoon, Dr. Augustus Cain and Henry Young were standing in the road talking when two black men, John Clark and Josephus Washington, came walking up. Young recalled Washington having "a gun in one hand and a paper in the other." The apparently illiterate Washington asked, "Doctor can you read the paper to us?" The notice from Samuel Williams contained the names of Gorsuch's fugitives, and a warning that "kidnappers" were coming up, "and they must be prepared to meet the Marshall, and also to notify the people." That same afternoon a neighbor saw Josephus Washington go by "with a gun and a shotpouch." John Long and another black, Lewis Reynolds, appeared at the farm of Lewis Cooper and spoke with three blacks who were ploughing.[2]

When Parker came home from work that Wednesday evening he found a number of black people in his house, including two of Gorsuch's fugitives, "all of them excited about the rumor" that slave catchers were on the way. Parker says, "I laughed at them, and said it was all talk." Parker, writing some years later, says casually that the two fugitives "stopped for the night with us, and we went to bed as usual." But Frederick Douglass, writing a few days after seeing Parker, not long after the event, reports that the black people at Parker's

> sat up late in apprehension of an attack, but finally went to bed, but sleep—they could not.

Seven black people stayed together at Parker's that night—waiting. The group included Parker; his wife, Eliza; his brother-in-law, Alexander Pinckney; Pinckney's wife (Eliza's sister), Hannah; Parker's friend, Abraham Johnson; and two of Gorsuch's fugitives, whose names Parker gives as Joshua Kite and Samuel Thompson.[3] These seven black people had decided to resist.

Sarah Pownall, wife of Levi Pownall, Parker's Quaker landlord, reports a conversation she had with the black leader, the night before the battle. She urged Parker

> if the slaveholders should come, not to lead the colored people to resist the Fugitive Slave Law by force of arms, but to escape to Canada. He replied that if the laws protected colored men as they did white men, he too would be non-resistant and not fight, but would appeal to the laws. "But," said he, "The laws for personal protection are not made for us, and we are not bound to obey them. If a fight occurs I want the whites to keep away. They have a country and may obey the laws. But we have no country."[4]

(top) The Parkers' Home. (Courtesy the late Walter Miller, Christiana)

(above) A side view of the Parkers' home. (*Lancaster County Historical Society Papers*, Vol. 10, No. 10 [1906])

"No country." No protection. The words echo Parker's feelings in his youth: "No home, no protector, no mother, no attachments."

But the adult Parker now had attachments, to family, to friends, to his people; he was determined to protect them.

Just before dawn on September 11, 1851, Joshua Kite, one of Gorsuch's fugitives, left Parker's and started out for work, apparently happy that the slave catchers had not come. As the Gorsuch posse moved up the lane toward Parker's, J. M. Gorsuch "heard someone singing." In the short lane leading to Parker's, Joshua Kite met the Gorsuch posse; racing back to the house, he "burst open the door," and ran upstairs to where the others were sleeping, crying, "O William! kidnappers! kidnappers!"

Having chased the black man to the house, Gorsuch and the marshal went inside, through the door which Joshua, in his haste, had left open. Marshal Kline demanded Gorsuch's fugitives. Then, says Kline, Edward Gorsuch called his slave by name, telling him to "Come down":

> "I know your voice, I know you;" he said, "If you come down and go home with me without any trouble I will look over the past." One of the negroes replied "If you take one of us, you must take us over our dead bodies." [5]

The Reverend J. S. Gorsuch was not present at the scene, but was informed soon afterward that his father called to one of his slaves

> that he saw him, and told him that if he would come down peaceably and go home with him, he would treat him as kindly as before he ran away. Resistance, he said, would do no good, for he came with the proper officer and authority, and he would not leave the premises without his property.[6]

Nicholas Hutchings, outside the house, heard Edward Gorsuch say that if his slave

> would come down and go home with him he would forgive him for the past. There was something thrown from the window and struck Pearce.

Dr. Pearce reports that "a missile" thrown from an upstairs window "resulted in giving me a very black eye, and quite staggered me. . . ." Joshua M. Gorsuch was struck on the

shoulder by a piece of wood thrown from above.[7] The resistance
had begun.

Inside the house, Parker stood defiantly at the top of the stairs,
looking down on Kline and Edward Gorsuch below, the other
black men and women in the room behind him. The slave owner
and the marshal heard guns being loaded in the room above.[8] A
parley began. "Who are you?" demanded Parker. "I am the
United States Marshal," answered Kline, making a move toward
the stairs. Parker says:

> I then told him to take another step, and I would break
> his neck.
> He said again, "I am the United States Marshal."
> I told him I did not care for him nor the United States.
> At that he turned and went down stairs.

Upstairs, Alexander Pinckney asked the other blacks, "Where is
the use in fighting? They will take us." He turned to go downstairs
and give up. Parker says that Kline heard Pinckney, and
exclaimed, "Yes, give up, for we can and will take you anyhow."
Parker urged the blacks "not to be afraid, nor to give up to any
slaveholder, but to fight until death."

> "Yes," said Kline, "I have heard many a negro talk as
> big as you, and then have taken him; and I'll take you."
> "You have not taken me yet," I replied; "and if you
> undertake it you will have your name recorded in history
> for this day's work."
> Mr. Gorsuch then spoke, and said,—"Come, Mr. Kline,
> let's go up stairs and take them. We *can* take them. Come,
> follow me. I'll go up and get my property. What's in the
> way? The law is in my favor, and the people are in my
> favor."
> At that he began to ascend the stair; but I said to
> him,—"See here, old man, you can come up, but you can't
> go down again. Once up here, you are mine."

When Gorsuch continued to mount the stairs, a five-pronged "fish
gig" came hurtling past him, followed by an ax.[9]
According to Parker:

> Kline then said,—"Stop, Mr. Gorsuch. I will read the
> warrant, and then, I think, they will give up."

He then read the warrant, and said, "Now, you see, we are commanded to take you, dead or alive; so you may as well give up at once."

"Go up, Mr. Kline," then said Gorsuch, "you are the Marshal."

Kline started, and when a little way up said, "I am coming."

I said, "Well, come on."

But he was too cowardly to show his face.

Safely downstairs Kline again demanded that the blacks surrender. To Parker, Kline said:

"I'll not trouble the slaves. I will take you and make you pay for all."

"Well," I answered, "take me and make me pay for all. I'll pay for all."

Edward Gorsuch put in his usual refrain. "You have my property." Parker answered:

"Go in the room down there, and see if there is anything there belonging to you. There are beds and a bureau, chairs, and other things. Then go out to the barn; there you will find a cow and some hogs. See if any of them are yours."

He said,—"They are not mine; I want my men. They are here, and I am bound to have them."

When Parker denied that men could be property, Gorsuch declared he didn't want to hear the black man's abolition lectures.[10]

According to Parker, Marshal Kline now told the blacks, "I am tired of waiting on you; I see you are not going to give up." The marshal loudly called out an order to one of his men: "Go to the barn and fetch some straw. . . . I will set the house on fire, and burn them up." Parker replied, "Burn us up and welcome . . .":

"None but a coward would say the like. You can burn us, but you can't take us; before I give up, you will see my ashes scattered on the earth." [11]

Suddenly, the trumpeting of a horn sounded from a garret window of the house. Parker's wife, Eliza, had asked "if she should blow the horn, to bring friends to our assistance." Parker agreed:

> It was a custom with us, when a horn was blown at an unusual hour, to proceed to the spot promptly to see what was the matter.

"What do you mean by blowing that horn?" asked the marshal nervously, ordering his men to shoot the trumpeter. Parker's wife sounded the horn again. From their position in a peach tree, two of the marshal's men fired at Eliza Parker. Eliza knelt down beside the window, and, says Parker, with "the horn resting on the sill, blew blast after blast, while the shots poured thick and fast around her." She was fired at ten or twelve times. But the thick stone walls and deep windows of the house protected her. These shots, claims Parker, fired by the marshal's men at his wife, were the first exchanged in the encounter.[12]

"I want my property," said Edward Gorsuch, "and I will have it." The slave owner had gone outside the house, and looked up at Parker who was leaning out a second-story window. Parker says that the marshal, instigated by Gorsuch, then fired a pistol at him. The shot broke the glass in the window above the black leader's head. Parker says he then

> seized a gun and aimed it at Gorsuch's breast, . . . but Pinckney caught my arm and said, "Don't shoot." The gun went off, just grazing Gorsuch's shoulder . . . another one of the party fired at me, but missed. Dickinson Gorsuch, I then saw, was preparing to shoot; and I told him if he missed, I would show him where shooting first came from.[13]

Marshal Kline says that Gorsuch had just gone outside when the slave owner was fired on by Parker in what Kline claims was the first shot exchanged in the confrontation. The marshal says he *then* fired straight up in the air, as a warning.[14]

Whoever fired first, Joshua M. Gorsuch saw a shot pass close by Edward Gorsuch's hat:

> Edward Gorsuch observed, you have shot at me; and demanded they should give his property up out of the house.

Gorsuch told the marshal he was determined to have his slaves and would not go home without them.[15] William Parker then asked the whites

> what they would have done, had they been in our position. "I know you want to kill us," I said, "for you have shot at us time and again. We have only fired twice, although we have guns and ammunition, and could kill you all if we would, but we do not want to shed blood."
>
> "If you do not shoot any more," then said Kline, "I will stop my men from firing."

It was now about sunrise. According to Parker, Edward Gorsuch called out:

> "Give up, and let me have my property. Hear what the Marshal says; the Marshal is your friend. He advises you to give up without more fuss, for my property I will have."

When Parker denied having Gorsuch's property the slave owner persisted: "You have my men." "Am I your man?" Parker asked, leaning out the window. "No," Gorsuch replied. Parker then called his brother-in-law, Alexander Pinckney, to the window. "Is that your man?" asked Parker. "No," was the reply. Abraham Johnson went to the window next, and "Gorsuch said he was not his man." Says Parker:

> The only plan left was to call both Pinckney and Johnson again; for had I called the others, he would have recognized them, for they were his slaves.[16]

Going to the window again, the twenty-six-year-old Abraham Johnson called out to the fifty-six-year-old Gorsuch:[17]

> "Does such a shrivelled up old slaveholder as you own such a nice, genteel young man as I am?"

"At this," says Parker,

> Gorsuch took offence, and charged me with dictating his language. I then told him there were but five of us, which he denied, and still insisted that I had his property. One of the [Gorsuch] party then attacked the Abolitionists, affirm-

ing that, although they declared there could not be property in man, the Bible was conclusive authority in favor of property in human flesh.

"Yes," said Gorsuch, "does not the Bible say, 'Servants, obey your masters'?"

Parker agreed it did. But, he asked, did not the same Bible say "Give unto your servants that which is just and equal"? Then began a "mutual Scripture inquiry" in which William Parker, the black "preacher," and Edward Gorsuch, the Methodist slave owner, "bandied arguments in the manner of garrulous old wives." Gorsuch quoted Scripture in defense of slavery, Parker quoted Scripture in defense of liberty. "Where," asked Parker, "do you see it in Scripture, that a man should traffic in his brother's blood?" "Do you call a nigger my brother?" asked Gorsuch. "Yes," said Parker.

Samuel Thompson, one of Gorsuch's fugitives, recalled that the slave owner was a "class leader" in his church. At this, says Parker, Gorsuch "hung his head, but said nothing." The blacks then taunted the religious slave owner by singing a popular spiritual, a song whose call and response routine recalled its African origin:

> "Leader, what do you say
> About the judgment day?
> I will die on the field of battle,
> Die on the field of battle,
> With glory in my soul." [18]

"Then," says Parker,

> we all began to shout, singing meantime, and shouted for a long while. Gorsuch, who was standing head bowed, said, "What are you doing now?"
> Samuel Thompson replied, "Preaching a sinner's funeral sermon."

"You had better give up, and come down," said Gorsuch. Parker then addressed the slave owner:

> "I see the sword coming, and, old man, I warn you to flee; if you flee not, your blood be upon your own hand."

Gorsuch answered:

> "You had better give up . . . and come down, for I have
> come a long way this morning, and want my breakfast; for
> my property I will have, or I'll breakfast in hell."

The slave owner "then started up stairs," says Parker, "and
came far enough to see us all plainly." Dickinson Gorsuch "was
standing on an old oven," outside the front door, "and could see
into the up-stairs room through the window. . . ." The blacks
"were just about to fire" on the old slave owner when Dickinson
yelled out:

> "O father, do come down! do come down! They have guns,
> swords, and all kinds of weapons! They'll kill you! Do
> come down!"

When the "old man" turned, and went down to join his son,
Parker noticed that "young Gorsuch could scarce draw breath,
and the father looked more like a dead than a living man."

> The old man stood some time without saying anything; at
> last he said, as if soliloquizing, "I want my property, and I
> will have it."

It was now about seven o'clock in the morning. Dickinson
Gorsuch addressed the marshal:

> "Don't ask them to give up,—*make* them do it. We have
> money, and can call men to take them. What is it that
> money won't buy?"
> Then said Kline,—"I am getting tired waiting on you; I
> see you are not going to give up."

Intending to "intimidate" the blacks, the marshal wrote a note
and gave it to Joshua Gorsuch. In a loud voice Kline pretended to
send to the sheriff in Lancaster for one hundred reinforcements.[19]
Parker spoke up defiantly:

> "See here! When you go to Lancaster, don't bring a
> hundred men,—bring five hundred. It will take all the men
> in Lancaster to change our purpose or take us alive."

About this time, says Parker, a large number of white men were "coming from all quarters," and the marshal, under authority of the fugitive slave law, was enrolling them as special constables. It is possible that local kidnappers had been informed of the Gorsuch posse's attack and had accompanied them to Parker's. It was rumored that a local gang of kidnappers was lurking in the background during the confrontation, hoping to get hold of the black leader who had interfered with their business.[20]

Some of the blacks again gave signs of hesitating in their resistance. A ten- to fifteen-minute armistice was arranged. Upstairs in the house Alexander Pinckney and his wife, Hannah, wanted to surrender. "We had better give up," said Pinckney. Downstairs, Marshal Kline, hearing Pinckney, called up to Parker:

> "Yes, . . . give up like men. The rest would give up if it were not for you."

Pinckney told Parker, "I am not afraid, . . . but where is the sense in fighting against so many men, and only five of us?" (Pinckney evidently did not count the two women.) The number of white men outside alarmed Pinckney. Parker says he commanded his brother-in-law to be seated, but Pinckney said,

> "No, I will go down stairs."
> I told him, if he attempted it, I should be compelled to blow out his brains. "Don't believe that any living man can take you," I said. "Don't give up to any slaveholder."

By this time, says Parker, Hannah Pinckney had also "become impatient of our persistent course. . . ." Hannah urged her sister, Eliza, to urge Parker to surrender. Furious at her sister's weakening Eliza Parker "seized a corn-cutter, and declared she would cut off the head of the first one who should attempt to give up." Parker asked Abraham Johnson what he wanted to do. "I will fight till I die," said Johnson.[21]

7 "Freedom's Battle"

EARLY THAT MORNING, a fifty-six-year-old black farmer named Isaiah Clarkson, who lived near Parker's, had been passing the leader's house. Seeing the yard full of strangers Clarkson "halted, and was met by a man who presented a pistol to him, and ordered him to leave the place." Clarkson hurried on to the shop of Elijah Lewis, the Quaker postmaster and storekeeper. Lewis was just opening his door when Isaiah Clarkson came up and told Lewis that

> Parker's house was all surrounded by kidnappers; that they had broken into the house and were about to take him away. . . .

Clarkson "insisted" upon Lewis's "going down to see that justice was done." [1]

On his way to Parker's, Elijah Lewis stopped at the home of the white miller, Castner Hanway, who had moved there with his new wife just a few months before. Lewis told Hanway and his helper, Henry Burt, that "William Parker's house was surrounded by kidnappers, who were going to take him." Continuing on his way, Lewis came upon a black man, Jacob Woods, working in a field. Lewis told Woods

> it was no time to take up potatoes, when Mr. Parker's house was all surrounded by kidnappers.

92

Elijah Lewis. (Forbes)

Jacob Woods dropped his work and proceeded to Parker's. After managing to swallow a quick breakfast Castner Hanway, who was feeling "a little unwell," rode to Parker's on his "bald-faced, sorrel horse." Hanway arrived at the scene before Lewis.[2] Upon Hanway's arrival, the Gorsuch posse members all noticed a change in the spirits of the blacks upstairs at Parker's. Dr. Pearce recalls the blacks had seemed to be giving in, but when Hanway rode up "they raised a yell, and became fully confirmed . . . to repel to the very last." Nicholas Hutchings says that before Hanway's appearance, the blacks had "appeared to be rather intimidated"; after the white man's arrival "they appeared to be in great spirits—all of them hallooing and shouting and singing." Nathan Nelson reports that when Hanway rode up "the negroes seemed to rejoice at it, they made a great jumping and a great noise." Dickinson Gorsuch swears that before Hanway's appearance "the negroes seemed as if they would have given up"; after Hanway's appearance Dickinson's father told him the blacks now "seemed to be determined." J. M. Gorsuch declares that when Hanway rode up "the colored people in the house stated they felt like dying . . . they appeared to be inspired. . . . They appeared to rally." [3]

The whites in the Gorsuch posse perceived the elation of the blacks as a reaction to the arrival of a white man, Castner Hanway. But the blacks' rejuvenated spirits seem to have had a significantly different origin. Immediately after Hanway's arrival at the scene, a number of armed blacks had first begun to appear.[4]

Parker says that Hannah and Alexander Pinckney had just spoken of giving up when from their position at the second-story window, those inside the house noticed the approach of at least one familiar black ally:

> Another one of Gorsuch's slaves was coming along the highroad at this time, and I beckoned to him to go around. Pinckney saw him, and soon became more inspirited.

Nicholas Hutchings reports that he

> saw one of Mr. Gorsuch's slaves named Noah Buley, ride up on a grey horse, near where Hanway was, and get off his horse, fasten it in the lane and load his gun. It was a fine looking horse he had, and a handsome gun.

It was no doubt for Buley, described by the Gorsuch family as "a copper colored mulatto . . . of a treacherous disposition," or for other black reinforcements that the cheer went up from those upstairs in the house, not for the white man, Castner Hanway.[5] The whites' very perception was distorted by their idea that the black resisters *must* owe their renewed inspiration to a white man.

Numbers of armed blacks now began to appear, summoned by the trumpeting of the horn and by word of mouth. Earlier that morning a local Paul Revere, the Quaker Joseph Scarlett, had galloped on horseback around the neighborhood warning that the kidnappers had come. Scarlett had informed a black man, John Roberts, that kidnappers were at Parker's and told Roberts to warn any other blacks he knew. Roberts went to Joseph Moore's, where Samuel Thompson (allegedly one of Gorsuch's fugitives) lived, but no one was home. Roberts went to borrow a gun from a white man, Joseph Townsend. Roberts told Townsend that kidnappers were at Parker's. The white man loaded his gun and gave it to the black man.[6]

From out of the woods and across the fields armed black men began to converge on Parker's. They came with stones, rails, canes, clubs, rifles, revolvers, pistols, pitchforks, scythes, and corn cutters. Their everyday means of work were taken up as weapons. Some were said to have come with swords. The seven blacks in the house were joined by at least eight others, perhaps by as many as 15. Altogether, from 15 to 25 blacks probably actually partici-

Ezekiel Thompson, known as "The Indian Negro." (Hensel, *Christiana*)

pated in the resistance. Later estimates of from 60 to 75, to more than 150 were, no doubt, greatly exaggerated.[7]

Marshal Kline saw a group of "ten to twenty" blacks approach. Among these blacks Kline especially recalled five: "an Indian-looking fellow, with long-looking and bushy hair, curious look out of his eyes"; another "very dark, big whiskers, a good-sized man"; another, "a light mulatto, round full face, with a straw hat on; another black-looking fellow with blue nankeen pants, straw hat on; another yellow-looking fellow with military cut whiskers, in shirt sleeves," with "a shot bag over his shoulders." [8]

These blacks gathered near where the marshal was talking with Castner Hanway and Elijah Lewis. The Quaker had just walked up, "in his shirt sleeves, with a straw hat on." Some of the blacks were carefully loading their guns, in full view of the whites. The marshal says:

> They were armed with guns, scythes, and clubs; all had something, nearly all of them. . . .

The "Indian negro," old Ezekiel Thompson, says Kline, had "a scythe [or 'corncutter'] in one hand and a revolver in the other." The marshal says this "Indian negro"

> came up to me, and I said, "You _____, if you come up to me, I'll blow your brains out;" and I took my revolver and held it up towards him; his revolver was in his right hand, and the corncutter in his left; he stood there while I was arguing with Hanway and Lewis. . . .

Marshal Kline says he showed Hanway and Lewis his warrants for Gorsuch's fugitives, and asked them to assist in the arrests, as the law required. Hanway and Lewis allegedly refused, telling the marshal that

> the colored people had a right to defend themselves, and I had better clear out, otherwise there would be blood spilt.[9]

Elijah Lewis says that the black men near where he, Hanway, and the marshal were talking

> had guns and threatened to shoot. Castner Hanway was sitting on his horse, and he beckoned with his . . . hand, "don't shoot! don't shoot! for God's sake, don't shoot!" and advised Kline that it would be dangerous to attempt making arrests, and that they had better leave.[10]

Posse member Pearce heard Hanway say something about "blood."

While the marshal, Hanway, and Lewis stood arguing outside in the lane, at the house, Parker says he came downstairs

> and stood in the doorway, my men following behind.
> Old Mr. Gorsuch said, when I appeared, "They'll come out, and get away!" and he came back to the gate.
> I then said to him,—"You said you could and would take us. Now you have the chance."
> They were a cowardly-looking set of men.
> Mr. Gorsuch said, "You can't come out here."
> "Why?" said I. "This is my place. I pay rent for it. I'll let you see if I can't come out."
> "I don't care if you do pay rent for it," said he. "If you come out, I will give you the contents of these";—presenting, at the same time, two revolvers, one in each hand.
> I said, "Old man, if you don't go away, I will break your neck."
> I then walked up to where he stood, his arms resting on the gate, trembling as if afflicted with palsy, and laid my hand on his shoulder, saying, "I have seen pistols before to-day."
> Kline now came running up, and entreated Gorsuch to come away.
> "No," said the latter, "I will have my property, or go to hell."
> "What do you intend to do?" said Kline to me.
> "I intend to fight," said I. "I intend to try your strength."
> "If you will withdraw your men," he replied, "I will withdraw mine."

I told him it was too late. "You would not withdraw when you had the chance,—you shall not now."

Kline then went back to Hanway and Lewis.[11]

One main group of blacks stood, armed, across from the end of the lane leading to the house, near the marshal, Hanway, and Lewis. According to his own report, the marshal now "began to beg" Hanway and Lewis not to let the blacks fire on his men, and he would withdraw them. The marshal added that he would hold Hanway and Lewis liable for the value of Gorsuch's slaves. The marshal says:

> I began to beg again and coaxed, for God Almighty's sake that they should not fire on my men, and that I would withdraw them.

Hanway and Lewis said they had no control over the blacks. The marshal then "hallooed" several times for his men to withdraw, and began to move quickly away.[12]

The battle's start is reported by a number of different witnesses, on both sides of the conflict.

The Christiana Resistance. (Still)

Quaker Elijah Lewis says, having established that the marshal had "authority," he and Hanway "had no further business" on the scene. Fearful of violence Lewis and Hanway began to move off. Lewis says Marshal Kline had followed him up the lane to the woods when the battle began. Lewis swears he

> had got alongside of the corn-field, and there was a shouting, with the colored people, I suppose, and presently I saw over the corn, a smoke raising near the house from the shots fired. . . . After the firing at the house . . . I could see or hear shooting and halooing, and could see smoke for some time.[13]

Marshal Kline, with certain duplicity, claims that he was close to Parker's house just before the final battle began. The marshal says the firing started when Hanway walked his horse over to the blacks gathered near the lane, stooped over, and whispered something to them which the marshal could not hear. The blacks, says the marshal, "then gave one shout," and one of them, "military whiskers" (Daniel Caulsberry), called out that the marshal was only a Deputy, "and up the lane they went towards Parker's house and fired." [14]

Dickinson Gorsuch says the battle began when two of his father's fugitives

> came shouting around me, and one that was in the house said, "there he is! take him;" that was Josh. They were shouting around me. I raised my revolver and told them if they touched me I would shoot them. I told my father we had better go, for they intended to murder the whole of us. He said it would not do to give it up that way.

Dickinson saw one of the armed blacks who had arrived at the scene on horseback, with a gun (probably Noah Buley), pass by him:

> He did not look at me. It was soon after this I saw them strike my father. They struck him with clubs.

Dickinson went back toward his father

> and put up my revolver to shoot at them. I was struck

Dickinson Gorsuch, said to resemble his father, Edward Gorsuch. (Hensel, *Christiana*)

across the right arm with a club; and about the same time, I was shot in the side.

Dickinson's pistol was knocked out of his hand, and he made his way, bleeding, up the long lane toward the woods.[15]

Joshua M. Gorsuch reports that just before the battle he called his cousin, Edward Gorsuch, to come away:

says I to Edward: the Marshal says, come on now, your property is secured to you.

Hanway was to be held liable for the fugitives. J. M. Gorsuch heard Edward Gorsuch arguing with his fugitive slave named Joshua. "It is not worthwhile to go on that way," said the master. The slave, reports Gorsuch's cousin, was "going on like a savage." J. M. Gorsuch saw Edward Gorsuch struck on the head with a club by a black man, and knocked "on his hands and knees." Then the slave owner was struck again. J. M. Gorsuch recalls:

> I discovered that they were intending to kill the whole of us, and especially Edward, and as I did not like to see him murdered in that state, I aimed to shoot one of them. My cap burst and did not go off. I then was beat severely. I believe the first one that struck me I aimed to shoot him. I . . . am of opinion that I must have shot him. . . . All this time a thought flashed over my mind that I should run, . . . for I found they were determined to kill me. I run, and they made after me.[16]

Dr. Thomas Pearce says that the marshal had asked his posse to retreat "as there was no possibility of making an arrest." Pearce told this to his uncle, Edward Gorsuch, and the two began to retreat. The blacks, says Pearce,

> were coming from every quarter . . . Most every one I saw had something to defend himself with.

Pearce and old Gorsuch were moving away when Pearce looked back and saw his uncle turn again toward Parker's. Pearce saw "the imminent danger," moved a few steps further on, called for Marshal Kline, and looked for him up and down the lane, but "could see nothing of him."

Pearce never admitted this under oath, but two witnesses testify that Pearce told them that, just before the shooting, he had

> called on his uncle to come away, his uncle had come out a marked distance . . . and he saw his uncle's countenance change suddenly, [he looked calm and stern] and he turned back and says, My property is here, and I will have it or perish in the attempt.[17]

The blacks at the end of the lane advanced; those at the house moved down toward Edward Gorsuch. Pearce says the blacks then "raised a regular yell," and shouting or singing "we are free," they rushed upon the slave owner. Pearce tells of seeing "a bright yellow negro," one of Gorsuch's own slaves, running up to his old master, evidently intending to shoot.[18]

William Parker says that Marshal Kline had moved back to Hanway and Lewis at the end of the lane. Old "Gorsuch made a signal to his men" near the house

> and they all fell into line. I followed his example as well as I could; but as we were not more than ten paces apart, it was difficult to do so. At this time we numbered but ten, while there were between thirty and forty of the white men.
> While I was talking to Gorsuch, his son said, "Father, will you take all this from a nigger?"

Parker answered Dickinson

> by saying that I respected old age; but that, if he would repeat that, I should knock his teeth down his throat. At this he fired upon me. . . .[19]

The bullets passed through Parker's hat, cutting off his hair next to the skin, but drawing no blood. Parker then ran up to

> Dickinson Gorsuch and knocked the pistol out of his hand, when he let the other one fall and ran in the field.

Parker's brother-in-law, the formerly apathetic Alexander Pinckney, was standing nearby. Pinckney said,

> "I can stop him";—and with his double-barrel gun he fired.
> Young Gorsuch fell, but rose and ran on again. Pinckney fired a second time, and again Gorsuch fell, but was soon up again, and, running into the cornfield, lay down in the fence corner.

The black man Jacob Woods had just gotten to the scene when he saw Pinckney, "a good chunk of a yellow fellow, [with a] full face," come running out of Parker's house

> and they commenced shooting; there was a great deal of smoke; I was scared.[20]

Meanwhile, says Parker, near the house Gorsuch's fugitive Samuel Thompson was arguing with his old master. Both were angry:

> "Old man, you had better go home to Maryland," said Samuel.
> "You had better give up, and come home with me," said the old man.
> Thompson took Pinckney's gun from him, struck Gorsuch, and brought him to his knees. Gorsuch rose and signalled to his men. Thompson then knocked him down again, and he again rose. At this time all the white men opened fire, and we rushed upon them; when they turned, threw down their guns, and ran away. We, being closely engaged, clubbed our rifles. We were too closely pressed to fire, but found a good deal could be done with empty guns. . . .
> While in close quarters with the whites, we could load and fire but two or three times. Our guns got bent and out of order. So damaged did they become, that we could shoot with but two or three of them.

According to Parker:

> Old Mr. Gorsuch was the bravest of his party; he held on to his pistols until the last, while all the others threw away their weapons. I saw as many as three at a time fighting with him. Sometimes he was on his knees, then on his back, and again his feet would be where his head should be. He was a fine soldier and a brave man. Whenever he saw the least opportunity, he would take aim.

Parker says that Samuel Thompson "bent his gun" so badly on his old master "that it was of no use to us." Parker reports that Thompson, Gorsuch's ex-slave,

> struck him the first and second blows; then three or four sprang upon him, and when he became helpless left him to pursue others. *The women put an end to him.*

The emphasis is Parker's.

The slave owner, Edward Gorsuch, lay in Parker's yard, in a pool of blood, dead. The flies buzzed around the corpse. The Gorsuch posse was retreating at a rapid pace. The Christiana resistance had lasted about one hour.[21]

8 Inquest at Christiana

THE HASTY RETREAT of Hanway, Lewis, and the six Gorsuch posse members is described by a number of eyewitnesses.

Dr. Thomas Pearce had advanced a few steps toward old Edward Gorsuch when the firing began. "When I saw my uncle fall," Pearce told one witness, "it was time to leave." Pearce was no doubt anxious at finding himself surrounded by a group of milling blacks. He "walked through the crowd however." As Pearce started away, he saw the armed Dickinson Gorsuch run to his father's assistance, and fire. Thinking he saw Dickinson clubbed or struck, Pearce began to run down the lane, away from Parker's, as the sound of gunshots filled the air. Pearce recalls: "the fire was kept up during the whole rout along the lane."

Pearce joined the fleeing Joshua Gorsuch, and both moved down the lane, "running as hard as they could go." Pearce and Joshua Gorsuch caught up with Castner Hanway, who was riding away from the scene. Pearce remembers the fear-crazed Joshua Gorsuch asking Hanway

> to loan him his horse and he begged of him to stop and arrest the negroes. . . .

Joshua Gorsuch only recalls

> a man came riding by and I asked him to let me get up behind him, I said for God's sake don't let them kill me.

Hanway turned on his horse, and placed himself between the blacks, Pearce, and Gorsuch, saying something to the blacks. Pearce later admitted that Hanway might have turned back his pursuers, saving Pearce's life.[1]

From his position on the hill above the scene of battle, neighbor Isaac Rogers saw Hanway riding away from the scene, and Pearce running alongside. Rogers saw a black man, Abraham Johnson, "with a gun some few yards behind." When they were near him, says Rogers,

> I hallooed to the colored man not to shoot; he didn't mind me. . . . The black man stopped and took aim. I hallooed to Dr. Pearce to take care. . . .

Rogers says that Hanway then

> turned on his critter and he says several times, "don't shoot, boys."

But the black man fired. Rogers thought he heard one of the blacks ask the black man with the gun why he didn't shoot again. The man with the gun "said he had no more powder and shot." [2]

As William Parker describes it, one of "our men" ran after Pearce. Dr. Pearce caught up with Hanway, who rode his horse between the black man and the doctor, to shield him:

> Hanway was told to get out of the way, or he would forfeit his life; he went aside quickly. . . .

The black man fired at Pearce, "but missed him,—he was too far off." Parker did not know if Pearce was wounded, "but I do know, that, if it had not been for Hanway," Pearce "would have been killed." [3]

Pearce says that Hanway told Joshua Gorsuch and himself that

> he could do nothing for us, and he hurried off and left us at full speed.

As Pearce and Joshua Gorsuch continued running up the lane they were chased and fired upon again by the blacks, some of whom apparently still had ammunition. Pearce admits that he

> ran with Joshua for a time, but finding they were over-

> taking us rapidly, I ran off as quick as possible, and left
> Joshua behind.

Looking back, Pearce saw a black man strike Joshua Gorsuch
over the head with a gun.[4]

William Parker had chased a posse member up the lane, and
was returning to his house, when he saw Joshua Gorsuch running
down the road toward him, with Alexander Pinckney following
behind. Parker reminded Joshua Gorsuch that he had earlier said

> he would like "to take hold of a nigger," told him that now
> was his "chance," and struck him a blow on the side of the
> head, which stopped him. Pinckney came up behind, and
> gave him a blow which brought him to the ground; as the
> others passed, they gave him a kick or jumped upon him,
> until the blood oozed out at his ears.[5]

Joshua Gorsuch remembers running down the lane, the black
men

> hollaring from behind me, "kill him," "kill him," and
> everyone apparently that could get a lick at me, struck me.

Joshua reports:

> I had on one of those fur hats, that fit close to the head, it
> didn't get knocked off . . . until I received the last
> blow,—there were two handkerchiefs in that hat and it was
> lined, and if it hadn't been the case, I should not be here
> to-day; I must have got over a dozen blows.

When later that morning Marshal Kline met Joshua Gorsuch
wandering a good distance from Parker's, Gorsuch "was as crazy
as a bed bug; he didn't know where he was." Dazed by the
beating, Joshua Gorsuch went on with the marshal to a store, and
immediately bought himself a new hat. Joshua Gorsuch reports:
"My nervous system appeared to be very much impaired" for
some time after the battle. He was not able to attend to business
for a month.[6]

After leaving Joshua Gorsuch behind, Dr. Pearce made his way
to the home of Isaac Rogers, on the hill above the scene of battle.
Rogers says he saw a man coming up the hill:

> I was going down to help him, when some of my neighbor's boys said I shouldn't, . . . that they [presumably, the blacks at Parker's] would kill me.

"After that," says Rogers, the man "got up and went away. Don't know where." [7]

One of the more mythological-sounding stories of the Gorsuch posse's retreat was told to R. C. Smedley years after the battle:

> When the Southern men with the United States Marshal and his aids fled from the fight, a gentleman from Baltimore, ran precipitately across a field to the house of Thomas Pownall, and without stopping to knock, or to ask permission to enter, rushed in, got under a bed, and begged one of the women to bring him a razor to shave off his beard, that the negroes might not recognize him. His beard was dark and very heavy. He removed it, wrapped it in a paper, and left it under the bed. The paper was discovered next morning and opened, and lo! the beard was white!
>
> In the evening he went to Levi Pownall's. He was very nervous, and apprehensive of every noise. During the night he became alarmed. He thought the negroes were marshalling near by to attack them. He could hear the toot of horns and the answer. He aroused those who were sleeping in the room with him, and his fears could not be quieted until it was discovered that the noise he heard was the sound of water dripping down a spout from the corner of the house.[8]

Marshal Kline called for his posse to retreat, and rapidly followed Elijah Lewis up the long lane toward the woods, accompanied by Nicholas Hutchings and Nathan Nelson. William Parker says he

> ran after Nathan Nelson, but could not catch him. I never saw a man run faster.

Nelson and Hutchings, says Parker,

> could outrun any men I ever saw. They and Kline were not brave, like the Gorsuches. Could our men have got them, they would have been satisfied.

Marshal Kline disappeared into a cornfield, some distance off from Parker's.[9] Although this was later a major point of contention, Kline undoubtedly ran from the scene among the first, and was already a safe distance away when the battle began.

After the firing, the wounded Dickinson Gorsuch wandered away down the lane, and was "bleeding out of his mouth," when Marshal Kline appeared out of the cornfield. Kline led the slave owner's wounded son

> up to the woods and I set him down on a stump and there he kind of fainted.

Kline called to the retreating Quaker, Elijah Lewis, to stop and help, "that there was a man shot." But Lewis continued on, accompanied by a boy. Later, asked why he didn't go back and assist, Lewis declared:

> It is a hard question to answer—I felt repugnant to going there.

Asked if he was alarmed for his own safety, Lewis admitted, "I was . . . quite alarmed." [10]

Marshal Kline continued on, and met Joseph Scarlett "coming very fast on horseback, the horse seemed to be in a sweat." The marshal accused Scarlett of alerting the blacks, then asked him where to find a doctor. Scarlett rode off without answering.[11]

Marshal Kline continued on to a nearby brick mill, where Hanway's assistant, Henry Burt, and the short, stoutly built Thompson Loughead were sitting outside. The marshal announced that some men were wounded, and asked about a doctor. Thompson Loughead rebuked the marshal for his posse's delayed retreat: "Says I, you had better left before so many darkies gathered." The marshal answered, says Henry Burt, that he had told his posse "it was impossible to do anything with the darkies they were after, there were too many against them. . . ." The marshal said he wanted his posse "to come away, but they would not mind him, and he came away and left them." [12]

Near Penningtonville, Marshal Kline met Joshua Gorsuch, who didn't know where he was, and was talking "nonsense." Kline led Joshua on to a store and gave him some water. The marshal offered a man one dollar to take him and Joshua Gorsuch by wagon to Penningtonville. The man took the dollar, hesitated a moment, then gave the money back to the marshal, and said he would not go. Kline and the wounded Joshua Gorsuch were forced to walk to Penningtonville.[13]

"A little after sun-up" on the morning of the battle, a white man, Miller Knott, had been reading the newspapers when he was "aroused by some sharp hallooing." His "little boy" John ran in the direction of the noise. Knott tried to call his fourteen-year-old back, but the boy had already gone too far to hear. Knott went after him. Young John Knott got to the scene some minutes before his father. From his position on the road above Parker's house, the boy witnessed the angry actions of the blacks:

> They broke out of the house . . . and commenced a terrible shouting and battering with clubs, and then they dispersed up the little lane, and run up towards the creek, and shot at one time there, at a tremendous rate.

The boy's father, Miller Knott, arrived at Parker's a few minutes after the firing. Knott saw "an old colored man," Isaiah Clarkson, come along the road past him. Knott reports:

> I said to him what have you been doing this morning? He said he had not been doing anything. He said he hadn't heard the horns blow.
> I told him I did not hear any horns. He then was passing towards his house. He lived close by there. I told him stop till we see a little further about this. He turned and went back with me pretty close to Dickinson Gorsuch. . . .

The Knotts and Isaiah Clarkson were approaching the wounded Dickinson Gorsuch when young John Knott saw a group of angry blacks "coming up with corn-cutters, guns and scythes." Miller Knott saw "twelve to fifteen" black men "coming up the lane" toward the wounded Dickinson Gorsuch:

> They were coming on him in a rage like manner. I told the old black man "they will kill him, save him, save him." He did not pay attention to that. . . . Says I, "save him or mind what is before you."

Old Clarkson signaled to the angry resisters and they went off into the cornfield, apparently not even seeing Dickinson lying on the ground. The Knotts heard the angry George Thompson say, "I would as soon die now as live," apparently meaning he would as soon die fighting as live to be returned to slavery.[14]

Miller Knott saw the blacks return to Parker's house where they were called to order by old Isaiah Clarkson. Knott recalls that Clarkson, who was "said to be a preacher,"

> got up on something a little higher than they were. He took his hat in his hand and waved it round and called "Order, men." They were still making a noise, and when he had come down to the third order, they were entirely quiet.

Knott emphasizes:

> They became very quiet, you would not have known there was anybody there.

Unfortunately for history, old Isaiah Clarkson's speech was not reported. Whatever Clarkson said, Knott reports the blacks "scattered very soon" after.[15]

The battle was over and the posse had retreated. Edward Gorsuch was dead. His son Dickinson lay critically wounded in a nearby field, with eighty "squirrel shot" in his arm and side. Nephew Thomas Pearce had had "a very severe blow over the eye" which had blackened it; he had a shot in his wrist and shoulder blade, two in his back, and his clothes had been perforated in twenty or thirty places; he also had a scalp wound, and a bullet hole through his hat. Cousin Joshua M. Gorsuch, as he says, had been "knocked out of my mind," and was wandering dazedly through the woods with a scalp wound. Marshal Henry H. Kline, and neighbors Nathan Nelson and Nicholas Hutchings, being the first to leave, escaped without injury. Two black men, Henry C. Hopkins and John Long, had received gunshot wounds, one in the thigh, the other in his arm, and later had their injuries attended to by a sympathetic doctor. No other blacks appear to have been seriously wounded.[16]

After the battle, William Parker returned to his house with a group of other blacks:

> Having driven the slavocrats off in every direction, our party now turned towards their several homes. Some of us,

however, went back to my house, where we found several of the neighbors.

The scene at the house beggars description. Old Mr. Gorsuch was lying in the yard in a pool of blood, and confusion reigned both inside and outside of the house.

Levi Pownall said to me, "The weather is so hot and the flies are so bad, will you give me a sheet to put over the corpse?"

In reply, I gave him permission to get anything he needed from the house.

"Dickinson Gorsuch is lying in the fence-corner, and I believe he is dying. Give me something for him to drink," said Pownall, who seemed to be acting the part of the Good Samaritan.

When he returned from ministering to Dickinson, he told me he could not live.[17]

Long after the resistance it was said that Parker and twenty-three-year-old Levi Pownall, Jr., had run "to get a horse and wagon" to bring the badly wounded Dickinson Gorsuch to the Pownall's. But

before they geared up, a neighbor brought the wounded man over in a dearborn.

The wounded Dickinson Gorsuch recalls Joseph Scarlett standing near him after the battle. Dickinson asked the Quaker

to hold my head. I asked him several times, as I felt very weak, . . . he wouldn't do it; I afterwards asked him to go and get me some water. After asking him several times he went and got me some water.

Later, the slave owner's son reportedly told Scarlett: "I did not think our boys would have treated us in this way." [18]

Joseph Scarlett was holding Dickinson's head and keeping the sun from shining on him when neighbor Lewis Cooper got to the scene. Cooper and Scarlett brought Dickinson to Levi Pownall's where Dr. Ashmore Patterson dressed his wounds. That evening it seemed to posse member Dr. Thomas Pearce that Dickinson Gorsuch was dying: "his pulse was scarcely perceptible, the fever high, and the pain intense." Dickinson's lungs appeared to be injured and there seemed "very little hopes of his recovery." Eighty "squirrel shot" were removed from Dickinson Gorsuch's body. When, thirty-one years later, Dickinson did finally pass away his body was found to be "pitted like a sponge." [19]

Back at Levi Pownall's house, Levi Jr. reportedly told Parker and Pinckney

> that they were up against the government of the United States and there was no safety for them in the country. They went away and concealed themselves someplace until that night.[20]

It was said that Levi Pownall, Jr., had gone to Parker's house later on the day of the resistance

> to look after clothing, etc. To his surprise he found a great number of letters put away in safe places. He carried them

Levi Pownall's House. (Courtesy LaVerne D. Rettew, Christiana)

home, and on examination they proved to be from escaped fugitives many of whom Parker had assisted. Had these letters been found by the slaveholders or the United States Marshal they would have led to the detection of the slaves, and would have divulged the means by which they escaped. He destroyed them all.[21]

At about six o'clock on the morning of the battle, abolitionist and underground railroad conductor Dr. Augustus W. Cain had heard from a black man, Francis Hawkins, that "kidnappers" were at Parker's. Later, it is said, Cain had seen Henry C. Hopkins, a black man who lived in a small tenant house of the doctor's, walking rapidly down the road toward Parker's. The black man was carrying an iron rod in his hand. Seeing the doctor, Hopkins said hurriedly: "Kidnappers at Parker's!" and walked quickly on. Hopkins was reportedly

> very much excited and his usual calm, peaceable, inoffensive disposition was at once aroused to the ferocity of an enraged lion. After the lapse of about two hours he came [back] to the doctor's holding one arm, and said he was shot. The doctor found a bullet lodged in the flesh of the forearm, removed it and dressed the wound.

So anxious was the black man to describe the battle that when Dr. Cain declined hearing him Hopkins reportedly "shed tears freely." There was good reason for the doctor's caution. Cain

> knew the event would create an intense excitement, and he did not want to learn of it through any of its participants. He would then have no knowledge to convey from them to a court in case there should be a trial; but he told the colored man that unless he made his escape he would certainly be arrested.

About an hour later, John Long, a short, thin, light-skinned, twenty-two-year-old black man, came to Dr. Cain's with a bullet in his thigh. "The doctor extracted it and dressed the limb." Dr. Cain then went to Parker's "to see for himself" the extent of the battle. When he returned that afternoon, Cain found that Henry C. Hopkins and John Long had disappeared from his tenant house. The doctor was wise not to listen to Henry Hopkins's tale of his part in the resistance. In the trial that followed, when the prosecution called Dr. Cain to testify, he could truthfully deny knowing anything of the event; Cain was not a cooperative witness. But many years later, when a Quaker friend asked, "Augustus, did thee have anything to do with the Christiana riot?" Cain admitted:

> Yes, indeed; I was surgeon to the insurgent army on that day.[22]

Sixty years after the battle, the black man Peter Woods, who was seventeen years old at the time, recalled:

> The day the fight happened I was up very early. We were to have a "kissing party" that night. . . .

Someone, it seems, was getting engaged. Woods continues:

> as I wanted to get off early I asked my boss, Joe Scarlett, if he would plough if I got up ahead and spread the manure. I started at it at two o'clock. The morning was foggy and dull. About daylight Elijah Lewis's son came running to me while I was getting my work done, and said the kidnappers were here.

Peter Woods says he got to Parker's just in time to see the posse's retreat:

> The morning of the riot I got there about seven or eight o'clock. I met some of them coming out of the lane, and others were on a run from the house. I met Hanway on a bald-faced sorrel horse coming down the long lane, and his party with him. The other party, the marshal and his people, took to the sprouts, licking out for all they could. . . . There were about sixty of our fellows chasing them. The strange party got away. I got hurt by being kicked by a blind colt on the hip. The shooting was all over. Gorsuch had been killed before I got there. The Gorsuch party was riding away as fast as they could.[23]

George Steele, Parker's white neighbor, recalls:

> On the day of the Riot . . . I had planned to go to Lancaster on business and to walk over to Christiana to

Peter Woods, aged eighty. (Hensel, *Christiana*)

take the cars. I heard the racket at Parker's house and determined to go that way and see what was the matter, but when I got as far as the Noble Road, I met some colored men that I knew and they told me what had happened, that one white man was killed and another of the slave holders badly wounded. They seemed exultant.

" 'Wictory,' one of 'em says," putting the up-country Pennsylvania Dutch accent on the word "victory."

> I told them they were in great danger and if anyone who had anything to do with it had any sense at all, they would leave the country before night.[24]

Having walked to Penningtonville Marshal Kline "offered five dollars a-piece" to "several gentlemen" to go and fetch the wounded in a wagon. At first the men were afraid to go, but finally, says Kline,

> One or two did start, providing I would not go with them—they were afraid to be seen with me.

Charles Smith accepted five dollars "to go and fetch Edward Gorsuch and his son to Penningtonville . . ." Smith found the body of Edward Gorsuch

> laying in the orchard. . . . Laying as he was dressed—just laid out on a board.

It was claimed that sometime after the battle $200 to $300 disappeared from the body of Edward Gorsuch, rumor having it that the blacks at Parker's had divided it among themselves.[25]

Gorsuch's remains were still lying unattended when neighbor Lewis Cooper returned to the scene of the battle with his wagon. Cooper says:

> As there was no other conveyance, and no machine for to carry him along, my dearborn was brought forward to take the corpse to Christiana.

The slave owner's body was brought to town and put in a side room of Fred Zercher's Hotel. A postmortem examination was performed by two local doctors, John Martin and A. P. Patterson. The doctors report that Edward Gorsuch's death was caused by a single gunshot wound. They also mention a minor "incision," and a "fracture of the left humerus," produced by a blow from some blunt weapon. The doctors' report describes no general mutilation of the body, such as southerners would later suggest had taken place.

Hearing that Edward Gorsuch was dead, Marshal Kline came

to Christiana, where the inquest was to be held. That afternoon
when the inquest began Marshal Kline was indignant. He told
those in charge that

> it was a very curious inquest, as there were no witnesses
> examined. . . .

The marshal insisted that he

> should be heard before they gave their verdict, but they
> didn't hear no witnesses but passed the verdict themselves.

Lewis Cooper was on the jury of inquest. Cooper had been in
Christiana and heard Marshal Kline offering various versions of
the battle. Later, asked why the inquest had not examined the
marshal, Cooper answered that the other jurors said it was "not
necessary, because they said they didn't believe what he would
say." The marshal, said Cooper, "had told numerous different
tales." [26]

The jury of inquest was organized and headed by Squire Joseph
D. Pownall, a Christiana justice of the peace. Although John
Beard, said to be Nelson Ford, a Gorsuch fugitive, lived at
Pownall's, neither the squire nor any of the jury members seem to
have been active underground railroad agents. They probably
represented more moderate abolitionist opinion, or were neutral
on the slavery question.[27]

In their summary statement the jury of inquest declared

> upon the view of the body of a man then and there lying
> dead, supposed to be Edward Gorsuch, of Baltimore
> county, Maryland,

they being "good and lawful men" of Lancaster County,

> charged to enquire . . . when, where and how the said
> deceased came to his death, do say . . . that on the
> morning of the 11th . . . the neighborhood was thrown
> into an excitement by the above deceased, and some five or
> six persons in company with him, making an attack upon a
> family of colored persons . . . for the purpose of arresting
> some fugitive slaves as they alleged. . . .

The Grave of Edward Gorsuch. (Hensel, *Christiana*)

The jury continued:

> many of the colored people of the neighborhood collected, and there was considerable firing of guns . . . by both parties. . . .

The jury stated that "after the riot had subsided" neighbors had found "the above deceased, lying on his back or right side dead." They concluded that the deceased "came to his death by gun shot wounds . . . caused by some person or persons to us unknown." Maryland's Attorney General Brent later charged that this jury of inquest had, without hearing witnesses, "stigmatized Edward Gorsuch, with having participated in a riot" against an innocent family of blacks. The inquest ignored the fact that Gorsuch's "slaves, his property was there . . ." said Brent. That evening, Marshal Kline arranged for some gentlemen "to get a coffin and shroud made," and had the corpse of Edward Gorsuch shipped home by train to Maryland.[28]

Sixty years later, in 1911, Pennsylvanian W. U. Hensel visited Edward Gorsuch's last resting place in Maryland. The grave was enclosed by a low stone wall, and the slave owner's plot stood between two other unmarked stones. Hensel notes:

the little graveyard is overgrown with myrtle. Human hands have not desecrated it in any way, but there is evidence that the gnawing teeth of rodent vandals have been at work on the graves.[29]

9 Arrests

IT WAS NOT UNTIL THE DAY after the battle, Friday, September 12, that Marshal Kline went before Christiana Justice of the Peace Joseph D. Pownall to begin the first official proceedings against the resisters. On that morning the marshal, on oath, named and charged seventeen men, fifteen blacks and two whites, with "aiding and abetting in the murder of Edward Gorsuch." Warrants were issued for the arrest of the seventeen men named. It is not clear how Kline could identify by name so many blacks. Later, Kline admitted it was difficult for him to recollect the names of the blacks present at the battle, claiming he "only knew them by sight." [1]

It was at Frederick Zercher's Hotel in Christiana that Marshal Kline, appearing before Justice of the Peace Pownall, swore out affidavits against the two white men Castner Hanway and Elijah Lewis. Justice of the Peace Pownall said he could not write fast enough to take down Marshal Kline's deposition, so Alderman J. Franklin Reigart wrote out the affidavits. The warrants for the two were served on them outside Zercher's tavern by Constable William Proudfoot some fifteen minutes after being issued. Hearing that they were to be arrested, Hanway and Lewis came to Christiana, and voluntarily surrendered themselves. Proudfoot reports the two alleged murderers asking him "whether they could

120

not get off till next morning," to make "family arrangements." But Constable Proudfoot did not want to take the responsibility.[2]

The surrender of the two "murderers" was witnessed by Lancaster Alderman J. Franklin Reigart, who saw Marshal Kline confront the two prisoners. Reigart thought Kline "a very singular looking man," with his "formidable" whiskers and moustaches. Kline's "feelings seemed much warmed at the time," says Reigart, the marshal's expression "seemed serious and sharp," and he spoke "in a loud tone of voice." As Reigart describes it:

> When Hanway and Lewis were first arrested and brought to the Hotel of Mr. Zercher, and when Hanway and Lewis were placed on the porch, Mr. Kline came up to them and said, "You white-livered scoundrels, you yesterday, when I plead for my life like a dog and begged you not to let the blacks fire upon us, you turned round and told them to do so." Mr. Lewis instantly replied, "No, I didn't." Mr. Hanway said nothing, he didn't deny it, I didn't hear him

Zercher's Hotel and Tavern. (Courtesy LaVerne D. Rettew, Christiana)

> make any reply. I then took Kline by the shoulder, and said, "I hope you will say nothing to produce a disturbance, we wish to do our business legally and in order." He replied that he would obey me, but he could not suppress his feelings; he had had his men shot down the day before like dogs, and it was impossible for him to restrain his feelings. I insisted upon it and he remained quiet; and I didn't hear him say anything more to them.

Alderman Reigart remembers some heated comments being made at the time to Hanway and Lewis by several spectators (probably Marylanders who had come up at the first news of Gorsuch's death):

> Several others then spoke up, and I was fearful of an excitement, and I had to exert myself to prevent it. . . .

Fearing an attack upon Hanway and Lewis, Reigart told the constable to take them

> out of the view of the people, and he took them up stairs and put a guard upon them. Against the black persons nothing was said. . . .

The spectators "seemed much enraged against Hanway and Lewis." [3]

Another dispute, between Marshal Kline and Lieutenant Ellis, who was directing the police force sent to Christiana, is reported by John Bacon, a Maryland neighbor of Edward Gorsuch who witnessed it. Bacon recalls that Kline came into Zercher's, went up to Hanway or Lewis

> and caught one of the criminals on the shoulder, and told him he wanted to speak to him; Lieutenant Ellis forbid him to speak to him or move him; and Kline said, he had been there all the time and assisted in arresting them, and was there before Ellis and his posse came up, and he had as much right to speak to him as anybody. Lieutenant Ellis and others said he had not and should not, and forbid him to do so. Kline went on to sneer at him, tantalizing him, that he hadn't any right there, that he was a small thing at any rate.

The dispute between the slightly built Ellis and Marshal Kline evidently ended with Kline having his coat torn off his back as he was forcibly ejected from the room.[4]

Later that afternoon Marshal Kline went to search the woods near Parker's for his two lost posse members, Nathan Nelson and Nicholas Hutchings, whom he hadn't seen or heard from since the retreat the day before. The marshal returned to Christiana without having found them. But back in town, says Kline,

> a young man came to see me and called me inside, and said don't make yourself uneasy, your two friends are safe and eat breakfast at our house this morning.[5]

The second day after the resistance, Saturday, September 13, numerous officials were present in and around Christiana. Among these were Lancaster District Attorney John L. Thompson and a "strong party of armed men." Thompson and Lancaster Alderman J. Franklin Reigart were apparently the most active officials at the scene. U.S. Marshal Anthony E. Roberts, from Philadelphia, was also present with a detachment of Philadelphia police. Roberts, an abolitionist, was doubtlessly less energetic about making arrests. Also present were U.S. District Attorney from Philadelphia John W. Ashmead; the notorious U.S. fugitive slave commissioner Edward D. Ingraham, "a strong force of U.S. Marines from the Philadelphia Navy Yard," a lawyer representing the Gorsuch family, and numbers of volunteers who had been deputized for the occasion. Armed posses began (in the often repeated contemporary phrase) to "scour the country" for participants in the resistance. The actions of these search parties were reported to be of the most arbitrary and violent nature.[6]

Abolitionist C. M. Burleigh, who reached Christiana the day after the resistance, saw black people "hunted like partridges upon the mountains" by a "relentless horde" of whites.[7]

A letter dated September 12, from a correspondent in Columbia, Pennsylvania, warns:

> About 50 of our citizens are now, 10 o'clock at night, waiting to start down in the cars in company with some Marylanders, to make arrests. Wo to them who resist! [8]

A letter from Baltimore, dated September 13, reports that in Gorsuch's neighborhood

> the feelings of some have led to a deep-seated and burning desire for revenge. . . . Numbers of young men have left, with the avowed purpose, it is said, of proceeding to the locality of the outrage, and capturing, at all hazards, the perpetrators and instigators of the dreadful act.[9]

A dispatch from Lancaster, dated September 15, in the *Anti-Slavery Standard*, reports:

> Gangs of armed ruffians from Maryland, assisted by the lowest ruffians this region can furnish, are prowling around the country, . . . arresting indiscriminately all colored persons whom they meet. . . . Cyrus Burleigh while passing by, was seized and treated very rudely. . . .[10]

The careful Pennsylvania lawyer W. U. Hensel admits that after the Christiana resistance, with numerous posses making arrests throughout the neighborhood,

> a local reign of terror ensued; "the valley" was in a state worse than subjection to martial law . . . the class of persons easily secured for the service then required of temporary officers of the law was not one as to secure delicacy of treatment or tender consideration for the objects against whom their summary processes were directed. Whites and blacks, bond and free, were rather roughly handled; few households in the region searched were safe from rude intrusion; many suffered terrifying scenes and sounds.[11]

David R. Forbes, editor of the *Quarryville* (Pennsylvania) *Sun*, and a chronicler of the Christiana case, says:

> there never went unhung a gang of more depraved wretches and desperate scoundrels than some of the men employed as "officers of the law" to ravage this country and ransack private houses, in the man-hunt which followed the affray.[12]

Peter Smith, an Irish immigrant, was a barkeeper at Fred Zercher's tavern when the Christiana resistance occurred. A railroad track curved sharply by Zercher's, and Smith recalls a group of Irish railroad workers were then engaged in relocating this track. Smith remembers that nearly all of these forty railroad workers were deputized as U.S. marshals, to hunt those blacks thought to have taken part in the resistance. Alderman Reigart recalls that "we got some hundred and fifty men from the railroad" to help local officers make arrests. Peter Smith remembers one of these railroad men holding a "horse pistol" in his hand, saying that he would shoot "the first black thing" he spotted, even if it was a cow.[13]

Francis M. Lennox, a schoolmaster, was in Christiana the evening of the day of the "riot":

> I was in the Red Lion Hotel; there were a number of United States Marines; I asked one what they were doing here; he said, "We are going to arrest every nigger and d----d abolitionist. . . ." I walked away. Sure enough they scoured the country for miles around, arresting every colored man, boy and girl that they could find.[14]

Jeremiah Moore, a Quaker, and a conductor on the underground railroad, lived near Christiana. Moore's daughter, Sarah, recalls that following the resistance

> twenty-two "kidnappers," or Southern sympathizers, came to father's to take the colored man [then living with the family] who had not been near the Riot. He heard of their coming, and was hidden under a pile of straw. They searched the premise over and threatened to shoot father because he didn't tell where the man was. He put down his hands, straightened himself up, and told them to shoot. They didn't dare do it, for they hadn't even a warrant for searching. With pitchforks they at last found the man and dragged him off.[15]

The arrest of one local black named John Morgan is described by Marshal Kline and his two deputies. When he approached Morgan to arrest him, Kline says Morgan "had an ax, and struck at me with it. I avoided the blow." George Jordan, one of Kline's deputies, says that as they approached, "Morgan raised the ax—he resisted." Jordan says he seized Morgan "by the neck, and Kline thrust his revolver in his face, and threatened to blow his brains out; Kline said to him, 'You were there, I can swear I saw you.'" Morgan denied being near the scene of battle when it occurred, and this seems to be the truth; a number of witnesses corroborate his alibi.

Deputy George Jordan's economic status is probably typical of many deputized for the occasion. Jordan resided at Parkesburg. He was, he said,

> not doing anything particular at Parkesburg; I am waiting for a job; I have been there for three months, doing nothing that whole time. . . .[16]

A few days after the battle seventeen-year-old Peter Woods saw officers come to arrest his "boss," Joseph Scarlett, one of the whites charged. Although he had arrived at Parker's after the shooting, Woods says he was scared:

> When Scarlett was arrested they were rough in arresting him. They took him by the throat, and pointed bayonets at him all around him. I said to myself if you arrest a white man like that, I wonder what you will do to a black boy? The arrests were made a day or two after the riot. I was plowing or working the ground, and when I saw the officers come to make the arrests, I quickly got unhitched, and went towards Bushong's, and soon there was six of us together and we went to Dr. Dingee's graveyard and hid. We heard a racket of horses coming and then we jumped into the graveyard. This was two days after the riot. We hung around Wm. Rakestraw's too; and he said we could have something to eat, but we couldn't stay around there. Then they got us. They asked George Boone and James Noble who we are. The man with the mace, the marshal I guess, said "I got a warrant for Peter Woods." They pointed me out and then he struck me and then they tried to throw me. They arrested me and took me up a flight of stairs, and then they tied me. Then they started away with

me and tried to get me over a fence. They had me tied around my legs and around my breast, and they put me in a buggy and took me to Christiana.

At Christiana, young Woods saw lawyers Thaddeus Stevens, David Paul Brown, and a Mr. Black, who all had quarters in Zercher's Hotel. The blacks did not know that Stevens and Brown were well-known abolitionists, and the lawyers do not seem to have introduced themselves. Woods says:

> We did not know who they were counsel for, and we thought they were threatening us, and trying to make us give ourselves away. Thad. Stevens or someone said to me: "Who do you live with?" They had just brought me down from the Harrar garret, and Fred Zercher was there. Mr. Brown asked me again how I got up there into that garret, who put me there? I made up my mind not to talk, and Brown said, "If you don't tell we will send you to jail." Then a mutiny broke out there.

Unfortunately, the nature of this "mutiny" is not clear from Woods's rather disjointed description; he says only:

> George Boone and [Constable] Proudfoot and others got into it. George commenced striking and I got knocked over. Boone was taking my part.

Later, says Woods, "they took me to Lancaster, and put me first in the old jail and then in the new prison." [17]

Among the other black people arrested was the mother of Eliza Parker and Hannah Pinckney. The fifty-one-year-old woman, named Cassandra or Catherine Warner, had been "taken by the negro hunting officers from her home, kept all night locked in the garret of the Christiana tavern," and finally claimed as a slave "by one Albert Davis of Harford Co., Maryland." A story was circulated that the old woman, "called 'Cassy,' by the slaveholders," had said she desired to return to slavery.

A reporter from the abolitionist press was present at the black woman's hearing before Commissioner Ingraham. The reporter, "having seen the slave catcher's story" of Cassandra Warner's "anxiety to go back," but noticing that the old woman "appeared very sad," took the opportunity to question her on the subject:

She acknowledged that she had told the officers that she wished to go back, but said she was terrified by their violence and threats and feared a worse fate, if she refused to go. Her house had been searched by armed men, for her daughters. She had been questioned, threatened and insulted, to extort from her information of them; she feared they had been carried off into slavery; she was alarmed at the military and police force she saw; and was told that the "light horse would be brought up from Philadelphia and cut the niggers all to pieces," and, said the poor old woman, with a sadness in her tones and countenance which touched our heart—"I thought I might as well go back as to live so. But now" said she with a wo-begone look, "I don't want to go back; O, I don't want to go back."

Cassandra Warner was awarded to the Maryland slave owner who claimed her, "and was not heard from afterward" in the Lancaster County area.[18]

Several newspapers report the arrest of other fugitive slaves in the aftermath of the Christiana resistance. A notorious Philadelphia slave catcher, George Alberti, may have gone to Christiana after the resistance to look for fugitives among those arrested. At least one well-known local kidnapper was active in the posses making arrests. Smedley reports that

William Baer was now on hand, elated with the opportunity of legally rendering his professional services to the government and was notably in the height of his importance.[19]

George Williams, one of those blacks arrested, is identified by Parker as "one of our men, and the very one who had the letters brought up from Philadelphia by Mr. Samuel Williams." Parker says that George Williams

lay in prison with the others arrested by Kline, but was rendered more uneasy by the number of rascals who daily visited that place for the purpose of identifying, if possible, some of its many inmates as slaves.

One day, says Parker, a notorious Philadelphia lawyer

whose chief business seemed to be negro-catching, came with another man, who had employed him for that purpose, and stopping in front of the cell wherein George and old Ezekiel Thompson were confined, cried out, *"That's him!"* At which the man exclaimed, *"It is, by God! that is him!"*

George Williams, and his part Indian cell mate, the forty-seven-year-old Ezekiel Thompson, reportedly jumped to their feet, Williams "frightened and uneasy," Ezekiel Thompson "stern and resolute." The lawyer and his client then hurried off

to obtain the key, open the cell, and institute a more complete inspection. They returned in high glee, but to their surprise saw only the old man standing at the door, his grim visage anything but inviting.

A quick conversation between the two black cell mates had resulted in Williams' lying down and covering himself with Thompson's blanket—to prevent a more positive identification. The lawyer and his client

inserted the key, click went the lock, back shot the bolt, open flew the door, but old Ezekiel stood there firm, his eyes flashing fire, his brawny hands flourishing a stout oak stool furnished him to rest on by friends, . . . and crying out in the most unmistakable manner, every word leaving a deep impression on his visitors, "The first man that puts his head inside of this cell I will split to pieces."

The men leaped back, but soon recovered their self-possession; and the lawyer said,—"Do you know who I am? I am the lawyer who has charge of this whole matter, you impudent nigger. I will come in whenever I choose."

The old man, if possible looking more stern and savage than before, replied,—"I don't care who you are; but if you or any other nigger-catcher steps inside of my cell-door I will beat out his brains."

It is needless to say more. The old man's fixed look, clenched teeth, and bony frame had their effect. The man and the lawyer left, growling as they went, that, if there was rope to be had, that old Indian nigger should certainly hang.

George Williams remained in prison for four months, accused of participating in the Christiana resistance. When finally discharged he was immediately arrested as a fugitive slave.[20]

Luckier than some others arrested was a black man named Lewis Christmas, who "drove team" for Christiana resident George Steele, a forgeman. Some time before the resistance, says Steele, Lewis Christmas "told me to write to a gentleman" at Elkton, Maryland, "who knew all about him."

> The Elkton man replied that Lew Christmas was a free man, that his father was Jerry Christmas, a free man who was a fiddler, and in demand at dance parties and for that reason was named Christmas. Lew's wife sewed this letter in a bag and Lew always carried it around his neck.

On the morning of the resistance, says Steele,

> Christmas and I were together at the mule stable a few minutes after the firing was heard and I knew he could not have been there, but he was arrested. I went before the Commissioner and Lew produced his letter and they let him go.[21]

R. C. Smedley reports that the Quaker abolitionist Thomas Whitson, upon hearing that a party of "special constables" was carrying off a black man who had worked for him, pursued and overtook the posse, and asked for the black's release. He was refused. On being told Whitson's name, one of the "constables" advanced toward him, flourishing a revolver, asking if he was not an abolitionist. "I am," said Whitson, staring at his opponent as directly as his one crossed eye would permit, "and I am not afraid of thy shooting me. So thee may as well put thy pistol down." The officer, turning to another, asked, "Shall I shoot him?" "No," was the response, "let the old Quaker go." The posse reportedly left, "convinced that Whitson was not a man to be frightened by bluster or to renounce a principle in the face of an enemy." The next morning Whitson and a neighbor who had seen the accused black at the time of the resistance, several miles away, went to see the officers, and obtained the black man's release.[22]

Thomas Whitson. (Smedley)

Two days after the battle on Saturday, September 13, in Christiana, U.S. fugitive slave Commissioner Edward D. Ingraham began to hear the charges against those indicted for participating in the resistance. The major witnesses against those arrested were Marshal Kline and a young black man, George Washington Harvey Scott, making his first appearance as a prosecution informer. When Kline named a number of black men who, he claimed, had been present at the battle, Scott's testimony supported the marshal's.[23]

On this first day of the Christiana hearings George Washington Harvey Scott testified that he

> was present when the man was killed, but had no hand in it; was there over night and staid out of doors in the road.

Scott swore that he had been "persuaded" to go over to Parker's by John Morgan and Henry Simms, two of the black men named by Marshal Kline. Scott swore that when he saw Morgan and Simms at Parker's:

> they had arms; . . . saw them shoot—saw the old gentleman shot; he fell in the lane; he was shot by Henry Simms; John Morgan cut the old gentleman in the head with a corn-cutter after he (Mr. Gorsuch) had fallen. . . .

Scott said that he himself

> went away as soon as the old man was killed; I left the
> other colored people there; they had pistols, muskets, and
> other guns; they wanted me to help, but I would have
> nothing to do with it; that is in taking their part in the fight,
> which was to kill the slave holders; the mob was to resist all
> slave holders. . . .

Later in the hearing George Washington Harvey Scott confronted "a mulatto," William Brown, accused by Marshal Kline of
being a ringleader, "one of the most active." Scott who had earlier
testified that he did not know any blacks at the scene except
Morgan and Simms, now swore:

> I saw Brown at Parker's on the morning of the murder;
> . . . he was armed with a gun. . . .

The accused, William Brown, pleaded with Scott:

> Did you see me there George?

and George Scott answered:

> I saw you there, in the yard, pretty soon in the morning.

The hearings closed that evening, about nine o'clock. Informer
Scott, whose testimony was said to have been "given in a straight
forward manner," was committed as a witness. Joseph Scarlett,
the white man said to have alerted the neighborhood, and William
Brown found themselves charged with treason against the United
States in forcibly resisting the execution of the fugitive slave law.
Others were detained. The females who had been arrested were all
released, a bit of male chauvinism definitely to the advantage of
Eliza Parker and Hannah Pinckney who were among them.[24]
    When the hearing continued the next day, Sunday, September
14,

> The excitement was very great. Several hundred persons
> were present and the deepest feeling was manifested
> against the perpetrators of the outrage.

When a number of prisoners and witnesses were taken to
Moyamensing prison in Philadelphia,

The excitement attending the conveying of the prisoners was tremendous, an immense crowd of people following the officers and the marines.

On Monday, September 15, the third day of the Christiana hearings, the seventeen-year-old black Peter Woods testified, but did not name any of those he had seen at Parker's. The hearing ended at ten o'clock that Monday night. Further hearings in Christiana were temporarily postponed, because, it was explained, Marshal Kline had to appear as a witness in Lancaster; the real reason was probably to give the United States authorities time to prepare and coordinate treason charges against the prisoners. Twenty-four blacks and three whites were committed to the Moyamensing jail in Philadelphia to await further proceedings.[25]

Thomas Whitson reports that Joseph Scarlett, and a number of black prisoners from Christiana, "enjoyed the distinction of . . . being shipped to Philadelphia in a cattle car. . . ." Whatever the mode of transportation, George Steele reports:

> The scene at Christiana when the prisoners were taken to Philadelphia was one to be remembered. The marines were getting on the train. Some Philadelphia politician, I forget his name, was addressing the crowd, protesting against the marshal's removing the marines and declaring that the country was in a state of insurrection. No one seemed to be listening to him. The Clemson gang were very much in evidence. Two of them, Bill Baer and Perry Marsh, were drunk and quarreling and Clemson was trying to quiet them.[26]

One of those blacks arrested was Daniel Caulsberry, whom Marshal Kline had sworn he had seen at Parker's with "a gun and a shot bag, or flask over his shoulder; . . . with the military whiskers . . ." George Steele says that Caulsberry was one of several black men employed by him, cutting wood, burning charcoal, and driving teams for the two iron forges on the Octoraro river. Steele says that

> "Dan" Caulsberry was a forgeman who worked for me. I was talking to him at the car window, about taking some care of his family while he was away and gave him a small

amount of money that I owed him. Perry Marsh called out,
"Look at Steele, he's giving them money." And he came
running up to me and said, "If it had not been for the
damned Abolitionists like you and yourself, these men
would not have got in this trouble." I said to him, "Perry
Marsh, sneak thief and jail bird, what do you want with me
and myself?" Amos Clemson came waddling up and took
Perry by the arm and led him away.

Perry Marsh calling George Steele an abolitionist is ironic.
Steele says that, although he knew William Parker, and employed
a number of black men,

> I was not at that time interested in the anti-slavery
> movement and I knew nothing of the underground rail-
> road.[27]

Steele's phrasing suggests he later became more intimately acquainted with abolitionism and the underground railroad.

The Christiana prisoners remained in the cold and drafty
Moyamensing jail in Philadelphia for three months. Fall turned
into winter. The prison was badly heated, airless, and unhealthy.
At one point the court ordered three prisoners moved to more
comfortable cells when the defense protested that their client's
health, and even the life of one individual, was in danger. George
Steele recalls:

> I visited the prisoners in Moyamensing Jail where they
> were waiting trial. . . . I am not certain but I think Dan
> [Caulsberry] came out of jail with some disease of the lungs
> and died soon after.[28]

Another visitor to Moyamensing was a reporter from the *New
York Daily Times*, the first edition of which had appeared just
seven days after the Christiana resistance. The *Times* reporter
found the white prisoners sitting in one large cell, being visited by
friends and family. As these friends supplied food, the only food
from the prison's commissary they were forced to eat was the
bread. The relatives and friends of the black prisoners were too
poor to travel from Christiana to Philadelphia simply for a short
visit. "The colored prisoners," the *Times* reporter says,

are confined in separate cells. . . . No two of these are together, and none of them are in cells with any other prisoners. They spoke well of the officers, and seemed satisfied with their fare, but complained much of loneliness, and said they should rather be at work.[29]

Another of those who visited the prisoners was Esther Moore, a dedicated white Philadelphia abolitionist whom William Still describes as "hating every form of oppression and injustice, and an uncompromising witness against prejudice on account of color." Oliver Johnson recalls how Esther Moore's "soul was fired with a righteous indignation" when the alleged Christiana resisters were imprisoned:

> Day after day did she visit the prisoners in their cells, to minister to their wants, and cheer them in their sorrow; and during Hanway's trial, her constant presence in the court-room, and her frequent interviews with the District Attorney, attested her deep anxiety as to the result of the impending struggle.[30]

While the prisoners were in Moyamensing, John Greenleaf Whittier wrote a poem "inscribed to Friends under arrest for treason against the slave power." The inscription refers to the four accused whites, all of whom were commonly thought to be Quakers. Although the poet exaggerates the heroism of these whites, the first stanza of Whittier's poem remains a bitter, biting comment on his society. The moving second stanza may be read as a tribute to all the Christiana resisters:

> The age is dull and mean. Men creep,
>   Not walk; with blood too pale and tame
>   To pay the debt they owe to shame;
> Buy cheap, sell dear; eat, drink, and sleep
>   Down-pillowed, deaf to moaning want;
> Pay tithes for soul-insurance; keep
>   Six days to Mammon, one to Cant.
>
> In such a time, give thanks to God,
>   That somewhat of the holy rage
>   With which the prophets in their age

On all its decent seemings trod,
  Has set your feet upon the lie,
That man and ox and soul and clod
  Are market stock to sell and buy! [31]

10 Reaction

IN THE DAYS FOLLOWING the battle the nation's press published news reports and editorials on what was generally called the Christiana "riot." The editorials interpreted the "riot" according to the political views of each party and faction, north and south. The Christiana resistance became propaganda.[1]

In the south, a secessionist faction called for the dissolution of the Union, condemned the 1850 Compromise, and questioned the effectiveness of the new fugitive slave law. The Christiana resistance provoked a South Carolina secessionist editorial to call on southerners to "throw off the accursed yoke which is galling us, at the risk of our fortunes, . . . and our lives." [2]

Southern moderates believed that the north-south conflict could be adjusted within the Union, supported the 1850 Compromise and the new fugitive slave law. This legislation, said a "moderate" Baltimore paper, had just begun to restore "good feeling between North and South" when the deplorable Christiana resistance "produced such an excitement—such a feeling of indignation in Maryland . . . as has seldom been witnessed." [3] Southern moderates hoped the resisters would be quickly brought to trial, and severely punished, as a demonstration of northern accommodation to the interests of the slave system. A Washington, D.C.,

137

paper advocated the death penalty for the "pestilent agitators" who had caused the resistance.[4]

Southern papers generally suggested that the black resisters had been incited by white abolitionists. A Louisiana paper hoped that Pennsylvania would take "resolute action to crush within her borders that desperate faction whose teachings have produced and encouraged these lawless acts." [5]

Southerners warned that disunion would surely follow if the north failed to punish and prevent fugitive resistance. A North Carolina editorial warned northerners to obey the fugitive slave law and threatened secession:

> If not, WE LEAVE YOU! Before God and man . . . if you fail in this simple act of justice, THE BONDS WILL BE DISSOLVED.

A Florida editorial on the resistance asked, "Are such assassinations to be repeated?" If so, said the paper, "the sword of Civil War is already unsheathed." [6]

In the north a large group of pro-Unionists strongly supported the Compromise and fugitive law, hoping these measures would bring peace, prosperity, and stability to the nation. They condemned the Christiana "riot" for disturbing relations between the sections. A Boston journal emphasized: the "unhappy differences between the north and south" had been adjusted by the Compromise, "harmony" reestablished. The Christiana resistance would "probe anew the half-healed wound." [7]

These pro-Compromise northerners criticized the "rioters" for challenging the sanctity of federal law. Slave owner Gorsuch, a Pennsylvania paper emphasized, "had all the necessary documents" to legally re-take his runaways. A New York paper condemned the resistance, saying, "The question is not what is the ethic of the matter, but what is the LAW of the matter." [8]

Many of these pro-Compromise northerners also blamed the "riot" on white abolitionists. A Boston paper declared that "the abolitionists thirsted for the blood of the Southerners," and had "urged their innocent dupes, the colored mob," to commit "a most foul murder." A New York paper declared: "The real murderers are the Abolitionists," whose "higher law" doctrine was like a "musket and bullet" in the hands of "the innocent negro." A

Lancaster, Pennsylvania, paper admitted there were in that county
a minority of "fanatical monomaniacs who justify armed resistance to the law." [9]

The tiny *Saturday Express* of Lancaster prophetically headlined
the Christiana resistance: "Civil War—The First Blow Struck."
The resistance, said the paper, had created

> a fever heat of indignation; not so much at the negroes as
> at those who instigated them to the deed. We have long
> foreseen such an issue; God grant that the future has
> nothing worse in store growing out of the same cause, . . .
> but we have an ominous premonition that this is not the
> end, but only the beginning. . . .[10]

An editorial in the Rochester, New York, *Advertiser* expressed
one of the most extreme northern reactions to armed black
resistance:

> A correspondent writes us, that "for a few days past, it
> has been observed that colored persons are pricing and
> buying fire-arms, such as pistols, revolvers, &c., with the
> avowed intention of using them against the ministers of the
> law, and our orderly citizens, should they be called upon to
> aid in the executing of the Fugitive Law in our city. . . ."
> Let the negroes buy as many revolvers as they please;
> but they may rest assured that the first one that is used by
> them against our citizens will be the signal for the
> extermination of the whole negro race from our midst. If
> they wish to provoke *a war of the races,* by re-enacting the
> bloody scenes of Christiana, they will find our civil and
> military authorities, and our citizens at large, prepared to
> defend themselves, and to put down their murderous
> assaults, with an avenging arm that will carry retributive
> justice home to such vile traitors and assassins. If the issue
> is to be forced upon us, to decide whether the white races
> are to maintain their rights and their position, or whether
> *negro mob law* is to govern and ride rampant over our laws,
> constitution and liberties—let it be known at once, that our
> people may be prepared for the emergency.[11]

Another less extreme group of northerners were ambivalent about the Christiana "riot." On the one hand they supported the Union, and welcomed the peace-keeping intention of the Compromise and fugitive law. But, they felt, in effect, this fugitive law would only lead to trouble. Some northerners also questioned the morality of the fugitive law, especially that provision commanding individuals to assist in an arrest. Their consciences were torn between the inhumanity of returning fugitives to slavery, and their respect for property, law, and order. The law must be obeyed, they felt, until it could be repealed. This conflict of feelings and beliefs caused what now seem some abrupt changes of editorial viewpoint.

The Boston *Christian Register* first declared:

> All the natural rights and claims and apologies are on the fugitive's side. He only did what any white man would be applauded for doing.

But, said the paper, violent resistance to the law was "bad, unlawful, impolitic and mischievous . . . and the offenders will have to suffer." [12] William Cullen Bryant's popular New York *Evening Post* declared the fugitive slave law "violated the moral instincts of the people." But, the paper concluded:

> it is better for one or a dozen men to suffer, than that the moral supremacy of the laws should be shaken.[13]

Horace Greeley's New York *Tribune*, America's most influential newspaper in the 1850s, in an editorial on "The Affray at Christiana" denied that white abolitionists had "advised the negroes to arm themselves and shoot down the slave catchers." The blacks had been counseled by Quaker friends to flee, rather than to fight. "It was good counsel and it is to be deplored that the negroes did not follow it." The *Tribune* continued:

> A great deal of horror is expressed . . . because white men perished attempting to execute a law of the United States. Had two of the resisting negroes fallen instead, comparatively little would have been thought of it, and we presume no arrests would have been deemed necessary.

The *Tribune* was "deeply shocked at the bloodshed" at Christiana, "but we cannot hold the negroes guilty of the crime of murder." The blacks had opposed the civil law, it was true, but a "divine law of Nature" was on their side. They had defended

> an inalienable right . . . to their own persons. . . . No act of Congress can make it *right* for one man to convert another into his personal property, or *wrong* for that other to refuse to be so treated.

"Slavery," said the *Tribune*, is a matter "of violence, and by violence," resistance to slavery was authorized "in the eyes of impartial and unsophisticated justice."

Then the *Tribune* concluded:

> But whatever be the absolute natural right in this case, it is plain that the blacks fell into lamentable error. They ought to have followed the advice of their friends and escaped from the country.

Had they fled instead of fighting, the blacks would have found "aid and comfort" on their journey:

> Now, by their act, they have changed the case and made themselves to be regarded as aggressors instead of sufferers. It is out of the question for fugitives to think of forcibly resisting the authorities, and being so, it is wrong for them to undertake it. . . . The only safety for such persons is to get out of this land of liberty as fast as they can.[14]

William Lloyd Garrison's Boston *Liberator*, representing the non-violent, "moral suasion" abolitionists, emphasized the provocative role of slavery, the fugitive law, and armed slave catching posses in causing violent resistance. The *Liberator* recognized that armed self-defense was a *legally* justified and generally honored American tradition, and felt the Christiana blacks were "fully justified in what they did by the Declaration of Independence." [15]

The *Pennsylvania Freeman*, like many abolitionist papers, also related the Christiana resistance to the ideals of the American Revolution. Had not Americans

> claimed "Liberty or death," "Resistance to tyrants is duty to God," as their National Creed? What wonder that the

negro fugitives think it is no crime . . . to defend their liberties by the same means for using which the "Revolutionary heroes" of our own and other countries are glorified? [16]

The National Anti-Slavery Standard declared:

> That Gorsuch should have been shot down like a dog seems to us the most natural thing in the world. . . .

The *Standard* had no doubt that the example set at Christiana "will be followed, and perhaps improved upon hereafter. . . ." The nation's editorial writers, said the paper, should not expect black people will "submit to Slavery even though the Salvation of the Union is dependent on such submission." [17]

A black New York newspaper, the *Impartial Citizen*, commented on the "ferocious malignity of sentiment" with which the nation's popular press had generally treated the Christiana resistance. The black paper was glad that a few voices had been raised in defense of the Christiana resisters and that principle of "liberty" for which Crispus Attucks, and other American revolutionaries, had died.[18]

The tactics of the Christiana resisters caused debate at abolitionist meetings. While the prosecution of the resisters was still in progress—

> in the midst of fiery trials—in a time of deepest excitement —near the locality of the late Christiana tragedy—the members and friends of the Pennsylvania Anti-Slavery Society held their Fourteenth Annual Meeting, at West Chester.

At this meeting a Mr. Aaron

> said he was sorry for the death of Gorsuch for a man whose heart was filled with tyranny . . . was not prepared to die—to meet his God.

But, Mr. Aaron added,

> he would have been more sorry had the slave-catchers got Parker and Pinckney and those other brave men, and carried them back into slavery. Those colored men were

only following the example of Washington and the American heroes of '76.

Their cause was righteous, if their means were not altogether right. We must pardon something to poor human nature, thus driven to its last extremity. Could we expect men so oppressed, so stripped of protection, when assailed by a band of armed kidnappers, to do better?

Mr. Aaron proposed that the Pennsylvania Anti-Slavery Society

let the world know that we sympathize with our brethren who are imprisoned on the charge of treason.

A more orthodox Garrisonian, Oliver Johnson, rose to publicly dissent "from the sentiments in favor of violence, avowed by Mr. Aaron." The Pennsylvania Anti-Slavery Society "had ever discouraged a resort to violence, and counselled reliance upon truth and moral power." Oliver Johnson added:

That men who believe in violence should act as they do at Christiana and Syracuse [where another fugitive slave rescue had occurred], was to be expected, and they who glorify the patriots of the Revolution can find no fault with them. But our weapons are only the mild arms of truth and love, weapons mightier far than sword or bayonet. Perseverence in the use of these must bring us success.

A resolution passed at the meeting blamed the fugitive slave law for the "Christiana tragedy and its consequences." It deplored those consequences "as most disgraceful to our country in the eyes of the world," and especially in the eyes

of those nations of Europe, who, while struggling for freedom against despotic power, have looked toward this nation as a model government, and a home of liberty.[19]

A number of more militant white abolitionists spoke eloquently in defense of the Christiana rebels. Joshua Giddings, the fiery abolitionist Congressman from Ohio, speaking at Worcester, Massachusetts, declared:

When I read the accounts of that terrible tragedy, recently enacted at Christiana, I could not but rejoice that the

Joshua Giddings. (Wm. L. Katz Collection)

despised and hunted fugitives, whom this unconstitutional enactment put beyond protection of the laws, had stood up manfully in defense of their God given rights and shot down the miscreants who had come with the desperate purpose of taking them again to the land of slavery. The time will come when the names of these men will be enrolled upon the list with those of the noblest warriors of the revolution.[20]

Gerrit Smith, a well-known political abolitionist, and a friend of John Brown, praised both the Christiana resisters and the blacks who had rescued a fugitive in Syracuse:

The half million of free blacks in this nation and Canada, hitherto patient beyond all parallel, under the insults and outrages heaped upon them, are at last giving signs that they will "stand for their life." Among these signs are the manly resistance offered to the kidnappers at Christiana, and the brave and beautiful bearing of the black men at Syracuse. . . .

Perhaps succumbing to some degree of wishful thinking, Smith assured blacks of white support for future acts of self-defense.[21]

In the aftermath of the Christiana battle Theodore Parker, the

Gerrit Smith. (Villard)

Theodore Parker. (Villard)

unorthodox Unitarian clergyman of Boston, discussed the effects of armed black resistance, and condemned the 1850 Compromise:

> It is now a very trying time with us all. It has long been plain, that the two Ideas of America—the Idea of Freedom and the Idea of Bondage—were entirely incompatible. . . . Peace measures, which seek a compromise between the two, will always turn out measures of war. . . . The question is not merely, "Shall there be slavery in one part of the nation? . . ." the question is, "Shall there be freedom in the other part?"

The Federal Government, the President, the Whigs, the Democrats, the leading merchants, and newspapers are all in favor of slavery, said the Reverend Mr. Parker. The leading clergymen

> have been true to the instinct of their class; they have sided with money, sided with power, and with the oppressor against the oppressed.

He continued:

> these are hard times; times of corruption, evil times. . . . Yet I think they are glorious times, also.

The anti-slavery movement could no longer be ignored. Every election was affected by the slavery issue. A great crisis was already underway. The clergyman was "glad the crisis has come; it will be over all the sooner."

Undoubtedly with the Christiana resistance in mind, Theodore Parker declared:

> I am glad some black men have been found at last, who dared to resist violence with powder and ball. They are driven to the elementary instincts of human nature. The law is against them; the Constitution is against them; public opinion is against them; and the kidnapper arms to take their bodies. Men who reverence our fathers for throwing British tea into Boston Harbor, and shooting to death the British soldiers at Lexington and Bunker Hill, cannot fail to do honor to negroes who repel violence by violence and shoot the kidnappers. . . . I say, I rejoice that a negro has shot a kidnapper. Black men may now hold up their heads before those haughty Caucasians, and say, "You see we also can fight. The power to kill is not a monopoly of the slave hunter!"

Then came a startling change of tone:

> But I deplore violence; let us do without it while we can, for ever if we can. I am no non-resistant; yet I am glad the leading anti-slavery men are so—that, great as is the right of liberty, they would not shed a drop of blood to achieve it for all mankind; for though I think their doctrines extreme, they are yet nearer right, I think, than the common notions. Let us have firmness without fight, as long as possible.[22]

Even this militant white clergyman felt it necessary to qualify his support of armed self-defense.

Some uncelebrated white people were unequivocal in their support. C. M. K. Glen of Macedon wrote to Frederick Douglass on September 27, 1851:

> Friend Douglass:
> I have just read the account of the battle at Christiana, . . .
> I want to say to you that I rejoice in the result. I *cordially approve* the conduct of the negroes, and hope that the blood shed, may be a good investment for freedom. I hold that the right of Revolution belongs to every man, to *black, as well as white,* that these men had as perfect a right to fight for their liberty as our revolutionary fathers did for theirs, and that any one who should join them in the struggle, should be placed side by side with Lafayette.

The writer compared the Christiana rebels and the exiled Hungarian freedom fighter Louis Kossuth, then due to make a fund raising tour of the United States. Glen asked:

> Will the people of this nation extend the hand of friendship and protection to Kossuth and his companions, and hang these men? [23]

On October 7, 1851, Frederick Douglass's white assistant editor Julia Griffiths wrote to Mary Botham Howitt, one of the day's most popular English novelists:

> The pro-slavery papers of the land designate the affair at Christiana "the Christiana tragedy," and the negroes concerned are called "traitors" or "assassins." I regard William Parker and his accomplices as true heroes. If they had been a little band of Hungarians or Poles, or Circassians fighting against a tyrant oppressor for their freedom, and having for their watchword, "Liberty or Death," their plaudits would have resounded from the shores of the Atlantic to the blue waves of the Pacific; but the men of Christiana were poor negroes, whose very manhood is disputed, and whose right to fight for their freedom is denied them!

It is an old saying that "even the crushed worm will turn at last," and I thank God that, at Christiana the tide of the slave-catchers onward march was "suddenly stopped and rolled backwards; that his dreams of invincibleness were broken," and that Eternal Justice there vindicated the right.[24]

The Christiana resistance was a significant event in Frederick Douglass's break with the Garrisonian abolitionists, and the black leader's adoption of a new anti-slavery philosophy. For his first ten years in the anti-slavery movement, Douglass had been a loyal Garrisonian. In February, 1849, an editorial in Douglass's *North Star* had first indicated his reservations about Garrison's non-violence and his refusal to participate in political activity. Douglass's editorial declared that slaveholders

> have forfeited even the right to live, and if the slave should put every one of them to the sword to-morrow, who dare . . . say that the criminals deserved less than death at the hands of their long-abused chattels?

In June, 1849, Frederick Douglass surprised an anti-slavery audience in Garrison's own Boston by declaring:

> I should welcome the intelligence to-morrow, should it come, that the slaves had risen in the South, and that the sable arms which had been engaged in beautifying and adorning the South were engaged in spreading death and devastation.

Hearing gasps of astonishment from his audience, Douglass asked them why, when they had hailed the 1848 barricades of the French Republicans,

> should you not hail with equal pleasure the tidings from the South that the slaves had risen, and achieved for themselves, against the iron-hearted slaveholder, what the republicans of France achieved against the royalists of France?

Douglass's disagreement with the Garrisonians came to a head at a public meeting of the American Anti-Slavery Society, at Syracuse, New York, in May, 1851, four months before the Christiana resistance. With Garrison himself in attendance, Douglass announced his conclusion that the Constitution might be interpreted, in light of its preamble, as an anti-slavery document. Douglass now believed in using the ballot for the overthrow of slavery, and his announcement caused great excitement. Garrison, intolerant of any dissent, cried out: "There is roguery somewhere." After what Douglass calls this "insulting remark," the break between the black leader and the Garrisonians became more pronounced.

A month later, in June, 1851, Douglass's newspaper, *The North Star*, merged with the *Liberty Party Paper*, and editor Douglass moved squarely into the camp of political abolitionists. The new *Frederick Douglass' Paper* began publication in Rochester, New York.[25] Four years earlier, in 1847, Douglass's home in Rochester had become an important station on the underground railroad. Rochester was a last main stop before Canada, and by 1850 Douglass was the leader of the busy underground in that city. On September 20, underground stationmaster Douglass personally implicated himself with the Christiana resisters by helping William Parker and two fellow blacks escape to Canada. On September 25, 1851, five days after William Parker had passed through Douglass's Rochester home *Douglass' Paper* carried an editorial headed: "Freedom's Battle at Christiana." In sarcastic and biting words Douglass wholeheartedly justified the armed resistance.[26]

"Everybody seems astonished," said Douglass, "that in this land of gospel light and liberty" men had been found "willing to peril even life itself" to gain freedom and avoid slavery:

> Pro-slavery men especially are in a state of amazement at the strange affair. That the hunted men should fight with the biped bloodhounds that had tracked them, even when the animals had a *"paper"* authorizing them to hunt, is to them inexplicable audacity.

That the blacks had killed the slave hunters might

> be explained in the light of the generally admitted principle "that self-preservation is the first law of nature," but, the

Frederick Douglass. (Wm. L. Katz Collection)

rascals! they killed their pursuers, when they knew they had *"papers!"* Just here is the point of difficulty. What could have got into these men of sable coating? Didn't they know that slavery, not freedom, is their natural condition?

Didn't they know that their legs, arms, eyes, hands and heads, were the rightful property of the white men who claimed them?

Did not these black men know, asked Douglass, that "in the seventy-fifth year of the freedom and independence of the American people *from the bondage of a foreign yoke,*" a new fugitive slave law had been decreed? Douglass addressed the black resisters:

Oh! ye most naughty and rebellious fellows! Why stand ye up like men, after this mighty decree? Why have not your hands become paws, and your arms, legs? Why are you not down among four-footed beasts with the fox, the wolf and the bear sharing with them the chances of the chase, but constituting the most choice game—the peculiar game of this free and christian country.

By signing the fugitive slave law of the United States, President Millard Fillmore himself had commanded that black men should cease to be men. But, "friends and brethren," said Douglass:

if the story gets afloat that these negroes of Christiana did really hear the words of the mighty Fillmore commanding them to be brutes instead of men and they did not change as ordered—why, the dangerous doctrine will also get afloat presently that there is a law higher than the law of Fillmore.

The Christiana resistance, declared Douglass, had demonstrated

that all NEGROES ARE NOT SUCH FOOLS AND DASTARDS AS TO CLING TO *Life* WHEN IT IS COUPLED WITH CHAINS AND SLAVERY.

This lesson, though most dearly bought, is quite worth the price paid. It was needed. The lamb-like submission with which men of color have allowed themselves to be dragged away from liberty, from family and all that is dear to the hearts of men, had wellnigh established the impression that they were conscious of their own fitness for slavery.

COLLEGE OF THE SEQUOIA
LIBRARY

Lack of resistance had only encouraged slave catchers, said Douglass. "The Christiana conflict was therefore needed," he said, to check these slave hunters. "Life and liberty," said Douglass,

> are the most sacred of all man's rights. If these may be invaded with impunity, all others may be. . . .

The resistance was right in terms of that

> justice which says to the aggressor . . . he that taketh the sword shall perish by the sword. The man who rushes out of the orbit of his own rights, to strike down the rights of another, does by that act, divest himself of the right to live; if he be shot down, his punishment is just.[27]

On November 5 and 6, Douglass, and the black leader Charles Remond, took part in a spirited debate on resistance, at a meeting of the Rhode Island Anti-Slavery Society. Remond, like Douglass, is said to have "justified the killing" at Christiana. *Douglass' Paper* reports that Remond

> exhorted his people to a brave and manly bearing . . . and reminded them that there was one avenue left to them— that they could be Traitors to the government that oppressed them, and if they died in heroic defense of their rights, posterity would reverence and cherish their memories while their oppressors would inherit an immortality of infamy.

This report adds that Frederick Douglass gave a long argument "in favor of forcible resistance to the Fugitive Slave Law." Another report has Douglass saying, of slave catchers, "that every one of them ought to be killed."

The white Garrisonian abolitionist Charles C. Burleigh followed Douglass

> agreeing with him in advocating a spiritual resistance to this diabolical law, but was opposed to physical violence and bloodshed, in all cases whatever, and went into a powerful argument to show them to be wrong in principle, and impolitic in practice.

Garrisonian pacifism, not Douglass's and Remond's opinion, triumphed in the meeting's resolution on Christiana.[28]

On November 20, 1851, Frederick Douglass, writing in his own paper, continued to support armed resistance:

> I insist upon it, that the only way to meet the man-hunter successfully, is with cold steel and the nerve to use it. The wretch who engages in such a business is impervious to every consideration of truth, love and mercy, and nothing short of putting him in bodily danger can deter him. The colored people must defend their rights, if they would have their rights respected. To shape their muscles for the fetters, and to adjust their wrists for the handcuffs at the bidding of the slaveholder, is an example of non-resistance, quite as radical as any class of men in the country could wish, and while it might excite the sympathy of a few, it could not fail to bring down upon the whole race to which they belong, the scorn and contempt of every brave man. I have but one lesson for my people in the present trying hour; it is this: *"Count your lives utterly worthless, unless coupled with the inestimable blessing of liberty."*

Other blacks were also unequivocal in their feelings for the Christiana resisters. Moral and financial support for all arrested came from many blacks throughout the country. In New York City the black leaders Dr. James McCune Smith, the Reverend Dr. J. C. Pennington, William Powell, Thomas Downing, and Charles W. Ray attended "a small but spirited meeting in Shiloh church basement" to "raise money to defend the Christiana Patriots." [29] In Columbus, Ohio, blacks honored the "victorious heroes at the battle of Christiana." [30] In Chicago, a meeting of black citizens, including John Jones, J. Barguet, H. O. Wagoner, William Johnson, and William Brown proposed "means to aid the Christiana sufferers on trial in Philadelphia." The "Ladies of Chicago Mutual Protection Society" contributed ten dollars on the spot.[31] In Philadelphia, the Special Vigilance Committee issued a financial appeal for the "Christiana patriots," signed by black leaders John P. Burr, J. J. G. Gould Bias, William Forten, and N. W. Dupee. In four months this Committee raised $663.41, of which $250 came from blacks in San Francisco, California.[32]

In Detroit, a large meeting of black people, including the Reverend W. C. Monroe, R. L. Baptiste, and William Lambert, appointed a "Committee of Vigilance," took a collection, and issued an appeal to all churches "in behalf of the Christiana sufferers." Five days later a second large Detroit meeting reported a good response to its earlier appeal from churches and "friends in all parts of the country." [33] Among these contributors, a group of Detroit black women raised thirty dollars, and sent it with a note to the "Special Vigilance Committee" of Philadelphia, "in behalf of our noble-hearted liberty-loving patriots of Christiana." The note said:

> We feel ourselves (females as we are) specially called upon to answer that portion of your appeal which relates to their suffering families.[34]

The reply from the Philadelphia Committee thanked the Detroit women for the money, but added:

> I by no means like the insinuation "females as we are" as though you were not a part of the great chain of humanity, and bound by every tie that links us to God our great father, and to our common destiny. In this case which is really and truly the cause of Christ, there is neither male nor female. . . .[35]

In the summer of 1851, the black minister Samuel Ringold Ward was touring the mid-west and north, speaking at abolitionist meetings about the fugitive slave law. Ward and his wife were in Ohio, and "about finishing that tour,"

> when we saw in the papers an account of the Gorsuch case, in Christiana . . .

Ward read of the arrest of the blacks said to have resisted, and their prosecution by a government which

> seemed determined to have their blood. Upon reading this, I handed the paper containing the account to my wife; and we concluded that resistance was fruitless, that the country

was hopelessly given to the execution of this barbarous [fugitive slave] enactment, and that it were vain to hope for the reformation of such a country.

With this in mind, and since the anti-slavery cause was not supplying bread and education for his children, Samuel Ringold Ward and his wife, on Monday, September 29, 1851,

> jointly determined to wind up our affairs, and go to Canada.[36]

11 Treason

On September 16, 1851, the Reverend John S. Gorsuch, the dead slave owner's eldest son, a clergyman in Washington, D.C., wrote a letter from Christiana to the Baltimore *Sun.* The Reverend Mr. Gorsuch had not been a posse member but had come to Pennsylvania after the battle. The Reverend's "History of the Christiana Tragedy," reprinted in many papers, described that event in lurid terms. As the Reverend Mr. Gorsuch reported it, the marshal had called for and begun a retreat when Castner Hanway "said something to the negroes," and "they set up a most hideous yell. . . ." According to the Reverend:

> the negroes in the house . . . rushing out, and whooping like savages, met the advancing gang around my father.

The Reverend describes four white posse members,

> all armed with pistols, it is true, opposed to about one hundred infuriated, blood-thirsty, howling demons.

The Reverend reported a black man striking his father on the head from behind, his father falling to his knees, and then being "shot several times, and cut over the head with corn-cutters." "The negroes," said the minister, conjuring up visions of black

156

barbarians, "were whooping and yelling with savage glee over their victim. . . ." [1]

Edward Gorsuch's Maryland sympathizers held a meeting at Slade's Tavern in Baltimore County on September 15. They recommended the formation of district councils "for the protection of the people in their slave and other property," resolved to contribute financially to the prosecution of Gorsuch's attackers, and agreed to employ a counsel to make sure Gorsuch's attackers received full punishment. [2]

An indignation meeting of reportedly 6000 people met at Monument Square in Baltimore City on September 15. Speakers called the Christiana "riot" an abuse of the "constitutional rights of every Southern man," and defended the Compromise and the Union. [3]

Another mass meeting of more strident tone occurred on September 17, in the north, in Philadelphia's Independence Square. Its purpose was "to ferret out and punish the murderers," those "guilty of the double crime of assaulting the Constitution" and taking "the lives of men in pursuit of their recognized and rightful property. . . ." It was proposed to take steps "for the protection of our own rights and the rights of our children," said to be

> daily imperilled and assailed by a race, who can never be our social or political equals. . . .

It was also proposed that blacks be prevented from settling in Pennsylvania. The abolitionists, described as "Utopian Philanthropists and insane fanatics," were said to have seen their doctrines exemplified at Christiana "in treason and blood." One speaker, John Campbell, was the author of *Negro-Mania*, "an examination of the falsely assumed equality of the various races," a book which demonstrated his own anti-black fanaticism. [4]

Philadelphia businessmen began to react. Pennsylvania newspaper editor Alexander McClure reports that

> the murder of a claimant for his property, acting in accordance with the laws of the nation, caused a very serious revulsion in the commercial and business circles of the State.

Philadelphia then had the largest Southern trade of any
of the Northern cities, and interwoven with it were large
business interests throughout the entire Commonwealth.[5]

An election for Pennsylvania governor was about to take place.
Whig candidate, Governor William F. Johnston, was running for
re-election against Democrat William Biggler. Governor Johnston
represented the moderate anti-slavery sentiment in the Whig
Party. As an elected official, Governor Johnston was pledged to
uphold the fugitive slave law, although he personally believed
every possible legal means should be used to repeal it.[6]

The Christiana "riot" alienated a large element in Governor
Johnston's own party, those who heartily supported the fugitive
slave law and the Compromise of 1850. These Whigs, known as
"silver-grays," or irreverently as "dough-faces," turned against
Johnston. These Whigs, says Alexander McClure, "regarded
commerce as more important than political faith, and they went
bodily" to the support of Democratic candidate Biggler.

McClure emphasizes that "the commercial classes" of Philadelphia

> were peculiarly sensitive about slavery agitation because of
> its probable effect upon the business of the city.

"Even Philadelphia," says W. U. Hensel, "was extremely conservative and desperately anxious not to lose the trade of the south." [7]

Among these commercial classes were also many Democrats
firmly opposed to the Whig governor's re-election. The Christiana
"riot" provided an occasion for a group of Philadelphia's most
prominent Democrats and businessmen to address an "open
letter" to Governor Johnston on September 14, three days after
the "riot." Signed by members of the city's most prominent
families, the letter asserted

> That citizens of a neighboring state have been cruelly
> assassinated by a band of armed outlaws at a place not
> more than three hours journey distant from the seat of
> government and from the Commercial metropolis of the
> State.
>
> That this insurrectionary movement . . . has been so far
> successful as to overawe the local ministers of justice. . . .

That your memorialists are not aware that any military force has been sent to the scene of the insurrection, or that the civil authority has been strengthened by . . . measures suited to the momentous crisis.[8]

Governor Johnston publicly replied on the same day that the guilty resisters had been arrested and would be given "the severest penalty" provided by state law. Johnston continued:

Permit me, gentlemen, having thus removed all just cause of anxiety from your minds, respectfully to suggest that the idea of rebellion or insurrectionary movement in the county of Lancaster or anywhere else in this Commonwealth, has no real foundation, and it is an offensive imputation on a large body of our fellow citizens. There is no insurrectionary movement in Lancaster County, and there would be no occasion to march military force there, as you seem to desire, and inflame the public mind by such strange exaggeration.

Johnston invited the "gentlemen" to abstain "from undue violence of language" and allow the law to take its course.[9]

The next morning, September 15, Johnston informed, perhaps for the first time, that leading participants in the Christiana "riot" were still at large, issued a proclamation offering a $1000 reward for the capture and conviction of the guilty parties. That same afternoon the prominent Democratic businessmen wrote a second open letter to the governor criticizing his absence from the seat of government (he was campaigning), and the fact that, shortly after the "riot," Johnston had passed by train through Christiana without paying his due respects to Gorsuch's corpse.

The governor's critics had a point. On the evening of the resistance, the train carrying Johnston on a campaign trip from Harrisburg to Philadelphia stopped at the Christiana station—at the very door of Zercher's Hotel where the body of Edward Gorsuch was laid out. While Johnston's fellow passengers had disembarked to view the remains, the governor himself had remained firmly in his seat. Johnston's disinterest had, no doubt, been a calculated political act, conveying his disapproval of the fugitive law and slave catchers.[10]

In their second letter the governor's critics also presumed that he would

> no longer treat the offense of the insurgents as though the homicide, which all deplore, had been committed by them, in an ordinary tumulty. . . . The crime which had been perpetrated in our immediate neighborhood was Treason. . . .

The writers claimed that forty-eight hours had elapsed before the police received enough reinforcements to safely visit the scene of the disturbance, and "the insurgents were then dispersed." The writers deplored the fact that the governor's "first act of State" was a proclamation issued four days after the battle. The Philadelphia gentlemen concluded:

> We believe that those enemies of the United States, whose acts you so charitably deny to be treasonable or insurrectionary, threaten and intend to re-enact them if a like occasion should arrive. We believe that your letter will afford them encouragement in their lawless designs.[11]

On September 18, the Reverend John S. Gorsuch got into the argument with his own open letter to the Governor of Pennsylvania. Although it was said the Reverend Mr. Gorsuch, "a preacher of the gospel, . . . never interferes in political affairs," the preacher's letter certainly added fuel to the anti-Johnston fires. The Reverend desired everyone to know the governor's "lack of official promptness" had resulted in the escape of slaves, allegedly the "principal murderers of his father." Gorsuch criticized Johnston for not viewing "the ghastly spectacle" of his father's remains. The Reverend reminded the governor that previously his brother Dickinson, "now so near death, was sent to you with a requisition from the Governor of Maryland" for the free black implicated in the Gorsuch grain theft; "but you would not deliver him up, and sent my brother home. . . ." This same black, the Reverend charged, had been among the Christiana rebels.

Gorsuch asked why the Pennsylvania governor had not issued his proclamation before "the murderers" escaped. Did the governor know "that not a magistrate or constable would act until compelled . . . ?" Gorsuch charged that the governor's Attorney

General, "true to his superior," would not aid Lancaster County officers in making arrests.[12]

On September 25, the Reverend Mr. Gorsuch sent "a card" retracting his charge against the Attorney General but reaffirming his accusations against the governor. Four days later, Attorney General Thomas E. Franklin himself replied to the Reverend Mr. Gorsuch—defending the governor and suggesting that the public determine whether Gorsuch's attack was attributable "to the evil instigation of some determined and unscrupulous political enemy of the Governor." [13]

This correspondence ended on October 6, with an angry rejoinder from the Reverend Mr. Gorsuch denying that his criticism of Governor Johnston had been instigated by anyone other than himself. Gorsuch thought it was extraordinary that when "my father was murdered by a band of negroes, encouraged by white abolitionists," the Governor of Pennsylvania had "showed an indifference that almost amounted to connivance." [14]

These public charges and countercharges helped to decide the election of the next Pennsylvania governor. The reaction to the Christiana battle, says Alexander McClure, "determined a most earnest and desperate contest for Governor. . . ." W. U. Hensel agrees; the Christiana resistance helped to "depress the campaign prospects of the Whigs." Johnston received 178,034 votes to Biggler's 186,499 and lost the election to Democrat Biggler by the small margin of 8465 votes. Democratic candidates also won four out of five Pennsylvania supreme court judgeships.[15]

While these political events were taking place in Pennsylvania, negotiations concerning the prosecution of the Christiana resisters were going on in Washington, D.C. The south was anxious that opponents of the fugitive slave law be punished and worried that Pennsylvania might treat the Christiana prisoners too leniently. On September 18, 1851, Governor of Maryland Louis E. Lowe wrote an open letter to President Millard Fillmore, pressuring the United States Government to take action in the case, emphasizing the dire consequences to follow if a "just punishment was not meted out to the Christiana prisoners."

Maryland had previously supported the Compromise, the Constitution, and the Union, wrote that state's governor: "It would be terrible indeed," if Maryland should be drawn to place herself at the head of a column of secession. Her declaration of disunion would be fatal. . . . The result is too terrible for contemplation. And yet, Sir, we must look the contingency right in the face.

The governor called for "retribution" upon the Christiana resisters, warning:

If passion and prejudice should control the verdicts of Pennsylvania juries, in the trial of this issue, I tremble for the Union.

Using a rather surprising metaphor, Lowe declared:

If the Union is to be merely a union of minority slaves to majority tyrants, . . . the sooner it is dissolved the better. This, I assure you, Sir, is the sentiment of the *patriotic South, the Conservative South, the Union-loving South.*

Referring to the Christiana battle, the Maryland governor declared:

I do not know of a single incident that has occurred since the passage of the Compromise measures, which tends more to weaken the bonds of union, and arouse dark thoughts in the minds of men, than this late tragedy. Nor will its influence and effects be limited within the narrow borders of our State. They will penetrate the soul of the South. They will silence the confident promise of the Union men and give force to the appeals of the Secessionists.

The governor concluded:

there is but a single corrective, . . . the most complete vindication of the laws and the fullest retribution upon the criminals.[16]

Such pressure, both from the north and south, caused the United States Government's action in the Christiana case. "The secret history" of the government's prosecution was told to H. G. Ashmead by his father, John W. Ashmead, Philadelphia U.S. Attorney at the time, and chief representative of the Fillmore administration's Law Department, headed by U.S. Attorney General John J. Crittenden.

In 1911 H. G. Ashmead revealed:

> As soon as the news of the troubles at Christiana reached
> Washington father was summoned there and had an
> interview with President Fillmore, Daniel Webster, then
> Secretary of State, and Attorney General Crittenden,—
> they were the three that he mentioned.

Ashmead "was loath to institute proceedings for treason in a case
in which he was confident" the verdict could only contradict

> the contentions of the general government. He was over-
> ruled, however, by the President, Mr. Webster, and Mr.
> Crittenden, who believed that while an acquittal of the
> defendant would be the only outcome of the trial possible,
> yet the authorities of Maryland were clamorous for some
> action on the part of the National Government, and the
> trouble and expense that such a proceeding would entail on
> the defendant would have the effect to deter others from
> like attempts to nullify provisions of the Fugitive Slave
> Law.

On November 14, 1851, in a letter to U.S. attorney John W.
Ashmead, the administration in Washington approved his course
in preparing for the Christiana prosecutions.[17]

The federal administration thus decided to prosecute for
treason, not expecting to win its case, but hoping that the
prosecution itself would placate southern opinion, and punish its
political opponents. That this political decision meant jailing a few
dozen blacks and several whites for months, and actually trying
one individual for an offense whose punishment was death, does
not seem to have disturbed the conscience of any lawyers or
politicians involved. The outrageousness of the United States
Government's prosecuting for political purposes is perhaps realized when one considers the mental anguish, physical distress, and
economic hardship caused those incarcerated and their families.

This political use of a treason charge was not new. Federalist
treason prosecutions of the Whiskey Rebels had also been
designed to impute disloyalty to the opposing faction's "Democratic clubs." Democrat charges of treason had helped make the

Hartford Convention the last blow to the then tottering Federalists. Effort had also been made to use treason prosecutions against opponents of the Jeffersonian Embargo. In a future case treason charges would be brought against leaders of the Homestead Strike, to break working class morale.[18]

The federal Constitution held that "Treason against the United States shall consist only in levying War . . . or in adhering to their Enemies, giving them Aid and Comfort." Two witnesses to the overt act of treason, or a confession in open court, were required for a conviction.

Prior to the trial of Hanway there had been seven incidents whose participants were actually tried for treason against the United States. Three of these incidents had occurred in Pennsylvania, seemingly a hotbed of subversion! In 1795, in the Pennsylvania Whiskey Rebellion cases, the defendants, Vigol and Mitchell, were convicted of levying war, based on their forcible resistance to the execution of a single federal statute; later they were pardoned. In 1799, in the Pennsylvania House Tax case, John Fries and others were also convicted of levying war by forcible resistance to the enforcement of a single federal law; they too were pardoned. In 1800, in other trials arising from the same incident, two defendants were acquitted of treason, two were found guilty. In 1807, in the Aaron Burr case, the judge directed a verdict of not guilty, based on the argument that levying war required an actual assemblage, not just a conspiracy. In 1808, in *U.S. versus Hoxie*, the judge directed that an organized, armed attack of smugglers on U.S. troops enforcing an embargo was a riot, not a levying of war. In 1814, in the *U.S. versus Lee*, the defendant who had sold provisions to the British was acquitted of intending to commit treason. Also in 1814, in a Pennsylvania case, *U.S. versus Pryor*, the judge directed that proceeding under a flag of truce with a British detachment, to help buy provisions, was not sufficient to establish adhering to the enemy. And in 1815, in the *U.S. versus Hodges*, the defendant was acquitted of adhering to the enemy in obtaining the release of prisoners to the British.[19]

The initial arrests and proceedings at Christiana had ended on September 15. Further hearings, scheduled for the next day, were postponed, apparently so the United States Government could prepare its treason case. Eight days later, on September 23, proceedings began again, this time in the Lancaster County Court House, before Alderman J. Franklin Reigart. Alderman Reigart, says W. U. Hensel, "mingled the pursuits of letters and law," and was the author of

> a somewhat bizarre biography of Robert Fulton, now [1911] something of a curio, once the ornament of many a center table in Lancaster County.

Whatever his literary attainments, Alderman Reigart was praised by the Reverend J. S. Gorsuch as one of the more resolute officials in the Christiana case.[20]

Prominent among the counsel for the prisoners at this Lancaster hearing was lawyer and anti-slavery Whig Thaddeus Stevens, then in his second term as the county's elected Representative in the United States Congress.[21] Among the lawyers for the prosecution were a number of prominent Lancaster County and Philadelphia officials, the Attorney General of Maryland, and a former U.S. Attorney General representing the friends of the late Edward Gorsuch. Lancaster County District Attorney John L. Thompson presented the case for the State of Pennsylvania, arguing that the Christiana resistance constituted the crime of "High Treason" against the United States.[22]

Marshal Henry H. Kline was the first and chief prosecution witness. References to the "niggers" liberally punctuated the marshal's accusations. He named several black men and three whites as present at the scene of battle. Another important prosecution witness, the young black man George Washington Harvey Scott, who had testified in a similar capacity at the previous Christiana hearing, again confirmed the accusations against the blacks named by Marshal Kline. The defense, in turn, produced several witnesses who swore to Scott's presence elsewhere at the time of battle.

Jacob Woods, another black prosecution witness, proclaimed his own innocence in going to Parker's, distinguishing his motives from the other blacks':

> I wouldn't have gone over there to be killed up—thought they were going to prove something.

No doubt under some behind-the-scenes pressure, Woods named seven black men as present at the battle, among these his own brother, Peter.

The defense presented sworn and detailed testimony that a good many of those blacks said to have been present at the battle had been elsewhere at the time. Despite these alibis Alderman Reigart, on September 25, sustained the charges against most of those accused. Their crime? Treason against the United States, and aiding and abetting in the murder of Edward Gorsuch. Those charged were taken to Philadelphia to await further proceedings. Several men who had been detained from the twelfth to the twenty-fifth of September were discharged. The day after Reigart's decision, on September 26, 1851, District Attorney Z. Collins Lee of Baltimore County, Maryland, wrote to President Fillmore, thanking him for the United States Government's action in the case.[23]

The complicated machinery of the law ground on; the case moved slowly through the judicial system, from village to town to city, from commissioner to alderman to judge. Two preliminary treason indictments had been handed down, one in Christiana by Commissioner Ingraham, one in Lancaster by Alderman Reigart. Now, in Philadelphia, the Christiana case came before a grand jury presided over by Judge John K. Kane.

As Judge Kane explained to this jury it was the duty of this "Grand Inquest" to inquire

> whether an offense has been committed, what was its legal character, and who were the offenders.

This grand jury would decide the indictment to be brought against the Christiana resisters in the U.S. Circuit Court. It was Judge Kane's duty to explain the "principles and rules of law" that applied in the case.[24]

Judge Kane's own strong "personal feeling" about enforcing the fugitive slave law was well known. Kane himself had been a district attorney and Attorney General of Pennsylvania. A year earlier, the judge had, instructing a grand jury, charged that abolitionist "fanatics of civil discord" were exalting in the power given them by the state's personal liberty law. Judge Kane had warned against forcible resistance to the new fugitive slave law,

Hon. John K. Kane. United States District Judge. (Hensel, *Christiana*)

asking that violations be strictly punished. That two of the judge's own sons were abolitionists, and one, at least, an active underground railroad agent, does not seem to have affected Kane's opinion.[25]

Kane's earlier charge, says W. U. Hensel, "did not afford a very encouraging outlook" for the Christiana resisters whose fate would be decided in the judge's court. "These very natural apprehensions," says Hensel, "were increased" when Judge Kane, on September 29, 1851, charged the grand jury sitting on the Christiana case.

Kane's instructions began with a survey of the alleged "facts." The "outrages" at Christiana were said to indicate a previous conspiracy to forcibly resist the United States Constitution's fugitive slave provision and law based on it. It was alleged, said Kane, "that for some months back gatherings of people, strangers as well as citizens," had taken place in the vicinity of Christiana. At these gatherings, it was said,

> exhortations were made and pledges interchanged to hold the law for the recovery of fugitives as of no validity, and to defy its execution.

Judge Kane assured the jury that "personally, I know nothing of the facts, or the evidence relating to them." As one of the justices before whom the Christiana prisoners would in future be tried, Kane said, "I have sought to keep my mind altogether free from any impressions of their guilt or innocence." But, stated Kane:

> If the circumstances to which I have adverted have in fact taken place,· they involve the highest crime known to our laws.

Since this was precisely one of the issues to be considered by the jury, the judge was using his authority to direct a decision.

"Treason against the United States," continued Kane, "is defined by the Constitution . . . to consist in 'levying war' " against the states. This included, said Kane, any combination to prevent the enforcement of a Constitutional provision or federal statute. The judge added that for "treason" to have taken place a "conspiring together to oppose the law by force, and some actual force must have been exerted. . . ."

The proof of a treasonous conspiracy, said the judge, "may be found in the declared purposes of the individual party before the actual outbreak; or it may be derived from the proceedings of meetings" in which he took part, "prompted," or "sanctioned," meetings "commending, counselling and instigating forcible resistance to the law."

"In treason," said Kane, "there are no accessories." All who advocated a treasonous act shared the guilt, whether or not they had bodily participated in the act. "There has been, I fear, an erroneous impression on this subject among a portion of our people," said Judge Kane, alluding to the unspeakable abolitionists. "If it has been thought safe," said Kane, "to counsel and instigate others" to acts of forcible resistance,

> to inflame the minds of the ignorant by appeals to passion, and denunciations of the law as oppressive, unjust, revolting to the conscience, and not binding on the actions of men,—to represent the Constitution of the land as a compact of iniquity, which it were meritorious to violate or subvert,—the mistake has been a grievous one. . . .

"He whose conscience," political or ethical theories forbid him to support the Constitution "in its fullest integrity, may relieve himself from the duties of citizenship" by leaving the country:

> But while he remains within our borders, he is to remember that successfully to instigate treason is to commit it.

Kane defended the law-abiding character of most Pennsylvanians:

> They have but one country, they recognize no law of higher social obligation than its Constitution, . . . they cherish no patriotism that looks beyond the Union. . . .

Kane admitted "that there are men here, as elsewhere, whom a misguided zeal impels to violations of the law. . . ." Referring to Pennsylvania's poor black population Kane acknowledged

> that we have not only in our alms-houses, but congregated here and there, in detached portions of the State, ignorant men, many of them without political rights, degraded in social position, and instinctive of revolt,—all this is true. . . . But it should not be supposed, that any of these represent the sentiment of Pennsylvania. . . .

Concluding his instructions to the grand jury, Kane added one last ominous reference to outside agitators:

> Your inquiries will not be restricted to the conduct of people belonging to our own State. If in the progress of them, you shall find that men have been among us, who, under whatever mask of conscience or of peace, have labored to incite others to treasonable violence, and who, after arranging the elements of the mischief, have withdrawn themselves to await the explosion they had contrived, you will feel yourselves bound to present the fact to the Court. . . .[26]

Early in October the grand jury began issuing indictments against individuals, and on November 13 collectively indicted thirty-six black men and five whites for treason against the United States. These forty-one citizens were (and as of 1974 still are) the largest number of Americans ever to be simultaneously charged with treason.[27]

Of the thirty-six black men charged, a few had definitely been active in the battle; some had served warning of the impending attack. Some of those blacks charged had quite definitely not been present at the time of battle, although they may have arrived at Parker's afterward. A number of blacks active in the resistance were not charged; these included Abraham Johnson, Alexander Pinckney, Hannah Pinckney, and Eliza Parker. Some twenty-seven of the thirty-six blacks charged were actually imprisoned; others charged, among them William Parker, and Gorsuch's fugitives, had escaped capture, and were to be tried *in absentia*.[28]

Besides those blacks imprisoned for treason, at least seven more were placed in the debtors' section of Philadelphia's Moyamensing prison, held at the government's expense, as prosecution witnesses. They received $1.25 a day for this allegedly voluntary service. No doubt a great deal of tough, behind-the-scenes bargaining had gone on to determine which of those blacks arrested would be accused of treason, and which would testify as witnesses for the prosecution.

The five whites charged with treason were Castner Hanway, Elijah Lewis, Joseph Scarlett, Joseph Townsend, and James Jackson. According to William Still, farmer James Jackson was an "aged member of the Society of Friends (a Quaker) and a well-known non-resistant abolitionist." W. U. Hensel reports that when Jackson was arrested, he "was so well known to Marshal Roberts that he was released 'on parole,' though subsequently indicted for treason." Although Jackson was one of those charged with the highest crime in the land, to be tried for his life, the Quaker was evidently never even imprisoned. Jackson had been nowhere near Christiana at the time of the resistance, and had no direct relation to it. The federal government apparently included the treason charge against Jackson simply to test the prosecution of any abolitionist whose speeches or writing might be interpreted as inciting resistance to the fugitive law.[29]

Joseph Townsend, being informed that "kidnappers" were at Parker's, had lent his loaded gun to a black man, John Roberts.

Joseph P. Scarlett, another of the accused whites, was a Quaker and a "man of mighty strength and brawn." It was said by a

Castner Hanway.   Elijah Lewis.   Joseph Scarlett.
Taken soon after the treason trial. (Hensel, *Christiana*)

neighbor that if Scarlett *had* been at Parker's during the confrontation,

> he doubtless would have proved a very good man for slaveholders to keep away from, notwithstanding his Quaker principles.

Another source identifies Scarlett as "a well-known abolitionist," who frequently gave employment and assistance to fugitives," but did not engage in underground railroad work "as a regular agent." He had helped to warn the area's blacks of the attack on Parker's. He had been present at the scene after the firing, and had ministered to the wounded Dickinson Gorsuch—some say had

Joseph Scarlett. (Forbes; The Library Company of Philadelphia Collection)

even saved the slave owner's son from attack by infuriated blacks.[30]

The two other accused whites, Castner Hanway and Elijah Lewis, had refused to assist in the arrests, and allegedly incited the blacks to violent resistance. Lewis was a storekeeper and a Quaker. Hanway, contrary to popular opinion, was not a Quaker. He had been born in the slave state of Delaware, and had lived in both Chester and Lancaster counties. He had moved to his home and mill near Parker's not many months before the Christiana resistance. Hanway, it is said, wrote to his wife from prison: "I do not regret my course; I have simply done my duty." [31]

Preparations for the Christiana treason trial were underway when, on Sunday morning, November 9, two black prosecution witnesses escaped from their cell in the debtors' section of Philadelphia's Moyamensing prison. A white man confined on other charges was said to have escaped with them. The two fugitive witnesses were Josephus Washington and John Clark. The day before the resistance Clark and Washington had been in possession of the message sent from Philadelphia with the names of Gorsuch's slaves, and had participated in warning the neighborhood. Clark and Washington had evidently indicated they would cooperate with the prosecution for they were held as paid, "voluntary" witnesses, rather than as prisoners charged with treason.[32]

Attorney General Brent of Maryland charged that these two black witnesses had disappeared "without breaking a lock or using any force." Another prosecution lawyer argued that the two black men would not have escaped on their own volition; as witnesses, he explained, they were receiving $1.25 a day, more than they could have earned if at liberty. The prosecution suggested that the vanished witnesses had been aided in their escape by some unnamed officer within the prison. The hint was directed at Marshal Anthony Roberts, the appointee and friend of the defense team's Thaddeus Stevens, and known, like Stevens, for his anti-slavery views. The defense indignantly responded that the vanished witnesses were more important to their own case than to the prosecution's, but this is doubtful.

The two black witnesses were never caught. One of the escapees, reports Smedley, was later rumored to have returned to the Christiana area, where he

> dug a cave in the woods, in which he lived for a long while, and was fed by the neighbors. His only object in thus escaping was to avoid being called upon to testify at the trial.[33]

Finally, twenty-one years after the two witnesses' escape, William Still, the black leader of the Philadelphia underground railroad, revealed the truth of the matter. The two black men had been identified in jail by their owners as fugitive slaves. Still reveals that the two had indeed "found a true friend and ally" in the U.S. marshal. In 1872 William Still recalled the prosecution's suspicions that the two witnesses' escape had been engineered by the abolitionist Marshal Roberts:

> to add now, that those suspicions were founded on fact, will doubtless do him no damage.[34]

II TRIAL

12 Prosecution

On Monday, November 24, 1851, the Christiana treason trial officially began. The courtroom was on the second floor of historic Independence Hall in Philadelphia, a city and a site both unavoidably calling forth thoughts of an earlier battle for liberty. The courtroom was almost immediately above that very hall in which, in 1776, the representatives of the rebellious American colonies had argued, adopted, and first proclaimed their Declaration of Independence—a fact whose symbolism could not be entirely lost on those attending the treason trial of 1851.

Only 75 years before there had issued forth from this very courthouse the manifesto of the revolutionary American colonists: "that all men are created equal," and endowed with "certain unalienable Rights," to "Life, Liberty, and the pursuit of Happiness." This was the courthouse in whose steeple then hung the prerevolutionary bell inscribed with the Biblical command: "Proclaim liberty throughout the land unto all the inhabitants thereof." It was this bell, in this steeple, which had rung to announce the colonies' declaration of independence. And it was this same Independence Hall in which the United States Constitution's fugitive slave clause had been adopted in 1787.

In 1851 the entire second floor of Independence Hall was leased by the United States Government for sittings of the Circuit and

177

District Courts. The courtroom, on the western portion of this floor, was said by W. A. Jackson, a young defense lawyer, to be "probably one of the most elegantly furnished for court purposes, in the country." Judge John K. Kane of the District Court was said to take "great pride in having everything about him conducted in the most polished style, and few Courts can boast of more urbane and polite attendants. . . ." Abolitionist lawyer D. P. Brown notes Judge Kane's "delicacy and refinement of manners," and says that Kane "is very particular in his costume, and exacts a most rigid observance of neatness and order from all concerned in the progress of a trial." For the occasion of the treason trial, the already elegant courtroom had been specially refitted. Jackson reports:

> Gas fixtures of the chastest design had been erected, in anticipation of evening sessions. Ventilators of the most appropriate patterns had been placed in the ceiling, controlled by cords terminating at the bench of the Judge, so that a uniform temperature could be preserved.[1]

The pending treason trial had aroused great public interest, and during the first ten days many were turned away for lack of space. Often, even standing room was unavailable. Policemen, stationed in the lobbies and stairway of Independence Hall, preserved order. Sometimes even those with authority had trouble entering. One of those who did attend a session of the trial was a Frenchman then making an American tour, Jean Jacques Antoine Ampère, son of the famous physicist. Also attending the trial were the Reverend John S. Gorsuch and the Quaker abolitionist and feminist Lucretia Mott. Other Quakers were also present in their plain, dark clothes. Reports indicate that no black people appeared in court except those brought up from prison.[2]

The array of lawyers on both sides was impressive. The prosecution counsel of seven included Attorney General of Maryland Robert J. Brent; U.S. Senator from Pennsylvania James Cooper; U.S. Attorney for the Eastern District of Pennsylvania John W. Ashmead; his cousin, an attorney of Philadelphia, George L. Ashmead; Philadelphia City Recorder R. M. Lee; District Attorney Z. Collins Lee of Baltimore; and Philadelphia lawyer James R. Ludlow.[3]

John W. Ashmead, U.S. Attorney for the Eastern District of Pennsylvania. (Hensel, *Christiana*)

The Governor of Maryland had "employed" his Attorney General, Robert J. Brent, assisted by Pennsylvania Senator James Cooper, to represent that state in the prosecution. The unusual participation of Maryland's Attorney General in the prosecution of a Pennsylvania case was the subject of some barbed comments by the defense suggesting that Maryland did not trust Pennsylvania justice. In reply, Attorney General Brent emphasized that he participated not only at the instruction of his state's governor, but "by sanction of the general government." [4]

There are hints that early in the case Maryland's Attorney General tried to supersede the U.S. Attorney in Philadelphia, John W. Ashmead, as "leading or controlling counsel" for the prosecution. Brent admits only that "an unfortunate question of etiquette" arose between Ashmead and himself. This "difficulty," says Brent, was "satisfactorily adjusted" at a meeting in Philadelphia on November 22, when Pennsylvania Senator James Cooper was made "leading counsel" for the prosecution. [5]

Attorney General Brent admits the preliminary difficulties with U.S. Attorney Ashmead were "prejudicial" to the development of the prosecution's evidence

> by preventing that early interchange of views and information, which was necessary to a thorough preparation of these important cases.

Thaddeus Stevens. (Hensel, *Christiana*)

Defense counsel Jackson agrees that the dispute among the prosecution lawyers accounted for a certain disorganization of their case.[6]

Most prominent among the five lawyers for the defense was Thaddeus Stevens, a Whig of the more aggressively anti-slavery variety, derisively called "Woolly Heads" in the openly racist political slang of the day. Stevens was known for his declarations of "unchangeable hostility to slavery in every form, in every place." But as a lawyer and duly elected and sworn member of the United States House of Representatives Stevens had also declared his "determination to stand by all the compromises of the Constitution and carry them into faithful effect."

Stevens had involved himself in the Christiana case soon after the resistance, appearing for the defense at both preliminary hearings in Christiana and Lancaster. Although Stevens was said to be "the brain of the defense," at this treason trial he had apparently agreed not to make the anti-slavery issue part of the defense argument. Stevens no doubt calculated he could best serve the anti-slavery cause by winning an acquittal, simply on the basis of Hanway's innocence. Such an acquittal would do more for the cause than using the trial as a forum for abolitionist speechmaking. For this reason, John M. Read, a prominent lawyer and respectable Democrat, was titular chief counsel for the defense, although Stevens did play a prominent role.[7]

The defense team also included Joseph J. Lewis, a leading Chester County lawyer, and Theodore Cuyler, a well-known

Philadelphian, who, with Stevens and Read, were "four of the most prominent lawyers of the State." The defense included the young W. A. Jackson as junior counsel. Jackson later wrote a short history of the case. Lawyer and abolitionist David Paul Brown sat with the defense as the special counsel for several prisoners.[8]

One of the two judges at the trial was Robert C. Grier, of the U.S. Circuit Court, described by abolitionist lawyer D. P. Brown as

> a man of large proportions; upwards of six feet high; apparently of great muscular power, and iron constitution, and somewhat corpulent; of sanguine temperament; ruddy complexion, and a most agreeable and good natured face.

Brown also mentions Grier's "occasional roughness of manner, and harshness of voice" occasioned by a difficult early life. Being a Pennsylvanian by birth, Grier was said to be looked upon more critically than a "stranger" when his federal post compelled him to make decisions counter to "the liberal policy of the State." Grier, says lawyer Brown,

> always appears to be swayed by a desire strictly to perform his duty, however he may sympathize with the oppressed.

It was Judge Grier who, just after the passage of the fugitive slave act, had declared: "As the Lord liveth and as my soul liveth" he would rigorously enforce the act "till the last hour it remains on the books." The second judge was the familiar John K. Kane, of the U.S. District Court, who had earlier charged the grand jury which brought the treason indictments in the case.[9]

On the first Monday of the trial Judges Grier and Kane took their seats at eleven in the morning. Eighty-one of the 116 citizens called for possible jury duty were present; nineteen of these were released on grounds of hardship or sickness. The number of jurors claiming to have difficulty hearing caused Judge Grier to comment on the sudden "epidemic" of deafness. Arrangements were made for two court stenographers to take down a verbatim transcript of the testimony—"phonographically"—apparently a rather new custom.[10]

The "propriety of restraining the publication of the testimony" in the newspapers was discussed, for fear that an unbiased jury could not be found for the following trials. The judges made no ruling on the matter, but a few days later warned the jury not to be influenced by anything they read in the newspapers. "Formerly," said Judge Grier,

> the press was disposed to wait until the Court had decided the case, . . . but it has got to be the principle in certain parts of the country that they pass upon it first.[11]

Boston abolitionists apparently mailed Judge Grier their written verdicts in the case. "This morning," said Grier,

> my hands, by the post-office, have been filled, from what is called the Athens of America, with a great deal of light upon the subject, for which I can't say I have any particular thanks to render. . . .

When Grier warned potential jury members to "avoid all papers coming from that direction," Thaddeus Stevens spoke up, hoping his honor "will extend your caution to missives from another quarter." [12]

On the first day of trial Judge Grier confessed his "extreme desire to be in Washington" in two weeks, to attend the U.S. Supreme Court, of which he was a member. Grier hoped to have at least one case disposed of before then. Thaddeus Stevens replied with sarcasm directed at the prosecution:

> I hope it will not take that time to get through with one case—in our country, we hang a man in three days, and I hope these gentlemen will not take so long a time.

To which Mr. Brent of Maryland indignantly exclaimed, "This is a civilized country." [13]

The next day, Tuesday, November 25, the court clerk read the indictment against the white miller, Castner Hanway, who was to be tried first. Each of the accused would be tried separately, Hanway's trial being, in effect, a test case, determining the character of the following prosecutions. The trial's outcome would determine whether resistance to the fugitive slave law could, in future, be prosecuted as treason. Hanway stood up for arraignment "side by side with his devoted wife," causing the prosecution

Castner Hanway, many years after the trial. (Hensel, *Christiana*)

to later warn the jury not to let their sympathy for this loyal female sway their judgment of the "traitor." [14]

The indictment against Hanway listed five specific charges:

1. That he, with a "large number" of armed persons, whose

purpose was to forcibly prevent the execution of the U.S. fugitive slave law, "did wickedly and traitorously levy war against the United States."

2. That Hanway and others did forcibly and "traitorously resist" Henry H. Kline, a U.S. officer, in the process of executing the laws of the United States.

3. That Hanway and others "liberated" from Kline's custody the fugitive slaves of Edward Gorsuch.

4. That Hanway and others did "meet, conspire, and consult" to forcibly resist the laws of the United States.

5. That Hanway, acting on his "traitorous intention," prepared and distributed various "books, letters, resolutions, addresses, etc.," inciting "fugitives and others" to forcibly resist the laws of the United States.[15]

Having read the indictment, the court clerk asked, according to the prescribed ritual: "How say you, Castner Hanway, are you guilty or not guilty?"

> Hanway: Not guilty.
> Clerk: How will you be tried?
> Hanway: By God and my Country.
> Clerk: God send you good deliverance.[16]

And more legal technicalities followed.

Wednesday, November 26, was spent in picking jurors. The President of the United States had previously ordered Judge Grier to instruct U.S. Marshal Anthony Roberts to summon for possible jury duty "men of the highest respectability of character, . . . intelligence, integrity and conscientiousness in the community." As Hensel says, the abolitionist

> Marshal Roberts had a delicate and difficult task . . . in view of his well known political opinions and . . . his personal and partisan affiliation with Thaddeus Stevens. . . .

Maryland's Attorney General Brent later claimed that "a large majority" of the potential jurors called by Marshal Roberts were "unfavorable to a conviction." But even Brent admitted that the final selection of twelve jurors included a majority who were "unexceptional and unbiased." Every possible precaution had been taken, admitted Brent, "to obtain a good and impartial Jury." [17]

The prosecution had proposed, and the court substantially accepted, six questions to be asked each potential juror. Since Hanway, if convicted, faced the death penalty, the first question asked was: did the juror have conscientious scruples against capital punishment; the second through fifth questions established whether the juror had formed an opinion in the case; the sixth established his opinion of the fugitive slave law.[18]

The prosecution and defense were both allowed a number of challenges "for cause" when a juror displayed obvious bias. Each side was also allowed a number of challenges without cause. Several times the defense was prevented from dismissing "for cause" a juror who, it was claimed, had shown obvious prejudice against Hanway. For example, the defense was not allowed to challenge "for cause" a juror who said he had "formed an opinion upon the outrage against the law" at Christiana. It was also no cause for defense challenge that a juror had "expressed an unfavorable opinion towards the course" of the defendants.[19]

The twelve jurors selected by the prosecution and defense included two "gentlemen," five farmers, a carpenter, a surveyor, a smith, and two merchants. The jurors' average age was fifty-three years. Their average weight was 178 pounds, a figure which caused great hilarity among the twelve solid citizens.[20]

Thursday, November 27, was Thanksgiving, and the court did not meet. As legal procedures would have required a completed jury to remain together in seclusion over the holiday, the last juror was not formally sworn in, and all twelve were allowed to spend Thanksgiving with their families. The "traitors" and "murderers" also received a special Thanksgiving banquet. An abolitionist newspaper reports the prisoners' being sent

> for their use six superior turkeys, two of them extra size, together with a pound cake, weighing 16 pounds. The turkeys were cooked with appropriate fixings, by order of Mr. Freed, the Superintendent, in the prison kitchen, by a female prisoner detached for the purpose. The dinner for the white prisoners, Messrs. Hanway, Lewis and Scarlett, was served in appropriate style in the room of Mr.

Morrison, one of the keepers. The U.S. Marshal, A. E. Roberts, Esq., several of the keepers and Mr. Hawes, one of the prison officers, dined with the prisoners as their guests. Mayor Gilpin coming in, accepted an invitation to test the quality of the pound cake. Mrs. Martha Hanway who has the honor to be the wife of the "traitor" of that name, and who has spent most of her time with her husband since his incarceration, served each of the 27 colored "traitors" with a plate of turkey, potatoes, pound cake, &c., and the supply not being exhausted, all the prisoners on the same corridor were similarly supplied.[21]

The participation of U.S. Marshal Anthony Roberts in this culinary incident caused Attorney General Brent of Maryland to censure the marshal's lack of "impartiality" and "decorum." Brent was shocked that Marshal Roberts admitted not only that he had assisted at the meal "but had set down and partaken sparingly" of the dinner with the white prisoners.[22]

According to William Still this "sumptuous dinner" was the "noble act of Thomas L. Kane," a clerk in the U.S. District Court and a son of the presiding judge. Many years after the event, Still revealed that long before that Thanksgiving dinner, the judge's son,

Mr. T. L. Kane had given abundant evidence that he approved of the Underground Railroad, and was a decided opponent of the Fugitive Slave Law; in short, that he believed in freedom for all men, irrespective of race or color.[23]

Despite Judge Kane's strong censure of anti-slavery agitators, one of his own sons was evidently an active abolitionist agent.

Dickinson Gorsuch does not appear to have enjoyed a very cheery Thanksgiving in the Quaker city. A terse entry in his diary says:

We went to Mr. Ashmead's office and stayed a while. John Bacon went home after the clothes I wore when I was shot.[24]

On Friday, November 28, the twelfth juror was formally sworn in, and the case of the *United States versus Castner Hanway* finally began with U.S. Attorney John W. Ashmead of Philadelphia opening for the prosecution. In a one-and-a-half-hour speech Ashmead outlined the prosecution's case against Hanway. Castner Hanway, said the lawyer, was not only implicated in the murder of Edward Gorsuch; he had also "wickedly . . . intended to disturb the peace and tranquility of the United States" and was thus charged with "high treason," the "most serious" crime "that can be perpetrated against a human government." [25] This was a crime of an "extraordinary character":

> In monarchical governments, it is true, crimes of this description are of frequent occurrence, but in a government like ours they are seldom committed. The tyranny to which the subjects of despotism are exposed, may so burden and oppress them that longer submission becomes intolerable. . . . In governments so constituted, the only hope for a change exists in revolution, and hence the attempt made is to overturn the whole fabric of government. Under such circumstances, treason may become patriotism, and the friends of liberty throughout the world may ardently wish for its success. No such excuse, however, exists with us; for our institutions are based upon the inherent right of the people to change and modify their form of government. . . . If obnoxious acts of Congress are passed they can be changed or repealed. Hence this defendant, if he has perpetrated the offense charged, . . . has raised his hand without excuse . . . against the freest government on the face of the earth.

The prosecution lawyer quoted the United States Constitution's fugitive slave clause and declared:

> It is almost needless to say, that without this provision, the Constitution of the United States never could have been adopted; the existing National Union never could have been formed, and the powerful, prosperous, and glorious Republic of the United States, never could have existed among the nations of the earth.[26]

This Union, Ashmead described "as one of those great blessings of Divine Providence. . . ."

The prosecution lawyer mentioned the personal liberty laws which Pennsylvania and other states had passed "for the protection of free people of color, and to prevent kidnapping." Such acts had weakened the federal fugitive slave law, and caused in the slave states:

> Deep feelings, intense excitement arising from wounded sensibility, mortified pride, and great personal interests believed to be placed in jeopardy.

At this time, said Ashmead, "our noble Union seemed to rock on its foundations." But the "Saving Spirit," the Compromise of 1850, and the new fugitive slave act, "rose bright and glorious above the storm." It was this federal law, said the lawyer, which had been attacked at Christiana. And when this law could not be enforced, warned Ashmead, "then, indeed, is the beginning of the end."

A number of judicial authorities were cited to support the argument that the Christiana resistance constituted "Treason" against the United States. Ashmead then asked the jury to consider "the influence your verdict may have on the future harmony and permanence of the National Union." They would decide, said Ashmead, whether the Constitution, and laws based on it, would be recognized throughout the Union as supreme. Ashmead hoped that

> this venerated hall from which the Declaration of Independence was first proclaimed to an admiring world, never can be the scene of the violation of the Constitution, the noblest product of that Independence.[27]

U.S. Deputy Marshal Henry H. Kline was the first and chief prosecution witness. Kline did not now, as he had at pre-trial hearings, refer to the blacks as "niggers." He had shaved off his "formidable" moustache—to look more civilized, a defense lawyer suggested. The marshal's appearance and testimony indicate careful preparation.[28]

Marshal Kline surprisingly detailed a number of minor incidents preceding the resistance which revealed him in a less than heroic light. Kline described his wagon breaking down, his delay and his meeting with the black man Samuel Williams who told Kline that he had missed his "horse thieves." This reference to the Gorsuch posse no doubt brought smiles to many a face in court. Kline mentioned his posse, just before the attack, stopping for "cheese and crackers" carried in a "carpet bag." Kline told of falling over a fence, his guns going one way, and he the other, as he chased a black man to Parker's.[29]

Such homey details, such unassuming testimony had the sound of truth. The marshal seemed to go out of his way to present himself in a foolish light, quite contrary to the heroic image he had displayed to the Gorsuch posse before the battle. Kline seems to have decided to sacrifice a heroic image for an (apparently) honest one. The marshal's testimony indicates a subtle attempt to convince the jury of his truth on major points, by creating a convincing sense of veracity on minor ones. It was a clever strategy. Either that, or the marshal was actually as foolish as he appeared.

The marshal's testimony, and the prosecution's questions, aimed to prove that the white miller Castner Hanway had led and incited the blacks to battle. Kline said he showed Hanway his warrants, and asked for his assistance, as provided by the U.S. fugitive slave law. Hanway, said the marshal, "allowed that the colored people had a right to defend themselves," and refused to assist.

Hanway, swore the marshal, said, "he did not care for any act of Congress or any other law." The marshal asked if Hanway would restrain the blacks, "and he said No,—he would not have anything to do with them." [30]

Kline described a group of armed blacks gathering at the scene, following Hanway's first appearance. Kline swore that Hanway rode over to these blacks, "stooped over and said something to them in a low voice, what that was I didn't hear." These blacks, testified the marshal, "then made one shout," and one of them "halooed out" that Kline was "only a deputy," and then advanced up the lane toward Parker's, and fired. The marshal claimed to have been present just before the firing, and to have witnessed

Hanway's incitement; the marshal's whereabouts at the battle's start thus became a major point of dispute between the prosecution and defense.[31]

At pre-trial hearings Marshal Kline had named a number of blacks as present at the battle. In his initial testimony at the trial the marshal identified only Parker, Harvey Scott, an "Indian negro," and another, "military whiskers," as present. Under cross-examination Kline admitted seeing only George Williams, John Morgan, and Henry Simms. Kline claimed he could identify the resisters only by sight, not by name. Thaddeus Stevens, for the defense, immediately asked that the black prisoners be brought into court, to be identified by the marshal. "If there is a war made," said Stevens, "we must see the soldiers." Stevens wished to have Kline identify a particular prisoner as present at the battle, then later contradict Kline's testimony by witnesses proving the prisoner had *not* been present.[32]

When the black prisoners were brought into court the next morning, Saturday, November 29, they presented a startling spectacle. As Maryland's Attorney General Brent indignantly describes the scene:

> these negroes were seen sitting in a row, supported on each side by white females, who to the disgust of all respectable citizens gave them open sympathy and countenance; each of the negroes appeared with new [red, white and blue] comforts around their necks—their hair carefully parted, their clothing in every respect alike; so as to present one uniform appearance to the eye, as far as possible—all done, doubtless, for the double purpose of giving "aid and comfort" to the accused murderers of a white man, and of confusing and perplexing so important a witness as Kline, in respect to their identity.[33]

Lawyer Jackson disclaims any attempt by the defense to confuse Kline, explaining the prisoners' similarity of dress by the probability that they had all been clothed from the same store by philanthropic Philadelphians. But it is hard to believe the defense did not intend to make Kline's identification of prisoners as difficult as possible. The marshal must have given a sigh of relief when Judge Grier ruled, on a technicality, that Kline did not have to make the identifications.[34]

The prosecution next called to the stand the other five members of the Gorsuch posse. Each told a fairly full version of the events at Parker's, suggesting that Castner Hanway had led and incited the blacks. The blowing of a horn and the gathering of armed blacks were cited as evidence of previous conspiracy. Unfortunately for the prosecution, the testimony of several of their own witnesses tended, especially in cross-examination, to cast doubt on the credibility of Marshal Kline, especially his claim to have been on the scene just before the battle.

Posse member Dr. Thomas Pearce reported hearing Castner Hanway warn the marshal: "You had better go home, you need not come here to make arrests, for you cannot do it." Pearce said he had called for Marshal Kline before the firing began, but "could see nothing of him." Cross-examined by Thaddeus Stevens, Pearce admitted declaring his "opinion" after the battle that Hanway had turned back most of the blacks who were chasing Pearce from the scene. Pearce admitted Hanway might have saved his life. Pearce also admitted saying he "considered it imprudent" for Edward Gorsuch to go into the fight.[35] J. M. Gorsuch remembered Hanway riding by as he attempted to escape from the angry blacks: "I asked him to let me get up behind him, I said for God's sake don't let them kill me." But Hanway had ridden off.[36]

Five posse members swore that, after having been "rather intimidated," dispirited, and ready to give up, the blacks in the house, upon Hanway's appearance, had seemed suddenly "inspired," and "appeared to rally." [37]

This testimony seems perfectly designed to prove the prosecution's contention that Hanway had conspired with and incited the blacks. It does not, however, seem to have been invented for prosecution purposes. The change in the spirits of the blacks is described a little differently by each posse member; the testimony would have been more uniform if it had been made up. Although several posse members had seen the blacks in Parker's looking out an upstairs window, it seems not to have occurred to them that the excitement of those in the house was due to the arrival, just after

Hanway, of other armed blacks. It is clear, however, that these black recruits caused the elation at Parker's.

The five posse members were followed on the stand by Miller Knott and his teen-age son John; their testimony barely mentioned Hanway. It was December 1, the second Monday of the trial, when the prosecution called Alderman Reigart and Constable William Proudfoot. The two officials told of Hanway's and Elijah Lewis's voluntary surrender. Lewis had denied Marshal Kline's accusation that they incited the blacks; Hanway had *not* denied the marshal's accusation, Reigart pointedly emphasized. Constable Proudfoot's testimony was similar.

Prosecution witness Charles Smith testified that Samuel Williams, the black Philadelphian, had told him of delivering a warning to some fugitive slaves near Christiana; Hanway was not mentioned.[38]

In a dramatic exchange, the next prosecution witness, the well-known abolitionist and active underground railroad agent Dr. Augustus Cain, cagily parried the questions of the prosecution. The prosecution had subpoenaed Cain to prove the Christiana "riot" had resulted from a previous abolitionist conspiracy to resist the fugitive slave law, in which Hanway was somehow implicated.

Questioned by G. L. Ashmead, Dr. Cain admitted that on the day before the battle two black men had shown him a note with some names on it—the doctor recalled "Josh" and "Ford," names of Gorsuch slaves. Dr. Cain identified his black informants as Josephus Washington and John Clark, the two who had previously and mysteriously disappeared from prison. Asked by Maryland's Attorney General Brent when he first heard of "the murder of Edward Gorsuch," Dr. Cain answered, "Not of the murder, I didn't hear, but I heard that the kidnappers had been at Parker's." Judge Grier interrupted:

> I suppose in the language of that region, any master seeking to recover his slave, is called a kidnapper. I want to know what the witness means by it. I know it is a cant phrase with some people—to say so.

Dr. Cain repeated: "I give the words as they were told to me by a colored man, that there were kidnappers at Parker's."

Questioned by Brent, Dr. Cain admitted knowing that a man had been killed at the time he dressed the wounds of two black men, before noon, on the day of the battle. Brent asked, "Did you give any information to have these men arrested?" "I don't know that I did," Cain answered. Brent asked, "Can you give the names of these colored men?" Cain named the two wounded black men, but they had also long before disappeared from the neighborhood.

Brent changed the subject. Did the doctor know of any meetings held in the area, "in regard to fugitive slaves?" "No, Sir," Cain answered. Brent asked: Have you knowledge of meetings "held in regard to the Act of Congress in regard to fugitive slaves?" "I don't know that I have, specially," Cain answered. Brent persisted: Had Cain knowledge of meetings, called for other purposes, in which the fugitive slave law was considered? "I think it likely I had," Cain answered. Brent finally drew from Cain the admission that he had attended such a meeting, "at Westchester, at the Horticultural Hall," about thirty miles from Christiana.

Brent asked: Were there speeches made at that meeting against the fugitive slave law? "There were speeches disapproving of the law, I believe," Cain answered. Brent asked, "Anything said about harboring the fugitive slaves?" "I don't recall anything was said of that kind," said Cain. "Who was the Chairman of the meeting?" Brent asked. "I don't recall that," Cain answered. Asked if Hanway was present, Cain said: "I don't—I don't recollect seeing him at it."

G. L. Ashmead asked, "Was it a society that met?" Cain answered: "I believe it was." "What society was it?" Ashmead asked, some impatience, no doubt, creeping into his voice at Cain's one-sentence answers. "I understood it to be the Anti-Slavery Society," Cain said. Judge Grier interrupted to ask if Cain was speaking of the Anti-Slavery Convention? This was a large, well publicized event, not easy to forget. "It was the Annual Convention," Cain admitted.

"You can't say whether Hanway was there?" Ashmead asked. Cain answered, "I don't recollect seeing him there." Ashmead asked, "Was that the only meeting you attended in regard to this subject?" "The only one I recollect," answered Cain. In what West Chester newspaper were resolutions of the Anti-Slavery Society generally published, Cain was asked. He was not aware of the resolutions being published in any newspaper, Cain answered, without revealing what papers he read. Asked how many from the Christiana area had attended the Anti-Slavery Convention, Cain answered, "I can't tell." Brent asked, "Can you give the names of some?"

Cain:	I don't know that I can; I don't recollect.
Question:	Was Elijah Lewis there?
Cain:	No, sir.
Question:	Was Scarlett there?
Cain:	I don't think he was.
Question:	Was Squire Pownall there?
Cain:	I can't recollect.
Question:	You can't state who was there beside yourself?
Cain:	I can't tell, I was there as a spectator; I didn't receive an invitation to go.[39]

Four black men were called as prosecution witnesses. All had been held for months in the debtors' section of Moyamensing prison. John Roberts, who had been held in custody seventy-two days, testified that a white man, Joseph Scarlett, had ridden up to warn his family "kidnappers" were at Parker's; Scarlett told Roberts to notify other blacks. Roberts told of borrowing a gun from Joseph Townsend. Townsend had loaded the gun. Hanway was not mentioned.[40]

Samuel Hanson, the next black witness, had early on the morning of the battle gone "to Christiana to get a pair of boots. . . ." The shoemaker had no boots and Hanson went to see if he could get some at a store "on the out-edge of Christiana." While Hanson was sitting on the front porch of the store, waiting for it to open, young George Pownall came walking by, and told him "there was kidnappers at Parker's." When Hanson got near Parker's "a while after sun-up" he heard firing and saw Hanway riding away from the scene. The next black prosecution witness, Samuel Thompson, also saw Hanway riding away from Parker's after the firing. The fourth black witness, Jacob Woods, had seen Hanway talking with the marshal before the firing; the witness had not heard the words.[41]

The prosecution then produced some of the clothes worn by members of the Gorsuch posse at the time of the battle. Dr.

Pearce's "low crowned, short-rimmed straw hat, with a piece of black ribbon around it, rather narrow," was seen to have a hole in it, "occasioned . . . by a bullet having passed through just above Dr. Pearce's scalp." Dickinson Gorsuch's vest "was very much torn." The coat of the deceased Edward Gorsuch "presented a shattered appearance near the left arm."

Then, as defense lawyer Jackson says, "to the surprise of everyone, the case of the United States was announced to be concluded." The prosecution had presented their evidence to prove that Castner Hanway had "treasonously levied war against the United States." The court adjourned early to await the return of the defense team's Representative Thaddeus Stevens and the prosecution's Senator James Cooper, who had gone to Washington for the opening of the thirty-second United States Congress.[42]

13 Defense

On Tuesday, December 2, Theodore Cuyler gave the opening speech for the defense. Cuyler had "listened with painful surprise" to the prosecution's treason case against Hanway, "that a charge so grave has been founded on evidence so weak." The defense would prove the case "to be the most absurd and groundless prosecution ever instituted in this or any other Court of Justice." The prominent role of Maryland's Attorney General in a Pennsylvania court was quite extraordinary, said Cuyler. It indicated that Maryland "thirsted for blood," and distrusted Pennsylvania justice.[1]

The prosecution had insinuated that to even dispute the question of Hanway's guilt somehow threatened the stability of the Union. While stressing his own concern for "the endurance of the Union" Cuyler declared:

> I have no sympathy with this mawkish squeamishness, this everlasting fear lest every exciting topic should disturb the Union. Let us hope that the Union rests . . . deep in the unchanging affections of all the people, and then we shall never fear the open and manly discussion of any question —however earnest the discussion, and however exciting the topic. . . .

196

Castner Hanway was an innocent man, unjustly charged with treason. Hanway did not intend, said his counsel, "to defend those sad deeds which disgraced the sweet and peaceful valley" near Christiana. Hanway did not intend

> to defend those who took part in that conflict. His defense is simply that he was in no way a party to those outrages. . . .

Hanway, said the lawyer, was known for his "peacefulness, quietness, and submission to the laws."

The Christiana "outrages," said Cuyler, did not amount to treason; no conspiracy against the fugitive slave law was involved. Previous illegal abductions had brought the area's blacks to Parker's:

> It was because of previous kidnappings that the blacks exercising but a fair and natural right armed themselves, and to some extent organized purely for their own protection.

Following this organization some whites had tried to pacify the excited blacks. Elijah Lewis, one of the accused, had been prominent among those "who nobly exerted themselves to soothe the justly excited feelings of the people. . . ." Seeing armed blacks at Parker's, Lewis and Hanway had warned the marshal not to attempt arrests. Riding away from the scene, Hanway had even shielded Dr. Pearce from the bullets of his angry black pursuers.

Do these facts, asked Cuyler, sustain the charge of "levying war" against the United States? With heavy sarcasm (although without great exactitude) Cuyler asked:

> Sir, Did you hear it? That three harmless, non-resisting Quakers, and eight-and-thirty wretched, miserable, penniless negroes, armed with corn-cutters, clubs, and a few muskets, and headed by a miller, in a felt hat, without a coat, without arms, and mounted on a sorrel nag, levied war against the United States.
> Blessed by God that our Union has survived the shock.[2]

The defense called Thomas Pennington, who had witnessed a kidnapping near Parker's nine months before the Gorsuch posse's attack. The prosecution objected that this kidnapping was irrelevant to the events at Parker's. Thaddeus Stevens stepped forth. The defense, said Stevens, denied the prosecution charge that blacks and whites had gone to Parker's because of a general, previous conspiracy against the fugitive slave law. Stevens explained:

> what we propose to show is this: That there were in that neighborhood a gang of professional kidnappers . . . some of whom had been confined in the penitentiary, and had come out. That they had not only upon one, but on two or three occasions, in the dead of night, invaded the houses of the neighbors, of white people, where black men lived, and [the houses of] black people, and by force and violence and [with] great injury and malice, without authority from any person on earth, seized and transported these [black] men away, and they have never afterwards been seen or known of in those parts. And that in consequence of this, there was a general feeling of indignation against these professional dealers in human flesh, not against lawful authority. . . .

Hanway had been informed that Parker's was surrounded by these kidnappers.

Judge Grier had earlier criticized the use, in the Christiana area, of the term "kidnapper" as a "cant phrase" covering even an authorized "master seeking to recover his slave." The defense now wished, said Thaddeus Stevens, to introduce testimony about previous kidnappings

> to show, may it please your honors, that if anybody should suspect in that neighborhood that there was a covert term or slang phrase used, and that kidnappers did not mean kidnappers, to show that it did mean those who followed that business for a living.

The defense wished to demonstrate "the reason why a whole neighborhood might be ready upon a notice given," that "kidnappers were at Parker's," to go to the aid of the black men under attack. Judge Grier ruled: "the evidence will have to be received." [3]

Thomas Pennington described the kidnapping of John Williams from the home of his son-in-law, William Marsh Chamberlain, about three miles from Parker's. Pennington's sad testimony revealed that no marshal had identified himself, no warrants or authority had been shown, and the black man's abductors had not identified him as a fugitive slave. Pennington named the local ruffian Perry Marsh as an armed participant in the kidnapping.

Prosecution cross-examination tried to establish that the black man abducted had, in fact, been a fugitive slave. Pennington denied knowing whether Williams was a free man or a fugitive; the black man had not been identified as a fugitive slave, Pennington emphasized. Pennington admitted that, a few weeks before John Williams's own abduction, Williams and other blacks, alarmed about a kidnapping at a house nearby, had left the neighborhood for a time. "There was a great panic among them," said Pennington. "What you call a 'stampede,'" put in Maryland's Attorney General.[4]

The next defense witness, Henry Rhay, swore that on the night of John Williams's abduction he had come upon an armed gang, and heard someone in the company say they were going to Chamberlain's "to take a black man." [5]

Rachel A. Chamberlain, Thomas Pennington's daughter, wife of William Marsh Chamberlain, was the next defense witness. When Thaddeus Stevens asked Rachel Chamberlain to describe the abduction she was suddenly unable to speak, due to "a disease of the heart to which she was subject." "When you feel well," said Stevens, "just state the facts to the jury." Rachel Chamberlain recovered herself and began:

> There was a set of men came into the house and knocked the colored man down and beat and abused him in a cruel manner.

She had been

> upstairs at the time, and by means of a stovepipe hole I saw all that was done. I saw them present a pistol to him. . . .

The shock of witnessing this event had stayed with Rachel Chamberlain: "I have been very much injured by it, and I have never been well since." [6]

The defense called Elijah Lewis to the stand. The prosecution objected, this time on the ground that Lewis, accused of the same crime as Hanway, had a personal interest in Hanway's acquittal. The objection was overruled. Elijah Lewis testified that a black man had told him that "Parker's house was surrounded by kidnappers; that they had broken into the house and were about to take him away." The black man had insisted on Lewis's "going down to see that justice was done." Lewis had notified Hanway of the "kidnappers." Marshal Kline had claimed that, before Lewis's arrival, Hanway had declared his opposition to all the laws of Congress. Lewis claimed that Hanway had gotten to the scene "about a minute perhaps—a very short time" before him. Lewis had not seen any discussion between Hanway and Marshal Kline, or heard the remarks attributed to Hanway. The marshal asked Hanway and Lewis to assist in arresting some slaves, showing them his warrants. Lewis had left his spectacles at home and could only make out the signature "Edward D. Ingraham," which assured him the marshal had authority to make arrests. Lewis swore that Hanway then "said he would have nothing to do with it. . . ."

Marshal Kline had testified that Hanway incited the blacks. Elijah Lewis testified that Hanway, while sitting on his horse, called out to a group of armed blacks: "Don't shoot! don't shoot! for God's sake, don't shoot!" Hanway, said Lewis, warned the marshal of danger, and told the officer he and his posse "had better leave." Lewis told of Marshal Kline calling several times for his men to retreat. Lewis swore the marshal had begun to retreat *well before* the first firing, and thus could not have seen Hanway incite the blacks near the house just before the battle. "Kline was up in the woods" when Lewis heard "shooting and halooing," and "saw over the corn a smoke raising near the house."

Cross-examined by the prosecution, Lewis's answers were evasive as to his abolitionist leanings. Lewis denied hearing any warning of kidnappers the evening before the resistance. Lewis did not know why Isaiah Clarkson had come to him to "see justice done." Asked if he had told the blacks the marshal had authority

to arrest fugitives Lewis answered, "I did not speak to them."
Asked why not, Lewis answered:

> I don't know that I can give any reason; I felt myself in
> danger and I wished to get away.

Asked if he had sold any powder or shot in his store the day
before the resistance, Lewis said he did not remember. Asked if he
had ever sold ammunition "to colored persons" Lewis answered,
"I sell to any who ask me." The prosecution persisted: "Then you
have sold to colored persons?" And Lewis answered, "Yes, to
colored, and to white, too." Asked if he had named to the
authorities those black men he had seen at Parker's, Lewis
answered, "I did not." Asked why not, Lewis said, "I don't know
that I can give any reasons." [7]

Henry Burt, the next defense witness, lived at Hanway's, and
told of Lewis's bringing Hanway news of "kidnappers." Immediately after the battle, Burt had asked Marshal Kline why he had
waited so long before retreating. The marshal had answered that
he wanted to withdraw, but the posse "would not mind him, and
he came away and left them." [8]

Defense witness Samuel Loughlin described a conversation with
Marshal Kline the day after the battle. Loughlin swore the
marshal said "he had seen there was going to be a fight. . . ." The
marshal said if the posse "had went" when he had ordered them to

> they would not have got hurt. He said he went into the
> woods and heard a gun go off. . . . [9]

Defense witness Isaac Rogers testified that after the firing he
had seen

> Castner Hanway riding on his horse, and Dr. Pearce
> running along side, and a colored man with a gun some few
> yards behind.

After Rogers had "hallooed to the colored man not to shoot,"
Hanway had "turned on his critter and he says several times,
'don't shoot, boys.' " [10]

Four defense witnesses testified to hearing posse member Dr.
Thomas Pearce relate his version of the confrontation, shortly
after the battle. The talkative Dr. Pearce seems not to have

considered at the time what effect his story might have when later repeated in a courtroom.

Defense witness John C. Dickinson swore that Pearce had said the posse's attack

> was the rashest piece of business he ever knew, the old gentleman [Edward Gorsuch] caused his own death, and his son's wounds. He also blamed Kline, he said, very much. . . . Kline, he said, left. . . . [Pearce] called, he said, for the Marshal two or three times, but there was no Marshal answered.

Dr. Pearce had told the witness of persuading Edward Gorsuch to withdraw; he and the slave owner had begun to retreat, when Pearce saw Gorsuch's

> countenance had changed; he looked calm and stern, and he wheeled round and said, he would have his slaves, or he would die in the attempt. The old gentleman stepped three or four paces—advanced towards the negroes, and received a wound and fell.

The same witness recalled Pearce's saying "he believed he owed his life to Hanway," for having "turned around and put up his hand" to stop the blacks, telling them "for God's sake" not to shoot.[11] The second of these defense witnesses, Dr. Ashmore Patterson, also testified Pearce had said

> that he believed he owed his life to Mr. Hanway, in giving defense against the infuriated blacks who were pursuing him.

Patterson swore that Pearce had spoken of Marshal Kline

> before the attack was made, having been boasting all the time of his former feats of valor and induced them to believe he was a man of great courage, but when they got on the ground, as soon as there was evidence of danger, that his courage seemed to forsake him and he left the ground.

James G. Henderson, the third of these defense witnesses, had

also heard Pearce blame the marshal for leaving the scene of
battle.[12]

The fourth of these witnesses, Lewis Cooper, heard Pearce say
that the attack on Parker's

> was one of the most imprudent acts his uncle [Edward
> Gorsuch] ever undertook, in fact it was the most imprudent
> one he ever saw in his life.

Pearce said he had

> called for his uncle to come away, his uncle had come out a
> marked distance . . . towards him, and he saw his uncle's
> countenance change suddenly, and he turned back and
> says, my property is here, and I am bound to have it or
> perish in the attempt.

Pearce had also called Marshal Kline "a monstrous poor thing."
Pearce said the marshal had left "at the first intimation of
danger." This defense witness, Lewis Cooper, had sat on the jury
of inquest at Christiana. Under prosecution cross-examination
Cooper was asked why Marshal Kline had not been allowed to
testify at the inquest. Cooper answered, "because no one would
believe what he would say. He had told numerous different
tales." [13]

Defense witness John Houston, a butcher who arose very early
"to see to killing the meat," testified that since June, when work
began on a new railroad track near Christiana, a horn had been
blown "in the morning, to call the hands to work. . . ." Houston
described this horn as "about sixteen or eighteen inches long. . . .
A tin horn with a reed for a blower." The defense suggested it was
this horn the posse had heard as they approached Parker's.[14]

Twenty-five defense witnesses swore to Marshal Kline's bad
"character for truth and veracity." The first witness, Judge
William D. Kelley, testified that he had heard Kline's general
character for truth and veracity "much spoken of." It was "very
bad." The second witness, Francis Jobson, a collector of water
rents who had seen Kline "frequently, every week and every day,
perhaps, for ten years," swore that the marshal's general character
and reputation for truth were "notoriously bad." Jobson added

that he had "shunned" Kline "always, but his character is so notorious, that I could not help hearing it." The fourteenth witness, John Mackey, testified that when Kline's name came up, people said that they "would rather doubt him, as if they had no confidence in him." These witnesses also included a fireproof-chest maker, a ladies' shoemaker who had been a police officer and was then a "night inspector" for the government, and another man who identified himself as "an officer of the Marshal's police, and a constable." [15]

The defense also called thirteen witnesses who swore to Castner Hanway's good character.[16] One of these witnesses, Enoch Harlan, a Quaker, had known Hanway for twenty-eight years. Harlan said that Hanway had been "rather remarkably a quiet man; rather more so than most young men." He described Hanway as "peaceable and loyal." The prosecution asked Harlan if he considered an individual loyal "whose sentiments were opposed to the Fugitive Slave Bill of 1851, and [who] would refuse to assist in the execution of that law?" Thaddeus Stevens objected, and Judge Grier ruled the prosecution "must not catechise" the witness "in regard to his faith."

The prosecution was allowed to ask Harlan what *he* meant by "loyal." Harlan said he meant a man who believed in changing those laws he opposed "by any constitutional means." Under further questioning the Quaker explained that

> there are some obligations which my country would require me to do, which I could not conscientiously do. I might be required to fight the enemies of my country, which I could not do.

Asked if his idea of "a loyal citizen consists of one who would obey every obligation which the law puts upon him" Harlan answered defensively, "I believe myself to be a loyal citizen." The prosecution replied, "Answer my question. I have no doubt you are." Harlan admitted that if not performing all duties required by law made one disloyal, he could not be considered "a loyal citizen." Asked if he would consider loyal a citizen who, if ordered by U.S. officers to assist in an arrest, would not do it, Harlan answered that there might be such a case in which he himself could not assist. Harlan supposed this passive non-assistance should be distinguished from active obstruction of the law.

Thaddeus Stevens, no doubt anxious to clarify Castner Hanway's relation to the doctrines being propounded by his friend, Harlan, asked if Hanway belonged to Harlan's sect of Quakers. Harlan answered that Hanway was not then, and had never been, a Quaker. It was Thursday, December 4, when Stevens announced the defense testimony closed.[17]

14 Rebuttal

THE PROSECUTION BEGAN the rebuttal. The defense had called twenty-five witnesses to indict Marshal Kline's character for truth. Prosecution lawyer G. L. Ashmead, trying to explain how so many witnesses had been found to testify *against* the marshal, emphasized to the jury, some of whom were farmers from outlying areas, "the difficulties of the position of a police officer in a large city." In such a city, said Ashmead,

> the more faithful a police officer is, and the more boldly he discharges his duties, the greater is the number of enemies he has clustered around him.

The prosecution then called sixty-eight witnesses to confirm Marshal Kline's good character for "truth and veracity." Cross-examining the prosecution's first witness, a police officer, Thaddeus Stevens asked if he had ever heard that Kline "was a pickpocket in New York?" The prosecution quickly objected; the question was ruled improper by Judge Grier, and the interesting subject of Kline's criminal record was unfortunately never pursued.[1]

Under cross-examination by the defense, a number of these prosecution witnesses admitted that, though they personally would believe Kline under oath, they had often heard the

marshal's truthfulness questioned by others. Cross-examined by
Thaddeus Stevens about Kline's reputation police marshal John S.
Keyser admitted:

> There is very few men but what somebody has got
> something against.

"Then you have heard something against this man?" asked
Stevens. "Yes, sir," answered Keyser, "and most every man." The
character witnesses for Marshal Kline included ten lawyers, six
police officers, four innkeepers, two aldermen, a doctor, and a tax
collector.[2]
   The prosecution next proposed to call several witnesses to prove

> that in the month of September, 1850, the county of
> Lancaster, and particularly the neighborhood of Chris-
> tiana, was patrolled by armed bodies of negroes, after a
> report that slaveholders had come up there for slaves. That
> these armed bands of negroes went from house to house in
> that neighborhood, searching for the slaveholders, swear-
> ing vengeance against them, and expressing a determina-
> tion to kill them.

Prosecution testimony would also be offered to show that:

> for a long period of time, there has been a regular
> organization for the purpose of resisting, upon every and
> all occasions, the execution of the laws of the United
> States. . . .

   When the defense objected, Judge Grier ruled that the prosecution had already called its chief witnesses and could not now,
under the guise of rebutting testimony, offer new evidence. The
judge continued: even if the prosecution's new testimony was
allowed, it might well

> prove directly the contrary from what it is offered to
> prove—only tending to show that there is a band of
> runaway negroes, banded together to help each other to
> resist their masters, who came to reclaim them; it would
> not be such public resistance to the law as to be called
> treason.

The judge gratuitously added that such bands of resistant black men

> might put the State of Pennsylvania to the necessity of refusing entrance to all colored persons hereafter. Such may be the evil meted out to them in consequence of the acts they are put up to by imprudent friends.

The proposed prosecution evidence of previous black resistance was not allowed.[3]

Defense testimony had suggested that the Christiana resistance had been directed at unauthorized kidnappers, not a 'legally authorized slave owner. The prosecution next offered the testimony of slave owner Samuel Worthington, "one of the most respectable citizens of Maryland," who it was claimed, in April, 1851,

> went up into the immediate vicinity of Christiana, for the purpose of arresting a colored boy belonging to him by the name of Jacob Berry.

Although Worthington was said to be "accompanied by several respectable people of Maryland . . . when they got near the house of a man named Haines," where the fugitive was concealed, "a white man hallooed, 'we know who you are, we will take care of you. . . .' " Despite this warning the party proceeded on to Haines's; when they knocked at the door

> the window above was thrown open, and a negro appeared and pointed a gun at the party. He was told that if he attempted to fire that gun he would be shot. A white woman was beside this negro in the room with him, and when it was necessary for the negro to make reply to the white men, he would turn round to this white woman and take his cue from her. . . . We shall prove that almost immediately after they arrived, this same white woman rang a large bell out of the window of that house; that immediately after . . . a horn was blown from the same house, and that immediately succeeding that, bells were heard ringing, and horns blowing, all round the country. . . .

The slave owner had been forced "to fly for his life."

Worthington's testimony would be offered to show "preconcert and combination" among Hanway and others in the Christiana area to prevent a slaveholder from legally reclaiming his property. This testimony was offered to contradict defense witnesses who, over prosecution objections, had been allowed to describe the illegal abduction from Chamberlain's of a "free" black man. The prosecution wished to offer evidence of a fully authorized attempt to arrest a fugitive slave which had been resisted in the very same manner as at Parker's.

Thaddeus Stevens denied the defense had claimed the black taken from Chamberlain's was "free," but only that he had been "kidnapped" without legal authority. Judge Grier agreed with Stevens. Grier did not think the defense had shown what the black man's

> condition was, but simply that he was a negro. In using that phrase I do not mean it as offensive to anyone.

Grier ruled the testimony of slave owner Worthington could not now be introduced as a rebuttal.[4]

At pre-trial hearings Marshal Kline had sworn that the black man George Washington Harvey Scott had been present, unarmed, at the Christiana battle. Scott himself, at three previous hearings in Christiana, Lancaster, and Philadelphia, had sworn to his presence at the battle. Informer Scott had supported and confirmed Marshal Kline's testimony, naming those blacks he claimed to have seen murder Edward Gorsuch. Several defense witnesses at preliminary hearings had contested Scott's claim to have been present at the battle.

During his trial testimony Marshal Kline had again made a special point of placing Harvey Scott at the scene of battle— unarmed, the marshal had emphasized. Asked by Thaddeus Stevens whether he might not be mistaken about Harvey Scott's presence Kline swore:

> No, sir. I took a good look at him. He seemed scareish and backed off a little before the second firing.[5]

Earlier in the trial, the defense had called three witnesses to contradict Kline's assertion that Scott had been present. Over strenuous prosecution objections the defense had called to the stand John Carr, a blacksmith with whom Scott worked as an apprentice, and in whose home Scott lived, about three miles from Parker's.

Blacksmith Carr recollected that on the night before the Christiana "riot" his son-in-law and Harvey Scott had gone to Penningtonville, "to a store, and they came back together. It was then near about the time I intended to go to bed." Carr's son-in-law had called him "into the room to look at goods he had bought. . . ." Scott had also been present, and the three inspected the purchases together.

Carr testified that on the same night, "between eight and nine o'clock," he knew Harvey Scott had gone upstairs to his room in the "garret." Carr himself had "buttoned" the door of Scott's room, "on the outside." This unusual procedure was occasioned by the visit of two of Carr's granddaughters. For two weeks the girls slept in a room through which the black man had to pass to reach his own quarters. Every night while the girls were visiting, either they or Carr had, after Scott was in his room, locked the door on him from outside.

On the night in question, Carr recalled that one of his granddaughters had already gone to bed when Scott went up to his room. The girl had then called to her grandfather to "button" the black man's door because, as Carr explained, "I don't suppose she liked to get up after she had stripped."

Early the next morning, said Carr, "a quarter of an hour before sun-up," he had "unbuttoned" Scott's door, "and called him to come down, and he answered, and came down directly after, and made a fire. . . ." Scott then brought the cow to the place near the blacksmith's shop where she was milked,

> went into the shop, and went to work. He worked till breakfast time, and we had our breakfast, and he went back with me into the shop, and was not out of my employ from the shop all that day.

Asked how he could be so sure of the particular morning on which Scott had been present, Carr answered that on this morning

> there was a man brought me a quarter of veal just after we were done breakfast. Stocker Coates was his name, and

> Harvey Scott and me were standing in the yard, after breakfast, and Stocker Coates said he hadn't weighed the veal, and if I would have my steel-yards [scale] brought up to the house he would weigh it, and he sent Harvey Scott for them, and he brought them and we weighed it and the value I gave him credit for—we had dealings in the shop—from these circumstances I charged my mind with it. . . . The veal and the news of the murder was on the same day.

Carr had entered the date of the transaction concerning the veal in his account book, which, however, he had left at home.

Carr recalled that just after this transaction a man named William McClyman, "that hauled bark," had come along and

> got to telling us about the riot. Harvey Scott and I were in the shop—and Harvey Scott said, "I am one nigger out of that scrape."

Scott had even several times asked the location of Parker's house, said Carr—"he didn't appear to know anything about it." Scott's lack of knowledge had not prevented his arrest, however. Carr recalled:

> They did not take him from my house until the following Saturday—it was at the shop they took him.[6]

The next defense witness, Carr's son-in-law, John S. Cochran, confirmed the blacksmith's testimony, on cross-examination even producing the dated bill which he had received for his purchases the night before the battle.[7]

William McClyman, the next witness, said he had "left home at half past six" on the morning of the "riot," to take a load of bark to Penningtonville. After making several stops, when driving past the blacksmith's, McClyman remembered seeing Harvey Scott "blowing the bellows in the shop for Carr." McClyman testified:

> The reason I observed it I had been up some evenings before, and George [Scott] struck a man with a hammer, and that man told me he was going to prosecute George, and George told me he would run away. When I went up

there that morning I saw George at work. Thinks I he isn't gone yet.

McClyman said he left Carr's and went into Flood's Hotel. There he ordered a glass of whiskey and noticed it was about five minutes past seven in the morning.[8]

Now, during the rebuttal, the prosecution called George Washington Harvey Scott to the stand for the first time during the trial. "What is proposed to be proved by this witness?" asked John M. Read for the defense. "We offer to prove," said the prosecution's G. L. Ashmead, "that the testimony given on the part of the defense, by Carr and others . . . is not correct": Harvey Scott *had* been at the scene of battle, as Marshal Kline had sworn. The prosecution would ask Scott "to explain how he got out of the room and proceeded to the scene of action." The defense objected to witness Scott, rather feebly, perhaps. The defense argued that, if Scott's testimony was to prove anything about the actual battle, he should have been introduced previously, as a prosecution "witness-in-chief." The prosecution answered that it was now offering witness Scott only to rebut defense testimony that he was *not* at Parker's. Judge Grier affirmed the prosecution's right to show that Scott was present.[9]

Prosecution lawyer G. L. Ashmead now formally asked Scott, "Were you at the battle on the morning of the 11th of September last?" Scott answered:

> I gave my evidence that I was there, once. I was frightened at the time I was taken up, and I said I was there, but I was not.

One can only imagine Ashmead's surprise, and the gasp arising from those in court. Ashmead, apparently in a state of shock, simply repeated the question, "Were you there on the morning of September last?" Scott answered, "I was proved to be there, but I was not there." Doubtfully, still too stunned to do anything but repeat himself, the prosecution lawyer asked, "On the morning of September last?" "No, sir," said Scott, amplifying his first statement:

> Kline swore I was there, and at the time I was taken up I told the man I was not there; and they took me to

Christiana, and I was frightened, and I didn't know what to say, and I said what they told me.

Suddenly the spectators in the courtroom could no longer contain themselves. Some clapped and some laughed. Maryland's Attorney General later complained that Scott's recantation "was received with open applause in the Courtroom." The black witness, called by the prosecution to substantiate Marshal Kline's veracity, had recanted. Kline, the prosecution's chief witness, was contradicted by one of the prosecution's own witnesses. Kline himself was now possibly implicated in pressuring Scott to commit perjury.[10]

G. L. Ashmead declared, "I had a conversation with this witness three or four days ago, and he said he was there." "Yes," put in Judge Grier dryly, but "others have had a conversation later than you." Grier hinted that the witness had been tampered with. Counsel Ashmead turned to Scott and asked if he understood the question, had he been present and observed the battle? "That was what I *said*," Scott answered, referring to his pre-trial testimony. "Do you say so now?" asked Judge Grier. He did not say so now, Scott replied. "Have you had a conversation with anyone, since you conversed with me?" asked G. L. Ashmead. "No, sir," said Scott.

At this point, attorney John W. Ashmead, no doubt feeling that his cousin's questioning of Scott had continued long enough, interrupted. "In a case of this character," said the attorney, "I think I have a public duty to perform." The attorney felt "bound in justice to the Government and to the public" to ask that Scott now be "committed to take his trial for perjury."

John M. Read came to Scott's defense:

> I do not wish to interfere with justice, but here is a poor negro with a weak mind who was entrapped into saying what was untrue, and I think it is taking advantage of him under the circumstances; I think this should not be done now.

It could be proved, said Read, that Scott was "a man who is hardly responsible for his acts."

Obviously in a conciliatory mood, and no doubt anxious to end the discussion as quickly as possible, attorney Ashmead said he was willing that Scott "be kept in custody today"—the implication being that he would be freed the day following. "Poor devil," broke in Judge Grier, a rush of paternal feeling for the black man evidently welling up in his breast, "it is not worth while" for the United States to hold him. "Let him go, and if you owe him anything, pay him, that he may not be tempted to steal." As a prosecution witness, Scott was entitled to $1.25 for each day he had been held in custody.

"The truth is," put in Thaddeus Stevens in Scott's defense, "he is not in his right mind." "With that explanation," said attorney Ashmead, "I am perfectly willing he should depart." With these words, and undoubtedly to the prosecution's relief, George Washington Harvey Scott was discharged. The court adjourned after a long, eventful day.[11]

When the court opened the next morning, Friday, December 5, Judge Grier chastised the spectators for their previous evening's outburst at Scott's recantation. "I would wish to remark," said the judge,

> that no one shall show his approbation by attempting to clap or laugh. I felt much mortified that anyone should be found exhibiting such conduct as was evinced last night. It was disgraceful to human nature. A poor wretched negro has been committing perjury, . . . and I say it is disgraceful that any person should be found so base in their opinion as to clap their hands in exaltation; it is a taste which should not be encouraged and I should feel little difficulty in punishing it very severely.

Scott's testimony, said the judge, "did not affect this cause a straw." [12]

But the lawyers' discussion of Scott's turnabout had not yet ended. George Ashmead arose; the prosecution wished to introduce testimony of Alderman Reigart, before whom Scott had sworn to his presence at the battle. Reigart would relate Scott's testimony. The prosecution also wanted to show, "that yesterday," in the office of U.S. Marshal Anthony Roberts, Scott "was conversed with, by several negroes, who were required to be sent away from him." Also, that only three days before, George

Ashmead had himself conversed with Scott and heard him affirm his presence at Parker's.

Defense attorney Read admitted that Scott had "sworn first to one thing and then to another." But, said Read pointedly, there were "other parties upon whom may be fixed the cruelty of having committed this perjury in the first instance." The hint was directed at Marshal Kline. Scott had been frightened into being a prosecution witness, suggested Read. And now Scott's persecution was continuing, said the lawyer, "because he happens to be a poor, miserable negro." Read objected to any prosecution repetition of Scott's previous testimony. Scott, said the defense counsel, had "not the moral force to say what he pleases."

"I will merely state," said the prosecution's Senator Cooper, "that this negro is not so shallow-minded, he is a man that can tell a straight-forward tale." Cooper gallantly acquitted the defense of tampering with the black witness; the guilt lay elsewhere. The "ragged, dirty, and filthy" appearance of witness Scott, said Cooper, contrasted with the neat appearance of the black prisoners, indicating a certain favoritism in the prison. The hint was directed at Marshal Anthony Roberts.

"It is not possible to my weak perceptions," said Thaddeus Stevens, for the defense, to see the propriety of continuing such insults:

> The United States, (no, sir) the State of Maryland rises here, and through one of the honored citizens of Pennsylvania, imputes to the defense, tampering with their witness. . . .

Stevens denied the defense had had any access to prosecution witness Scott; the defense had not "approached Scott" or "bribed him. . . ."

If the prosecution believed Scott to have been at the battle, continued Stevens, "it was their duty" to have called him as a "witness-in-chief." "Why did they not produce him?" asked the lawyer:

> Why keep him back to the last moment? I would say, they distrusted his testimony. . . . But when Kline's testimony had been crushed to the earth, they seemed to be goaded to

frantic madness, and they brought him [Scott] to fill up their case.

Scott had perjured himself previously in testimony before Alderman Reigart. Stevens objected to Reigart's repeating Scott's false statements.

"We will withdraw the witness," abruptly declared George L. Ashmead for the prosecution. And thus ended the rebuttal.[13]

In retrospect, it seems safe to assume that the day before his recantation, Scott had, in Marshal Roberts's office, indeed been "conversed with by several negroes . . ." It seems likely that the same abolitionist marshal, who had had a hand in the escape of two witnesses, had also played some role in Scott's change of mind. "But," as defense counsel Jackson later asked, "if it were granted, for the sake of argument, that 'some negroes' had a conversation" with Scott,

> by what rule of right or principle of law, could they be condemned for entreating the unhappy man not to degrade himself by [again] committing the loathsome crime of perjury?

Whatever the cause of Scott's recantation, the evidence seems perfectly clear that the black man's last testimony was the truth. Although Scott did not directly implicate Kline in his earlier perjury, the black man's recantation no doubt cast further doubt on the character and veracity of the marshal.

George Washington Harvey Scott, it seems, had more in common than first appeared with his legendary namesake who also, it is claimed, could finally not tell a lie. Considering the turn of events, it would be interesting to know if George Washington Scott ever received the fee which was his due as a prosecution witness.

15 Summations

THE PROSECUTION'S SUMMATION began the day after Scott's recantation, with J. R. Ludlow leading off. Scott's turnabout was still not quite forgotten. Ludlow asked the jury to

> notice the scene, if I may so call it, which closes the evidence for the prosecution. A poor negro is brought upon the stand, and he swears directly contrary to what is supposed he would have sworn. Strange occurrence, it first seemed, and I was under the impression that it might overwhelm the case for the prosecution, from the fact that it had taken place and was not explained.
>
> But, I thank heaven a night has passed, and that cool, calm and collected men, have had an opportunity of thinking about that matter. A man, who on divers occasions swore to the mentioning of certain facts, suddenly changes his whole story. But he changes it methodically. Does he use negro language on that stand . . . ? No!

The lawyer magnanimously conceded his willingness to forget the whole matter: "In any event, I am willing it should weigh for nothing." But Scott's recantation was not yet disposed of. Marshal Kline might have been mistaken in identifying Scott as present at the battle, Ludlow admitted. Ludlow assured the jury:

217

I of course would not for a moment pretend to charge my
learned friends upon the other side with having bribed him
[Scott], and I would not say that there are any in the Court
house who would have done it, but I must confess, that
taken in connection with the circumstances that two of our
witnesses have escaped from the jail of this county, it is not
remarkable that he should have sworn as he did.

A good dinner, a tri-colored scarf, a new suit of clothing
or the almighty dollar, might have accomplished the result.

Reacting angrily to these suggestions of malfeasance, defense
counsel J. J. Lewis, in his own summation, termed the prosecution
insinuation "villainous and atrocious to the last degree, and I . . .
spit upon it and trample it beneath my feet." [1]

The summations, which began on Friday, December 5, lasted
seven whole days, with three prosecution and two defense lawyers
participating. When it was Thaddeus Stevens's turn to speak for
the defense a large crowd gathered to hear the abolitionist
congressman.

The crowd's "expectation was raised to the highest pitch . . ."
and there was much disappointment when Stevens announced he
would not speak. Stevens's reticence, no doubt, arose from the
decision not to make his well-known abolitionism part of Hanway's defense.

The official report of the summations, even though incomplete,
occupies more than seventy small-type, closely printed, double-
column pages of the trial record. Senior defense counsel John M.
Read's summation lasted three days.[2] The American public of
1851 appreciated the art of public speaking, and a flagging interest
in the trial picked up when the summations began. When, for
instance, on Saturday morning, December 6, J. J. Lewis began the
summation for the defense, an abolitionist newspaper reports:

> there was a great throng present at the trial. The room was
> overcrowded with women and Marshal Roberts was
> greatly embarrassed at his inability to find or to make a
> place for them. The special attention of the spectators was
> attracted to a row of colored men, seated on the north side
> of the room. . . . These were the colored prisoners alleged
> to have been engaged in the treason at Christiana, and

Lucretia Mott. (Still; Wm. L. Katz Collection)

numbered twenty-four. They were all similarly attired wearing around their necks "red white and blue scarfs."

The paper reports that the well-known Quaker abolitionist and feminist Lucretia Mott sat at the head of the blacks:

> This, we believe, is her first appearance in court since the trials have commenced. Her dignified and benevolent countenance ever attracts attention. . . . She sat knitting during the entire session of the court. . . . One of the colored persons, whose name is Collister Wilson, was too unwell to be brought from prison. . . . The two white men, Lewis and Scarlett, were also brought from prison, but occupied the rear or east end of the court room.[3]

Prosecution and defense summations comprise a complex dialectic of charges, responses, and countercharges. The prosecution charged that before the affray at Parker's, Hanway had conspired with and led the blacks to resist the fugitive slave law. This conspiracy could be inferred from the blacks' rejoicing when the white miller first rode up. The prosecution's Senator Cooper emphasized the "huzzas and other demonstrations of welcome by the besieged negroes" which greeted Hanway's arrival at Parker's. This "extravagant rejoicing," said Cooper, proved the blacks knew that Hanway would support their resistance. An additional proof of conspiracy, said Cooper, was that Hanway had been followed to Parker's by several groups of armed blacks.[4]

The blacks at Parker's had asked for "time to consider, and

were about giving up," emphasized prosecution counsel J. R. Ludlow. Then Hanway, "the leader in the conspiracy," made his appearance. "Instantly the scene is changed," the blacks "take courage and rush down the lane, and the result is, they murder a man in cold blood." Hanway "was known to the colored people as a man who would stand by them, in their resistance to the laws," stressed Maryland's Attorney General Brent.[5]

Defense lawyer J. J. Lewis admitted the blacks at Parker's house had been excited at the time of Hanway's appearance. But, for the first time during the trial, the blacks' elation was attributed not to Hanway, but to the arrival of other blacks. Lewis pointed out that

> just after Hanway arrived, a number of blacks appeared on the ground. These are stated by Dickinson Gorsuch to have come trooping from all quarters.

Those upstairs in Parker's, "being in a more commanding position than the persons around the house," must have seen the black recruits "at some distance off, as they approached. . . . Can it be doubted," asked the defense lawyer, that the aid which those in the house "most desired, being that of men whom they were certain of being their friends, was what inspired their courage?"

> Castner Hanway was a stranger, only a few months resident in the neighborhood, as far as appears, not known to one black man present. They could not know whether he would be an ally or an enemy, or indeed either. But they knew well on what side every African would array himself in case of difficulty.

Hanway had gone to Parker's thinking it was being attacked by illegal kidnappers, said Lewis. Finding this was not the case, Hanway had left.[6]

The prosecution charged that Hanway had refused to assist in the arrests, as the federal law required; this refusal was not only illegal, but also allegedly indicated general opposition to the fugitive slave law. The defense admitted Hanway's refusal to assist, but claimed it only indicated the miller's fear for his own life.[7]

The prosecution charged that Hanway's declaration (as reported by Marshal Kline) that he (Hanway) "did not care for any act of Congress or any other law" proved his treasonous intention. Hanway never made this declaration, the defense responded; Marshal Kline was lying.

The prosecution charged, again according to Marshal Kline, that Hanway had ridden over to the blacks, whispered something to them, after which the blacks had opened fire, and the battle began. Hanway's whispering to the blacks, said Attorney General Brent of Maryland, "was the signal." Then, said Brent, referring to Dr. Pearce's pre-trial testimony, the blacks "advanced singing the hymn 'We are free!' and fired." [8]

The defense again replied that Marshal Kline had lied; Hanway had not incited the blacks just before the battle. Moreover Marshal Kline had not even been present at the time he swore he saw Hanway incite the blacks; the marshal had already retreated some distance from the scene. Kline had not fled before the battle's start, the prosecution maintained.

Both sides admitted that as Hanway was riding away he had protected Dr. Pearce from the bullets of the enraged blacks. But, argued prosecution counsel Ludlow, Hanway saved Pearce's life only "to save his own"; Hanway had ordered the blacks not to fire because he himself, being in the way, was in danger of being shot. Hanway's order to the blacks, charged Ludlow, was additional evidence of Hanway's control over them:

> he raises his hand, and they were quiet. He but spoke the word, and the firing ceased. If they had shot their leader, it would have been a bad thing. . . .

Maryland's Attorney General Brent emphasized that Hanway had not stopped the blacks from going into battle, though "he could afterwards say, 'Boys, don't fire'; could call them 'boys,' in a familiar way. . . ." [9]

The defense replied that Hanway's having saved Dr. Pearce's life only proved the pacifistic intent of the miller's actions. In going to Parker's, Hanway intended to avert injury to the innocent. Defense counsel J. J. Lewis re-emphasized:

> no man regrets the lamentable events of the day more than Castner Hanway. We are here neither to justify, excuse or palliate it.

Hanway had asked his lawyer to declare his sympathy with the late slave owner's relatives. There was no evidence, said the defense lawyer, that Hanway "combined . . . for any purpose, with the blacks on the ground." Elijah Lewis's testimony in fact showed that Hanway had withdrawn

> to a sufficient distance, to be beyond all just suspicion of participation with the perpetrators of the outrage . . .[10]

Hanway belonged to no unpatriotic group opposed to the fugitive slave law, emphasized defense counsel Lewis. Hanway, said his lawyer, was

> a quiet humble citizen, whose whole time has been devoted to the pursuit of his lawful occupation; who has never mingled in the temporary excitements of the day, but who had been satisfied to pursue the even tenor of his way . . . always obedient to the laws.

Hanway, said the defense lawyer, was a man

> having no strong opinions or feelings upon any of the agitating topics of the day . . .

Had any testimony been offered on Hanway's opinion of the fugitive slave law? The lawyer asked the jury:

> can any of you say, from anything you have heard here, that Castner Hanway has any opinion either one way or another on the subject?

Defense lawyer Lewis pointed out that no witness besides Marshal Kline directly linked Hanway with any improper act. Should Kline's testimony be believed? asked Lewis. It was Kline's cowardice in retreating, and his desire to shift responsibility from himself, that motivated his accusations against Hanway. It was Kline's leaving and Edward Gorsuch's "return to make the intended arrests" that had "exasperated the negroes, and brought about the conflict."

The trial of Hanway could not even be taking place, said the defense lawyer, if the prosecution had permitted its main witness, Marshal Kline, "to slide back in the slime of his filthy track, to his condition of insignificancy and contempt." After the recantation of Harvey Scott, the lawyer added, "it was not necessary to produce evidence of Kline's character for truth." [11]

Prosecution counsel Cooper again tried to explain how the defense had found so many witnesses to indict Kline's reputation for truth. Cooper appealed especially to the farmers on the jury when he asked whether

> in this City—in any large city, do you suppose it is a difficult matter to find creatures, bred from its corruptions, like reptiles from the slime of the Nile, who are ready at need to asperse [slander] and drag down, if possible, to their own level of degradation, the character of the best and purest citizens in the community. [12]

The inclusion of Marshal Kline among "the best and purest citizens" must have seemed a fanciful conceit to many of those in court.

Attorney General Brent insisted the prosecution could explain its lack of *direct* evidence connecting Hanway with the blacks in a general conspiracy to resist the fugitive slave law. Brent explained:

> it is not to be expected (in a case like this) that direct proof shall be brought, where the whole region is infected, and where every white man in that immediate neighborhood . . . is leagued with the traitors.

It was not to be expected, said Brent,

> that we shall find in that horde of traitors, voluntary witnesses to implicate directly one who sympathizes with them . . . [13]

The existence of a general conspiracy was evident to the prosecution: Samuel Williams's warning the Christiana blacks proved to prosecution counsel Brent "some foul treachery in the city of Philadelphia" by which old Gorsuch was to "be ultimately butchered." Horns, heard by posse members, were said to have, by pre-arrangement, called armed blacks to Parker's. These horns, the defense answered, were sounded in the neighborhood every morning to call to work a group of railroad laborers; other horns daily awoke the area's farmers. [14]

Prosecution counsel Brent charged that an "organization"

existed in the Christiana area "to prevent any colored man, slave or free, from being carried into slavery." Brent emphasized that it was no more right

> for an assembly of refugee slaves to organize for the purpose of resisting the execution of the laws of the United States, than it would be for a company of white men; and that if there be an armed assembly of colored persons, whether free or fugitive slaves, to resist by open force and violence, the execution of the laws of the United States, that every one of them are guilty of treason.

Maryland's Attorney General raised a frightening specter: If "this armed resistance" at Christiana

> by a band of one hundred men, be not treason, . . . then an army of ten thousand blacks may be raised in the free States for armed resistance to this law of Congress, and it would not be treason.[15]

The defense argued that the "organization" in the Christiana area existed only to protect the neighborhood's blacks from kidnappings such as had occurred at Chamberlain's.

Prosecution counsel Ludlow doubted that the men who abducted the black from Chamberlain's "were kidnappers at all," but legally authorized slave catchers. And even if the black man was removed from Chamberlain's without proof of legal authority it "did not violate the laws of the land," argued prosecution counsel Brent; a "master can take his slave when and where he pleases." The Constitution "recognizes no right on the part of the slave to resist his master. . . ." Defense counsel J. M. Read denied the Constitution authorized "a band of kidnappers, man-stealers by profession," to take a black man into slavery against his will.[16]

If illegal kidnappings had taken place in Lancaster County, said prosecution counsel Ludlow, the inhabitants of the area, "instead of arming lawless negro bands to rid the country of such miscreants," should have taken legal measures, and had the kidnappers "arrested, tried, and convicted." [17]

White abolitionists had encouraged, incited, and led the resistance of Christiana blacks, argued prosecution counsel Brent. The blacks at Parker's, Brent claimed, sent Isaiah Clarkson "to get white advice, white counsel, and whites to be present." Hanway, said Brent, went to Parker's knowing the blacks "wanted white advice." Such a white man who would incite and encourage resistance was in fact "far guiltier" than "the armed negroes." Any blacks who resisted slave catchers were "but mere instruments"; the real guilt rested with the whites who incited them, especially "those in high places, who in the Congress of your nation and in the pulpit, preach treason, and incite men to rebellion . . ." [18]

Gorsuch's "slaves, his property was there," said Brent, by way of justifying the posse's attack. And "white men were there exciting these blacks to rebellion and murder." In such circumstances, said Brent, "well might a change come over" old Gorsuch's countenance,

> well might he, a brave man, become calm and stern, and utter those memorable words, "My property is here and I will have it, or perish in the attempt." [19]

Why, asked Brent, are there so many whites in the Christiana area so sympathetic to fugitive slaves? These whites, Brent charged, were not even "crazy [abolitionist] fanatics," but were interested in

> the labor of these runaway slaves to the exclusion of white labor; they get it cheaper than they could white labor, . . . that is their philanthropy and friendship to colored people.[20]

This was an old charge against those who harbored fugitives.

The prosecution argued that the Christiana resistance resulted from a general conspiracy to resist the federal fugitive slave law, and constituted treason or "levying war" against the United States. Maryland's Attorney General admitted, if the object of the Christiana resisters

> was merely to rescue the particular slaves of Mr. Gorsuch, . . . and there was not a general purpose to prevent the execution of the laws of the United States, upon any, and all fugitive slaves in the neighborhood, then perhaps it might not be treason. . . .

But if the resisters had acted toward Gorsuch's fugitives as they would have toward any runaways,

> then, I say, there is a conspiracy for a treasonable purpose, namely: to nullify and obstruct the execution of the laws of the United States.[21]

Defense counsel J. J. Lewis declared that the Constitutional definition of "levying war"

> was framed by men who, in the exercise of the right of revolution, had risked the penalties of treason, and studied the subject on the steps of the scaffold.

These American revolutionaries had purposely limited the definition of treason; the term was not intended to refer to "a mere tumult—a fight—" but to an insurrection "national in scope and object." A truly treasonous action, said Lewis,

> aims at the life of the government, or at least at the prostration of some branch of its power by an armed opposition.

For example, the lawyer said, with pointed irony:

> An attack on the negro population of a town or city, by an armed mob of thousands, such as has occurred in both Columbia and Philadelphia within a few years, has never been supposed to be treason.[22]

The defense denied any intent to dissolve the Union or "to overturn the government" was involved at Christiana, declaring it preposterous to dignify a mere "riot" with the name of "insurrection."

The majority of Pennsylvanians, asserted Maryland's Attorney General Brent, supported their forefathers' "solemn contract" guaranteeing the return of fugitives. An individual who opposed the return of fugitives had no right to set up his conscience, and

> say he will execute just such laws as he chooses . . . If there be such citizens among you, . . . let them, at least fly to some other land, and there preach those higher law sentiments . . . to sow the bitter seeds which bring forth

blood and massacre and may at some future date, end in civil war itself.

Hanway and others had no right *not* to assist in the recapture of fugitive slaves "because it was repugnant to their consciences. Conscience!" sniffed Brent. If every citizen was to follow his conscience, the United States Government would need a "standing army" to enforce unpopular laws:

> And such a standing army! An army that would have to be stationed in every town and county, so as by a sufficient display of force to execute the civil process. . . . Is that the sort of government we live under? A government of force and military terrors? [23]

Encouragement of fugitive slaves, and the struggles of southerners "to recapture our property," had held back "the process of gradual emancipation which was going on some twenty years ago, . . ." Brent argued. Abolitionist efforts to "force" emancipation on the slave states

> has retarded and reversed the progress of public opinion ·. . . until there is a wide spread opinion in the South, that no living man will ever see the day when slavery will be abolished.

Refusing to discuss the morality of slavery—"for we of the South do not argue such questions out of our own borders"— Maryland's attorney general contended that the proportion of blacks to whites in the section's population necessarily prevented emancipation:

> Are the white people of the South to emancipate those of a hostile caste? With the African caste there can be no social and practical amalgamation, except by a few degraded people. What is to become of them? Are they to be turned free . . . ?

Maryland did not have the wealth "to export" her entire black population, said Brent. In such a case, he asked, "Do you expect us by preaching abolition to turn loose this numerous and dangerous class in our midst . . . ?"

The escape of slaves, said Brent, threatened vital southern interests, especially in those states "where heat renders it impossible for white men to labor beneath the burning sun. . . . We of the South," said Brent, "most vitally interested in slave property" would not have signed the Constitution, and this "Union never could have been formed," without the Constitutional agreement to surrender fugitives.

Brent denied using the threat of disunion to influence the jury: "I do not come here to say that the Union depends upon your verdict. . . ." But, warned Brent, there could be no Union if southerners came to feel the Constitution was but a piece of parchment. Southerners would stand "as a unit to resist . . . oppression" from the north, and "maintain the rights which had been handed down to them by their Revolutionary forefathers."

The defense, said Brent, had described the Christiana battle as "too inconsiderable and trifling an affair to rise to the dignity of treason." The first battles of the American Revolution, he thought, "might have been disposed of in the same way in London." [24]

The Christiana battle, argued prosecution counsel Ludlow, was "not an isolated, disconnected instance." In recent years "bigots, fanatics, and demagogues" had "endeavored to stimulate the populace to illegal and monstrous acts." These agitators, warned Ludlow, "would bring upon this country of ours civil war, disunion, and all that is horrible." [25]

The prosecution's Senator James Cooper denounced the destructive abolitionist "religious principle"

> that for the sake of an abstract right, [Cooper here referred to *liberty*] whose very exercise were disastrous to the unprepared bondmen who inherit it, would tear this blessed confederacy in pieces, and deluge these smiling plains in fraternal blood, and barter the loftiest freedom that the world ever saw, for the armed despotism of a great civil warfare! [26]

In an even higher flight of poetic fancy, Maryland's Attorney General Brent expressed his concern for America's continued existence as a leader of the free world. Without the enforcement of the Constitution's fugitive clause there could be no American Union, said the slave state's official, no star-spangled banner to float in triumph over every wave, . . . no beacon lights, shining from every mountain top, to give light to the oppressed of other nations, and guide them to peace, happiness, and freedom.[27]

The summations ended on December 16, 1851.

16 Verdict

THE SUMMATIONS CONCLUDED, Judge Grier instructed the jury on the law and facts relevant to their verdict. This decision, said the judge, in a voice said to be shrill and piping, was an important one,

> not only because it is the first of a numerous series of cases of the same description which involve the issue of life and death to the parties immediately concerned, but because we know that the public eye is fixed upon us. . . .

Grier continued:

> Without intimating any opinion as to the guilt or innocence of the prisoner at the bar, it must be admitted that the testimony in this case has clearly established that a most horrible outrage upon the laws of the country has been committed.
> A citizen of a neighboring State, while in the exercise of his undoubted rights, guaranteed to him by the Constitution and laws of the United States, has been foully murdered by an armed mob of negroes. . . .

"It is now more than sixty years since the adoption of the Constitution of the United States," said Judge Grier:

230

> Under its benign influence we have become a great and powerful nation; happy and prosperous at home, feared and respected abroad. . . . here, the minority uphold the constitution and laws imposed by the majority. . . . We have not here pronunciamentos, rebellions and civil wars caused by the lust of power, by ignorance, faction, or fanaticism, which in other countries have marred every attempt at free government.[1]

The judge declared that, "with the exception of a few individuals of perverted intellect," and a few districts whose "moral atmosphere had been tainted and poisoned by male and female vagrant lecturers and conventions," no group could be found in America who had applauded the "disgraceful tragedy" at Christiana. Perhaps uneasily aware of some irony in the historic location of his courtroom, Judge Grier remarked:

> It is not in this Hall of Independence, that meetings of infuriated fanatics and unprincipled demagogues have been held to counsel a bloody resistance to the laws of the land.

Again alluding to the unmentionable abolitionists, Grier placed the "guilt for this foul murder" on those who advocated "doctrines subversive of all morality and all government." These subversives really objected "to the Constitution itself," whose clause concerning the return of fugitive slaves was, according to abolitionist heresy, voided by "some 'higher law.' " The fugitive slave law, instructed Grier, was based on the Constitution, and any "public armed opposition" to this law "is as much treason as it would be against any other act of Congress. . . ." [2]

Judge Grier reviewed the specific acts by which Castner Hanway had allegedly levied war against the United States. The judge then concluded:

> Two questions present themselves for your inquiry—1st. Was the defendant, Castner Hanway, a participant in the offenses proved to have been committed? Did he aid, abet, or assist the negroes in the transaction? . . .
>
> 2nd. . . . if he did, was the offense treason against the United States? . . .

The first question, of Hanway's participation, was a purely factual one. The second question was a problem of both fact and law. The judge would help the jury correctly define the law of treason, but it was their own responsibility to decide if Hanway's actions came within that category.[3]

The prosecution must have stirred unhappily when Judge Grier advised the jury "there is no evidence of any previous connection of the prisoner [Hanway] with this party of 'rioters' "; there was "no evidence, even" that Hanway was a member of any group opposed to the Constitution or the nation's laws. But, said the judge, Hanway *was* guilty if his acts or declarations "countenanced or encouraged, aided or abetted" a treasonous resistance.

For a treasonous levying of war to have taken place, ruled Grier:

> The conspiracy and the insurrection connected with it must be to effect something of a *public nature*, to overthrow the government, or to nullify some law of the United States, and totally to hinder its execution, or compel its repeal.

Grier explained:

> A number of fugitive slaves may infest a neighborhood, and may be encouraged by the neighbors in combining to resist the capture of any of their number; they may resist with force and arms. . . . Their insurrection is for a private object, and connected with no public purpose.

Such an insurrection would not be treason.

Grier carefully continued:

> Without desiring to invade the prerogatives of the jury in judging the facts of this case, the Court feels bound to say, that they do not think the transaction with which the prisoner is charged with being connected, rises to the dignity of treason or a levying of war.

One can only imagine the prosecution's dismay at this opinion from the bench. Their consternation must have grown as Grier continued: there was no proof of any "previous conspiracy to make a *general and public resistance to any law* of the United

States . . ." There was no evidence that anyone involved in the resistance

> had any other intention than to protect one another from what they termed kidnappers (by which slang term they probably included not only actual kidnappers, but all masters and owners seeking to recapture their slaves. . . .[4]

In the neighborhood of Christiana, said Grier,

> Individuals without any authority, but incited by cupidity, and the hope of obtaining the reward offered for the return of a fugitive, had heretofore undertaken to seize them by force and violence, to invade the sanctity of private dwellings at night, and insult the feelings and prejudices of the people. It is not to be wondered at that a people subject to such inroads, should consider odious the perpetrators of such deeds and denominate them kidnappers—and that the subjects of this treatment should have been encouraged in resisting such aggressions. . . .

In spite of such provocation it "cannot be denied," said Grier, that the Christiana resisters "are guilty of aggravated riot and murder. . . ." But, the judge clearly suggested, they were not guilty of treason.

Despite their innocence of treason, the government's prosecution of the Christiana resisters was justified, Judge Grier assured his listeners. Only recently meetings had been held in the north denouncing the fugitive law

> and advising a traitorous resistance to its execution: conventions of infuriated fanatics had incited to acts of rebellion; and even the pulpit had been defiled with furious denunciations of law, and exhortations to a rebellious resistance. . . .

The government was therefore perfectly justified in supposing that the transaction at Christiana "was but the first overt act of a treasonable conspiracy extending over many of the Northern States, to resist by force of arms" the nation's fugitive law:

> In making these arrests, and having this investigation, the

officers of the government have done no more than their strict duty.[5]

This charge of Circuit Judge Grier to the trial jury is particularly interesting in view of the clarity with which District Judge Kane, in his own earlier charge to the grand jury, had expressed totally contradictory views on the subject of treason. Kane had defined any violent attempt to prevent enforcement of a single federal law as levying war. Grier's charge revealed an evident distaste for Kane's legalistic and wider definition. What Kane thought of Grier's final charge is unknown.[6]

The Christiana treason case was committed to the jury which retired to deliberate at the nearby American House Hotel, where they had been lodged during the trial. Although it was rumored that the prosecution had abandoned all hope of conviction, there existed the possibility of a mistrial, if the jury could not agree on a verdict. After an absence of fifteen minutes the jury returned. When they had reassembled, the court clerk asked according to the prescribed ritual: "Gentlemen of the Jury, have you agreed upon your verdict?"

> Jurors: Yes, Sir.
> Clerk: Prisoner, stand up. Jurors look upon the prisoner. Prisoner look upon the Jurors. How say you, Jurors, is Castner Hanway guilty . . . or not guilty? [7]
> Jurors: NOT GUILTY.

Whether, morally speaking, Hanway might be called guilty for *not* aiding the blacks was an issue not discussed.

The prosecution was evidently prepared for the possibility of an acquittal. Immediately after the decision, U.S. Attorney Ashmead proposed: "Considering the circumstances of the case, and the ordeal through which he has passed," that Castner Hanway be discharged; the government would not prosecute on the four federal misdemeanor charges remaining against the prisoner. Judge Grier agreed, and Hanway left the courtroom a free man for the first time in four months, less one day. Treason charges against Elijah Lewis and Samuel Williams were also ignored. The two were admitted to bail of $2000 each, with four lesser federal indictments still pending against them. A number of blacks remained in jail.[8]

Five days later, on December 17, hearings continued on the fate of the remaining prisoners. United States Attorney J. W. Ashmead announced that, on the basis of Judge Grier's charge, further treason prosecutions would cease. But, said Ashmead, a clear case of riot and murder had been made out; the prisoners would be moved to Lancaster, to await trial in the State court. Fearing that the prisoners might escape punishment by lenient Lancaster authorities, Ashmead reserved the right, if they were not there convicted, to bring them back to Philadelphia to be tried for misdemeanor in the United States court.

Fourteen days later, on the last day of December, 1851, Marshal Anthony Roberts transported some of the black prisoners from Philadelphia to the Lancaster prison. U.S. Attorney Ashmead's fears of Lancaster County leniency were justified. Lancaster District Attorney John L. Thompson found the evidence insufficient to warrant the prisoners' detention. Nine black prisoners transferred to Lancaster on December 31 were discharged that very evening.[9]

George Williams, one of the blacks released, had, according to William Parker, been identified in the Philadelphia jail as a fugitive slave. The man who claimed to be George Williams's master, accompanied by a lawyer and Marshal Kline, had followed Williams to Lancaster. At midnight, on the day of the black man's release, he was re-arrested—as a "fugitive from labor"—handcuffed, and hurried away in a wagon. Williams's claimant and Marshal Kline, fearing a rescue, drove away "at a killing pace." The night was freezing, and the two white men drank heavily as they speeded on. Their horses needing rest, they were forced to stop for the night at a Parkesburg tavern. Here, overcome by heat and liquor, Williams's claimant and Marshal Kline soon fell asleep, leaving the tavern keeper to watch the black man, who was also apparently asleep. The tavern keeper himself was soon "snoring at a fearful rate."

George Williams now "opened first one eye, then the other . . ." Moving slowly to the snores of his captors, he "stealthily crawled towards the door" when suddenly he saw the tavern keeper's eye upon him. Williams "paused, knowing his fate hung by a single hair." When the black man whispered softly for a drink of water, the tavern keeper "pointing his finger to the door . . . closed his eyes, and was apparently lost in slumber." George Williams hurried off through the ice and snow.[10]

R. C. Smedley's version of Williams's escape assigns a more active role to the white tavern keeper who, seeing that the black man's captors

> were drowsy, went to the door, quietly unfastened it and beckoned to the slave who, seeing the opportunity offered him to escape, quickly left and ran across the fields to the house of William Williams, a colored Methodist minister. . . . The preacher filed off his fetters, which the slave put in his pocket as a memento of the occasion. . . .

According to Smedley, Williams and the preacher set out for Philadelphia. As they were crossing a stream they met some men, and the minister, "feeling apprehensive of detection," told Williams he had "better get rid of the cuffs." Williams "dropped them in a stream." Later, learning where Williams had left his handcuffs, it is said that Joseph Scarlett "went to the place, found them," and kept "those interesting relics" in his possession for several years.[11] According to Parker, Williams arrived safely in Philadelphia, where he was cared for "by his old friends" and Dr. J. J. G. Gould Bias, a black physician-clergyman of that city.

Parker adds that when George Williams's alleged master and Marshal Kline awoke to find their prisoner gone, the disappointed claimant "threatened to blow out the brains of Kline." The marshal, in turn, threatened to hold the tavern keeper responsible for the slave's loss. The tavern keeper, "seizing an iron bar," swore that they should both be "sent after old Gorsuch," and threatened to "raise the whole township on them." Kline and the southerner left quickly, knowing that the released blacks "were all in the neighborhood, and that nothing would please these brave fellows . . . more than to get a sight at them. . . ." Ezekiel Thompson, in particular, "had sworn by his heart's blood, that, if he could only get hold of that Marshal Kline, he should kill him and go to the gallows in peace." [12]

In January, 1852, "riot" and "murder" charges were still pending in State court against some of the Christiana resisters.

The lawyers for the accused now assumed the initiative and charged Marshal Henry H. Kline with swearing falsely at the pre-trial hearing in Lancaster. This indictment was signed by a large number of witnesses, and Kline was held in $1000 bail before Charles G. Freeman, a Philadelphia alderman, to appear before court in Lancaster. Kline's indictment apparently gave the lawyers for the Christiana resisters some bargaining power. On January 16, with Joseph McClure of Bart Township as jury foreman, the perjury indictment against Kline and the "murder-riot" charges against the resisters were both ignored. The "traitors" still in prison were released, and the bonds of those free on bail were canceled.[13]

Defense lawyer Jackson declares: "to avoid the imputation of imbecility" after abandoning the treason charges, the prosecution decided to charge the black Philadelphian Samuel Williams with a federal misdemeanor: obstructing the execution of the U.S. fugitive slave law. Earlier, when Williams was first arrested for his role in the Christiana resistance, the *Philadelphia Sun* had reported:

> He acknowledged to the officers, on his way to prison, that he did go . . . and convey word to the blacks . . . that the slave catchers were in pursuit of the fugitives, and said that he would do so again under the same circumstances.[14]

Despite this reported confession, on January 12, 1852, in the U.S. Court in Philadelphia, Samuel Williams pleaded "not guilty" to interfering with the arrest of Edward Gorsuch's slaves.

Among Williams's defense lawyers was one Robert P. Kane, whose brother had earlier arranged the Thanksgiving banquet for the imprisoned "traitors," and whose father, Judge John K. Kane, had co-presided at the treason trial. Black underground agent William Still reports that the judge's son, counsel

> R. P. Kane, Esq., although a young volunteer in the anti-slavery war, brought to the work great zeal, high attainments, large sympathy and true pluck, while, in view of all the circumstances, the committee of arrangements felt very much gratified to have had him in their ranks.

One of the special "circumstances" of Samuel Williams's trial to which Still, no doubt, alludes is the fact that the presiding judge was none other than the young defense counsel's father.

The familiar U.S. marshal, Henry H. Kline, was the principal witness against Williams. After several interruptions in the trial due to the judge's illness, on February 5, 1852, Samuel Williams was found "not guilty." With Williams's release the Christiana resistance prosecutions finally came to an end. The prosecutions are estimated to have cost the United States Government between $50,000 and $70,000. The Government got little for its money. Prosecutions which had begun with the charge of "levying war" against the United States ended without a single conviction, even on the lesser charges of murder and riot.[15]

After the treason charges were dropped, Hanway's attorneys asked the court to order the United States Government to pay the costs of his defense, claiming that the expense had ruined him. The court refused to so order. Later, after all the charges were dropped, the Christiana defendants directly petitioned the United States Government to pay the costs of their defense. This petition to the United States Congress states that those arrested had been

> charged with the highest crime known to our laws, and thrown into prison, where they were detained many months and subjected to great expense in making preparations to meet those charges, . . . after which they were discharged without a hearing, thereby tacitly admitting the charges were groundless. . . .

The petitioners asked

> the honorable representatives of the most magnanimous nation of the earth, to grant us some relief from our embarrassments. . . .

Congress did not grant the Christiana defendants' request. It should be noted that the lawyers who prosecuted the case against the Christiana resisters had early in the proceedings estimated the "maximum" fee for their services, and received written promise from the United States Government that it would be paid.[16]

Early in December, 1851, before the Lancaster "murder" and "riot" indictment had been finally dismissed, President Fillmore's annual message to Congress referred to the Christiana battle, and other recent fugitive slave cases:

> It is deeply to be regretted that in several instances officers of the Government, in attempting to execute the law for the return of fugitives from labor, have been openly resisted and their efforts frustrated and defeated by lawless and violent mobs; that in one case such resistance resulted in the death of an estimable citizen. . . . I have regarded it as my duty in these cases to give all aid legally in my power to the enforcement of the laws, and I shall continue to do so wherever and whenever their execution may be resisted.
> Some objections have been urged against the details of the act for the return of fugitives from labor, but it is worthy of remark that the main opposition is aimed against the Constitution itself, and proceeds from persons and classes of persons many of whom declare their wish to see that Constitution overturned. . . . Fortunately the number of these persons is comparatively small, and is believed to be daily diminishing. . . .[17]

Calculating quite differently, Garrisonian abolitionist Oliver Johnson, on December 8, 1851, wrote to the anti-slavery Congressman Joshua Giddings:

> The treason trials are making a great deal of talk here now, and thousands are ready to listen who have long been indifferent.[18]

On December 18, 1851, Congressman Giddings himself spoke at a large anti-slavery meeting in Philadelphia. At this or a similar meeting the Ohio congressman reportedly denounced the fugitive slave law

> which he said he would trample under his feet as an unholy thing, and an outrage upon the Constitution. His allusion to the Christiana affair, and to the efforts of the Government to hang peaceable citizens of Pennsylvania as traitors, were rapturously applauded. He made no secret of his admiration and approval of the conduct of the blacks in fighting for their freedom, and said that if he were a slave,

he would take his liberty if he had to walk over the dead bodies of slaveholders all the way from the borders of Kentucky to the Canada line. . . .

"When Mr. Giddings had concluded his address," Quaker Lucretia Mott reportedly arose,

and while expressing her dissent from those portions of his speech which sanctioned violence, thanked him . . . for his manly vindication of the rights of the slave.

The chairman of the meeting, the Reverend Mr. Furness, then said

he was glad to see that we had with us, on the occasion, two of the Christiana Traitors; whereupon there was a cry, "Let them come to the platform. . . ." Castner Hanway and Elijah Lewis, though naturally reluctant to exhibit themselves, took their place on the platform amidst the most tempestuous cheers. Mr. Giddings, standing between them, and taking them by the hand, said: "I declare to you, my friends, that I am far prouder in being able to grasp the hands of these brave men, than I should be to receive the applause of the mightiest prince that ever trod the footstool of the Almighty." The cheers which followed this were tremendous.[19]

On Christmas day, 1851, New York's anti-slavery senator William H. Seward sent an acid thank-you note to John W. Ashmead, of the Christiana prosecution:

My Dear Sir,

I thank you for the kind remembrance manifested by you sending me a copy of your opening argument on the late Trial for Treason. While I cannot but rejoice in the result of that trial as a new assurance of the security of Popular Liberty, I am not unable to appreciate the ability with which you have maintained the untenable position which the Government was made to assume. The argument is highly logical and eloquent, and I cannot better manifest my good wishes for you and for the Country than by expressing a hope that it may be the good fortune of the cause of truth and justice hereafter to enlist you on their side.[20]

On December 31, Philadelphia abolitionist and underground railroad agent James Miller McKim wrote to William Lloyd Garrison

the cause is in a very promising position just now. . . . These Treason Trials have been a great windfall.[21]

In January, 1852, Maryland's governor, Louis E. Lowe, discussed the Christiana case in a message to his State's General Assembly. The "trial of Castner Hanway was a farce," charged the governor. Now, after Judge Grier's instructions to the Christiana jury, no future fugitive slave resistance could be considered treason. The fugitive slave act had become "a mockery and a delusion."

Maryland's governor noted that "patriotic voices," both north and south, "have spoken out, in favor of the Constitution as the basis for the Union." He hoped these voices would prevail and hinted at the dire alternative of southern secession and civil war:

Shall domestic feuds destroy our power, when the eyes of all nations are turned to the star of our empire, as the harbinger of their deliverance? . . . May so incalculable a calamity be spared to the nations of the earth. And yet, when, American blood is made to flow upon American soil, as a grateful libation to American fanaticism; when, whole communities stand listlessly by, and a prostituted press and venal politicians are found, in the open day, to glory in the human sacrifice; when Law proclaims its own weakness from the Bench, and Treason stalks unpunished, through the halls of Justice; the Nation can judge of the probable remoteness of that calamity.[22]

Many years after the event, the black underground railroad agent William Still summed up the results of the Christiana resistance and treason trial quite differently:

At first even the friends of freedom thought that the killing of Gorsuch was not only wrong, but unfortunate for the cause. Scarcely a week passed, however, before the matter was looked upon in a far different light, and it was pretty generally thought that, if the Lord had not a direct hand in it, the cause of Freedom at least would be greatly benefited thereby.

And just in proportion as the masses cried, Treason! Treason! the hosts of freedom from one end of the land to the other were awakened to sympathy with the slave. Thousands were soon aroused to show sympathy who had hitherto been dormant. Hundreds visited the prisoners in their cells to greet, cheer, and offer them aid and counsel in their hour of sore trial.[23]

The Christiana case, says Still,

was doubtless, the most important trial that ever took place in this country relative to the Underground Rail Road passengers, and in its results more good was brought out of evil than can be easily estimated. The proslavery theories of treason were utterly demolished, and not a particle of room was left the advocates of the peculiar institution to hope, that slave-hunters in future, in quest of fugitives, would be any more safe than Gorsuch. The tide of public sentiment changed—Hanway, and the other "traitors," began to be looked upon as having been greatly injured, and justly entitled to public sympathy and honor, while confusion of face, disappointment and chagrin were plainly visible throughout the demoralized ranks of the enemy. . . .

Especially were slave-holders taught the wholesome lesson, that the Fugitive Slave Law was no guarantee against "red hot shot. . . ." In every respect, the Underground Rail Road made capital by the treason.[24]

"This affair at Christiana," says Frederick Douglass,

and the Jerry rescue at Syracuse, inflicted fatal wounds on the fugitive slave bill. It became thereafter almost a dead letter, for slaveholders found that not only did it fail to put them in possession of their slaves, but that the attempt to enforce it brought odium upon themselves and weakened the slave system." [25]

A final pecuniary result of the Christiana resistance is of interest. Several bills of expenses, rendered to Edward Gorsuch's estate, a few months after the slave owner's death, reveal a most practical, unsentimental side of the business. Gorsuch's posse members, it seems, were determined to be repaid for every cent spent on their fatal errand. Neighbor Nicholas Hutchings submitted a bill "for expenses incurred in accompanying the late Edward Gorsuch to Pennsylvania and back," including a 37 1/2-cent "supper in York," and a 25-cent "breakfast at Gallagherville." He "received in full' a total of $8.84. The expenses of George Gorsuch (a relative who came up after the battle) include 25 cents for "Refreshments," and total $4.55. The bill submitted by cousin Joshua M. Gorsuch totals $20.73 3/4, including $12.00 "to pistol, and hat lost," and $5.50 "to medical attendance." Cousin Joshua "received payment" on February 21, 1852.[26]

III FREEDOM-BOUND

17 Escape

IN THE DAYS immediately following the Christiana resistance, a number of its most active participants went into hiding or made their escape to Canada via the underground railroad. In 1872, Robert C. Smedley collected reminiscences of local families, who claimed to have aided the Christiana fugitives' escape. Other ex-underground agents wrote down their own recollections, and some recorded the underground railroad stories they had heard from friends or relatives. These accounts, recalled years after the event, when it had become popular to claim participation in the underground, must be read cautiously. But if these accounts differ somewhat on the route taken by Parker and the other Christiana fugitives, they do undoubtedly convey a fairly accurate general sense of the underground railroad in action.[1]

Smedley reports that one midnight after the "riot," three former slaves engaged in it came to Caleb C. Hood's in Bart Township, Lancaster County. These black men, William Howard, Charles Long, and James Dawsey, asked underground railroad agent Hood

> his advice about the best course for them to pursue. A good supper was given them, and after consultation it was decided that they should take shelter in the woods, as the

premises might be searched. They wanted to proceed at once to Canada; but their clothes were at their homes, and the money due them in the hands of their employers, and they dared not return for them lest they might be captured. At their desire, Caleb went next day, collected their money and clothing and delivered it to them that night. Howard's wife sent especial request for them not to attempt to leave the country then, as every place was so closely watched. Taking a woman's advice, proverbial for being best in emergencies, they gave up their plans of risking an attempt to escape in the midst of so much danger. The family gave them victuals, and saw no more of them for two weeks, when they returned one dark and rainy night at 12 o'clock, and called them up. They had been secreted during that time under the floor of a colored man's house in Drumore township, and now felt the time had come for them to "strike for liberty." Caleb took them that night to Eli Hambleton's. On the following night Eli took them ten miles to the next station. In ten days they reached Canada. Howard then wrote to his wife, who immediately sold their household goods and went to him.[2]

Early on the day of battle, after it was over, William Parker planned his next move. Warned by sympathizers that officers would soon come to arrest him, Parker says,

> I determined not to be taken alive, and told them so; but thinking advice as to our future course necessary, went to see some old friends and consult about it. Their advice was to leave, as, were we captured and imprisoned, they could not foresee the result. Acting upon this hint, we set out for home, when we met some female friends, who told us that forty or fifty armed men were at my house, looking for me, and that we had better stay away from the place, if we did not want to be taken. Abraham Johnson and Pinckney hereupon halted, to agree upon the best course, while I turned around and went another way.

Before parting temporarily, Parker, Pinckney, and Johnson evidently decided to leave that night for Canada.

Parker's "great trial" was to leave his wife and family:

Uncertain as to the result of the journey, I felt I would rather die than be separated from them. It had to be done, however. . . .

The three men, traveling together, had a better chance of reaching Canada than a larger group, but, says Parker, they "went forth with heavy hearts, outcasts for the sake of liberty."

Before setting out on his "long journey northward," Parker determined to have, if possible, one last visit with his family. Parting briefly with Pinckney and Johnson, Parker and several others went along the road until they found the place where his wife was hiding. On the way, Parker reports,

> we met men in companies of three and four, who had been drawn together by the excitement. On one occasion, we met ten or twelve together. They all left the road, and climbed over the fences into the fields to let us pass; and then, after we had passed, turned, and looked after us as far as they could see. Had we been carrying destruction to all human kind, they could not have acted more absurdly. We went to a friend's house and stayed for the rest of the day, and until nine o'clock that night, when we set out for Canada.[3]

On the evening of the Christiana resistance, Dickinson Gorsuch, the slave owner's badly wounded son, was being cared for in the home of Levi Pownall, William Parker's neighbor and landlord. The Quaker family carefully nursed the wounded but still conscious Dickinson, all the while assuring him that "they had no unity with his cruel business, and were very sorry to see him engaged in it." Dickinson's eldest brother, the Reverend J. S. Gorsuch, reports that the Pownalls bestowed on his brother "every attention that kindness can suggest and charity execute." [4]

George Steele, who later married Levi Pownall's daughter Elizabeth, recounts the events on the evening of the day of battle as his wife had no doubt recounted it to him. It was dark. Elizabeth Pownall's mother, Sarah, was in the sitting room tending the wounded Dickinson Gorsuch. The twenty-six-year-old Elizabeth and her twenty-nine-year-old sister, Ellen, were in the kitchen washing dishes. Friends and sympathizers of the Gorsuch family had arrived on the scene from Maryland. They, along with a number of Pennsylvanians, were in and about the house, and appeared to be guarding it. Some of them professed fear that the blacks would attack the slave owner's son.

Suddenly, Elizabeth and Ellen Pownall looked up from their dishes and saw William Parker and Alexander Pinckney at the kitchen door. The two men didn't seem to realize the danger they were in. Elizabeth Pownall quickly blew out the candles and motioned them inside. The young women quietly called their mother, whom George Steele describes as "the best and most capable woman I ever knew." Sarah Pownall, her two daughters, and the black men met in the darkened pantry. For a few moments the silence was dense. Then the capable Sarah Pownall whispered to Elizabeth and Ellen: "Get a clean pillow case and fill it with bread and meat." One of the daughters remonstrated with her mother: "All these people in the house to feed, and barely enough bread for breakfast." Sarah Pownall whispered a command: "Mix more bread!" The pillowcase was filled with food, and the eighteen-year-old George Pownall took it out to the orchard, leaving it at the foot of an apple tree.

A plan was devised to disguise the two black men in the broad-brimmed hats and big overcoats of gentlemen callers. Twenty-three-year-old Levi Pownall, Jr., who for years afterward sighed over the sacrifice of his beaver hat and big coat, provided the men with clothes. When the black men were arrayed, the two young Pownall women walked with them arm in arm down the dark pathway to the garden gate, where they waved the men farewell and wished them Godspeed on their long journey.[5]

Dickinson Gorsuch recuperated at the Pownalls' for three months and one day. Once, a rumor was heard that William Parker had been captured and killed on his way to Canada. Hearing this rumor, it is said that Dickinson told Elizabeth Pownall he thought Parker was safe in Canada. With dubious magnanimity the slave owner's son added: "I am glad of it, for he was a noble nigger." [6]

After leaving the Pownalls' on the night of the battle, Parker and Alexander Pinckney re-joined Abraham Johnson. "When we had walked as far as Christiana," reports Parker with his usual bravado, we saw a large crowd, late as it was, to some of whom, at least, I must have been known, as we heard distinctly, "A'n't that Parker?"

"Yes," was answered, "that's Parker." Kline was called for, and he, with some nine or ten more, followed after. We stopped, and then they stopped. One said to his comrades, "Go on,—that's him." And another replied, "You go." So they contended for a time who should come to us. At last they went back. I was sorry to see them go back, for I wanted to meet Kline and end the day's transactions.[7]

R. C. Smedley traces the route and lists the underground conductors said to have aided the Christiana fugitives' escape. According to Smedley two adventurous women, Elizabeth Coates and Ann Preston, an early graduate of the Philadelphia Woman's Medical College, in broad daylight drove the "well-covered" fugitives in a dearborn to the home of James H. Taylor in West Marlborough. Taylor is said to have taken the fugitives to the next station just in time. Returning home Taylor found

> the hunters had been at his place in search of any colored people who might have fled to him from the vicinity of Christiana.[8]

Luckily, Taylor had already delivered Parker, Pinckney, Johnson, and one other unidentified fugitive to the home of Isaac and Dinah Mendenhall, in Kennett township. Smedley reports:

> The four men slept in the barn at Isaac Mendenhall's at nights, but during the day they husked corn in the field, with all the appearance of regular farm hands. If pursuers came, the family were to give a certain sound when the men were to flee to the woods. One day a messenger came and said there was a party on the track of these men, and it would not be safe to keep them longer. During the remainder of the day they concealed themselves in the woods. Isaac decided to take them that night to John Vickers. . . .

In the meantime, Dr. Bartholomew Fussell, "then living near

(top left) Isaac Mendenhall. (Smedley)

(top right) Dr. Bartholomew Fussell. (Smedley)

(left) Dinah Mendenhall. (Smedley)

by, at Hamorton," heard that the fugitives were at Mendenhall's. Dr. Fussell went to consult with Isaac Mendenhall about the black men. Learning Mendenhall's plan, the doctor said,

"Isaac, I am better acquainted with the route than thee is; and beside, I have no property to sacrifice if I am detected and thee has. Thee start with them on the road and I will meet thee and go with them and thee can return." After

Graceanna Lewis. (Smedley)

some deliberation, Isaac accepted the proposition, and at an appointed hour in the evening, started.

Isaac Mendenhall's wife, Dinah, recalls her feelings on that evening:

"These were not only fugitives but participants in the tragedy, and harboring them subjected us to heavy fine and imprisonment. But we had always said we would never submit to carry out that accursed Fugitive Slave Law, come what might. But that night when they started, the poor quivering flesh was weak and I had scarce strength to get into the house. But I held to my faith in an Overruling Providence, and we came through it in safety." "These," she remarked, "were the times which tried men's souls, and women's too." [9]

Smedley reports that Dr. Fussell took the fugitives on to his niece, Graceanna Lewis. Graceanna and her two sisters, Mariann and Elizabeth R., were, according to William Still, "among the most faithful, devoted, and quietly efficient workers in the Anti-slavery cause." The three Quaker sisters' home, near Kimberton, Chester County, was "always open to fugitives," and "became an important center of Underground Railroad operations for the region. . . ." [10]

Smedley reports that Dr. Fussell, with Parker and his comrades, arrived at the Lewises' "before midnight." Leaving the fugitives in his wagon, the doctor went to the house, awoke the family, told them whom he had with him and what the danger would be in harboring them. They admitted them, however, and put them in a third-story room, the door of which locked on the inside. They were told not to unlock it unless a certain signal was given. As the girl then living with the family was not to be trusted, they borrowed food for the men from a neighbor, so as not to excite her suspicion. The following day arrangements were made with J. Pierce West, living near by, to take them to the house of a friend in Montgomery county, about a mile or more from Phoenixville. A little after dark he and his brother, Thomas, started with them in a market dearborn, throwing some old carpet over them, just as they would cover a butter-tub. Passing through Phoenixville, about midnight, they arrived at the friend's house, whose name is not now remembered, and there left them.[11]

William Parker traces his group's passage from Christiana to Penningtonville, to Parkesburg, to the house of a friend six miles past Downington, Pennsylvania. There, he says, they stopped to rest on Saturday night, September 13, two days after setting out. The next evening, they journeyed fifteen miles further. Here, says Parker,

I learned from a preacher, directly from the city, that the excitement in Philadelphia was too great for us to risk our safety by going there. Another man present advised us to go to Norristown.

At Norristown we rested a day. The friends gave us ten dollars, and sent us in a vehicle to Quakertown. Our driver, being partly intoxicated, set us down at the wrong place, which obliged us to stay out all night. At eleven o'clock the next day we got to Quakertown. We had gone about six miles out of the way, and had to go directly across the country.[12]

A more detailed account of the fugitives' escape from Norristown to Quakertown was given to Smedley by Dr. Jacob L. Paxson, an underground railroad conductor described by one

Dr. Jacob L. Paxson. (Smedley)

source as "a faith-healer, curing 'by laying on the hands,' an advanced thinker but unsteady . . ." [13] Dr. Paxson recalled that a few days after the Christiana "riot," Parker, Pinckney, Johnson, and one unnamed fugitive

> came on foot in the night to Norristown. . . . Dr. William Corson announced their arrival to John Augusta. The four men were concealed in a lot of shavings under a carpenter shop which stood three feet above ground on Church street, near Airy. There they remained four days, and were fed with food passed to them upon an oven-peal across a four-foot alley from a frame house in which Samuel Lewis, a colored man, lived. During this time the United States Marshal's detectives were watching every part of the town.
>
> On the fourth day a meeting was held by a few trusted friends in the office of Lawrence E. Corson, Esq., to devise means for their escape. Dr. Paxson proposed engaging five wagons for that evening, four to be sent in different directions as decoys to lead off the vigilant detectives. The plan was adopted, and the wagons and teams were engaged of Jacob Bodey, whose sympathies were known to be in favor of the fugitives. But he would accept no pay, saying he would do so much as his share.
>
> The first [wagon] was sent up the turnpike road and shortly after, the second was sent down that road; another was sent across the bridge toward West Chester, and the

fourth out the State road toward Downingtown. The
attention of the alert officers being now attracted in these
directions, the men after having shaved, and otherwise
changed their personal appearance, walked from the carpenter shop to Chestnut street and down Chestnut to the
house of William Lewis, colored, where the fifth wagon
which was to go directly through the town and up the Mill
creek road was waiting for them.

Dr. Paxson was there also, and saw the men with
William Lewis, colored, as their driver start safely for
Quakertown. Lewis was a little tremulous with fear at the
perilous undertaking, which, with the haste, somewhat
confused him at the start. On the road he became
bewildered, and went several miles out of the way, which
gave Parker the impression that he was partly intoxicated
—a condition in which Lewis never was known to be.[14]

In Quakertown, on Tuesday, September 16, after five days on
the road, Parker says he and his company rested, and then set out
again that evening:

A friend piloted us some distance, and we travelled until
we became very tired, when we went to bed under a
haystack.[15]

Although Parker does not say so, perhaps he and his company
were received at the Quakertown home of Richard Moore,
reportedly "the last important station of the Underground Railroad" in Bucks County. Moore's grandson was "quite confident"
that one of the fugitives carried north by his father's brave black
assistant, Henry Franklin, "was Parker, the principal hero in the
Christiana tragedy." [16]
Parker continues:

On the 17th, we took breakfast at an inn. We passed a
small village, and asked a man whom we met with a
dearborn, what would be his charge to Windgap. "One
dollar and fifty cents," was the ready answer. So in we got,
and rode to that place.

Wishing to make some inquiries, Parker went into the post

office, and to allay the postmaster's suspicions, asked for a letter
for John Thomas, which of course he did not get. The postmaster
scrutinized the black man closely, gave him directions, and then
evidently did not trouble himself further.

"After going about nine miles," says Parker,

> we stopped in the evening of the 18th at an inn, got supper,
> were politely served, and had an excellent night's rest. On
> the next day we set out for Tannersville, hiring a convey-
> ance for twenty-two miles of the way.

From Tannersville they took the train to Homerville, where after
an hour's wait they took a stagecoach.

> Being the first applicants for tickets, we secured inside
> seats, and from the number of us, we took up all of the
> places inside; but, another traveller coming, I tendered him
> mine, and rode with the driver. The passenger thanked me;
> but the driver, a churl, and the most prejudiced person I
> ever came in contact with, would never wait after a stop
> until I could get on, but would drive away, and leave me to
> swing, climb, or cling on to the stage as best I could. Our
> traveller, at last noticing his behavior, told him promptly
> not to be so fast, but let all passengers get on, which had
> the effect to restrain him a little.
>
> At Big Eddy we took the cars. Directly opposite me sat a
> gentleman, who, on learning that I was for Rochester, said
> he was going there too, and afterwards proved an agreeable
> travelling-companion.
>
> A newsboy came in with papers, some of which the
> passengers bought. Upon opening them, they read of the
> fight at Christiana.
>
> "O, see here!" said my neighbor; "great excitement at
> Christiana; a—a statesman killed, and his son and nephew
> badly wounded."
>
> After reading, the passengers began to exchange opin-
> ions on the case. Some said they would like to catch
> Parker, and get the thousand dollars reward offered by the
> State; but the man opposite to me said, "Parker must be a
> powerful man."

I thought to myself, "If you could tell what I can, you could judge about that."

Pinckney and Johnson became alarmed, and wanted to leave the cars at the next stopping-place; but I told them there was no danger. I then asked particularly about Christiana, where it was, on what railroad, and other questions, to all of which I received correct replies. One of the men became so much attached to me, that, when we would go to an eating-saloon, he would pay for both. . . .

Just before reaching Rochester, when in conversation with my travelling friend, I ventured to ask what would be done with Parker should he be taken.

"I do not know," he replied; "but the laws of Pennsylvania would not hang him,—they might imprison him. But it would be different, very different, should they get him into Maryland. The people in all the Slave States are so prejudiced against colored people, that they never give them justice. But I don't believe they will get Parker. I think he is in Canada by this time; at least, I hope so,—for I believe he did right, and, had I been in his place, I would have done as he did. Any good citizen will say the same. I believe Parker to be a brave man; and all you colored people should look at it as we white people look at our brave men, and do as we do. You see Parker was not fighting for a country, nor for praise. He was fighting for freedom: he only wanted liberty, as other men do. You colored people should protect him, and remember him as long as you live. We are coming near our parting-place, and I do not know if we shall ever meet again. I shall be in Rochester some two or three days before I return home; and I would like to have your company back.

I told him it would be some time before we returned.

The cars then stopped, when he bade me good by. As strange as it may appear, he did not ask me my name; and I was afraid to inquire his, from fear he would.[17]

It was nine o'clock on the morning of Saturday, September 20, that Parker and his comrades reached Rochester, after traveling all night. After walking two or three blocks from the train station,

Parker reports that he and his fellow fugitives "overtook a colored man, who conducted us to the house of—a friend of mine." Parker never mentions this Rochester friend by name, still fearful when his narrative was written that to do so might cause injury. Only many years later, when no harm could come from it, did Parker's Rochester friend Frederick Douglass, in his autobiography, reveal his own role in Parker's escape.[18]

Parker says only that his Rochester friend

> welcomed me at once, as we were acquainted before, took me up stairs to wash and comb, and prepare, as he said, for company.
>
> As I was combing, a lady came up and said, "Which of you is Mr. Parker?"
>
> "I am," said I,—"what there is left of me."
>
> She gave me her hand, and said, "And this is William Parker!"
>
> She appeared to be so excited that she could not say what she wished to. We were told we would not get much rest, and we did not; for visitors were constantly coming. One gentleman was surprised that we got away from the cars, as spies were all about, and there were two thousand dollars reward for the party.[19]

One of those who visited the Christiana fugitives in Rochester described it to a Syracuse newspaper reporter:

> A friend by our side says that he saw last Saturday evening, at Rochester, three of the colored men who killed Gorsuch and shot his son. . . .

The informant reported that the blacks had said the posse had fired first, and that "they begged the whites to desist." After the old slave owner

> had shot at them, and their own pistols were discharged, they kicked the elder Gorsuch's pistol out of his hands, and knocked him down with clubs and killed him—they had his revolver in their possession.

Parker says that "ten dollars were generously contributed by the

Rochester friends for our expenses; and altogether their kindness was heartfelt, and was most gratefully appreciated by us." [20]

A hastily scribbled note, dated "Sept. 1851," from Frederick Douglass to his white Rochester friend Samuel D. Porter probably refers to Parker and his two comrades, and conveys the excitement of that moment:

> There are three men now at my house who are in great peril. I am unwell, I need your advice. Please come at once.

The note was signed "D.F."—in case it was intercepted.[21]

It was Frederick Douglass's responsibility to send the three fugitives safely on their way from Rochester to Canada. In his autobiography Douglass describes his aid:

> The work of getting these men safely into Canada was a delicate one. They were not only fugitives from slavery, but charged with murder, and officers were in pursuit of them. There was no time for delay. I could not look upon them as murderers. To me, they were heroic defenders of the just rights of man against manstealers and murderers. So I fed them, and sheltered them in my house. Had they been pursued then and there, my home would have been stained with blood, for these men who had already tasted blood were well armed and prepared to sell their lives at any expense to the lives and limbs of their probable assailants. What they had already done at Christiana, and the cool determination which showed very plainly especially in Parker (for that was the name of the leader), left no doubt on my mind that their courage was genuine and that their deeds would equal their words. The situation was critical and dangerous. . . . The hours they spent at my house were therefore hours of anxiety as well as activity. I dispatched my friend Miss Julia Griffiths to the landing three miles away on the Genesee River to ascertain if a steamer would leave that night for any port in Canada, and remained at home myself to guard my tired, dust-covered, and sleeping guests. . . . Happily for us the suspense was not long, for it turned out that that very night a steamer was to leave for Toronto, Canada.

This fact, however, did not end my anxiety. There was danger that between my house and the landing or at the landing itself we might meet with trouble. Indeed the landing was the place where trouble was likely to occur if at all. As patiently as I could, I waited for the shades of night to come on, and then put the men in my "Democrat carriage," and started for the landing on the Genesee. It was an exciting ride, and somewhat speedy withal. We reached the boat at least fifteen minutes before the time of its departure, and that without remark or molestation. But those fifteen minutes seemed much longer than usual. I remained on board till the order to haul in the gangplank was given; I shook hands with my friends, received from Parker the revolver that fell from the hand of Gorsuch when he died, presented now as a token of gratitude and a memento of the battle for liberty at Christiana. . . .[22]

William Parker recalls spending one day in Rochester, and leaving "at eight o'clock that evening in a carriage, for the boat, bound for Kingston in Canada," not Toronto, as Douglass remembers it. Parker describes the scene at the dock with perhaps a certain exaggeration:

As we went on board, the bell was ringing. After walking about a little, a friend pointed out to me the officers on the "hunt" for us; and just as the boat pushed off from the wharf, some of our friends on shore called me by name. Our pursuers looked very much like fools, as they were. I told one of the gentlemen on shore to write Kline that I was in Canada.

But Parker's triumphant mood soon changed:

Once on the boat, and fairly out at sea towards the land of liberty, my mind became calm, and my spirits very much depressed at thought of my wife and children. Before, I had little time to think much about them, my mind being on my journey. Now I became silent and abstracted. Although fond of company, no one was company for me now.[23]

18 Canada

FUGITIVES SANG:

> Take me back to Canada,
> where de' cullud people's free.

Canada!—to many slaves a legendary free land; talked about, dreamed of, and sought after by those who fled from bondage to a new life "under the paws of the British lion." In his youth William Parker had heard of "the land far away in the North where the runaway was safe from pursuit . . ." [1] Now he had arrived—at the last stop on the underground railroad.

After his hopeful dreams of a promised land, Parker's arrival in Canada was something of an anti-climax:

> We landed at Kingston on the 21st of September, at six o'clock in the morning, and walked around for a long time, without meeting any one we had ever known. At last, however, I saw a colored man I knew in Maryland. He at first pretended to have no knowledge of me, but finally recognized me. I made known our distressed condition, when he said he was not going home then, but, if we would have breakfast, he would pay for it. How different the treatment received from this man—himself an exile for the

sake of liberty, and in its full enjoyment on free soil—and the self-sacrificing spirit of our Rochester colored brother, who made haste to welcome us to his ample home,—the well-earned reward of his faithful labors!

On Monday evening the 23rd, we started for Toronto, where we arrived safely the next day. Directly after landing, we heard that Governor Johnston, of Pennsylvania, had made a demand on the Governor of Canada for me, under the Extradition Treaty.[2]

The Webster-Ashburton Treaty of 1842 provided for the extradition of fugitive criminals, not runaway slaves. The return of runaway slaves from Canada might be accomplished only by claiming them as "fugitives from justice"; but no precedents for such criminal extradition had been set, due to legal technicalities or the disappearance of the accused blacks. In 1850, migration of American blacks to Canada had increased after the passage of the new U.S. fugitive slave law. Canadian abolitionists had warned their officials of renewed attempts to extradite runaway slaves on criminal indictments. But slavery had been officially abolished in Canada, and throughout the British empire, in 1833. Canadian courts, politicians, and public opinion were generally unsympathetic to the return of fugitive slaves.[3]

Hearing of the extradition request for Parker, his Christiana comrades were worried:

> Pinckney and Johnson advised me to go to the country, and remain where I should not be known; but I refused. I intended to see what they would do with me. Going at once to the Government House, I entered the first office I came to.[4] The official requested me to be seated. The following is the substance of the conversation between us, as near as I can remember. I told him I had heard that Governor Johnston, of Pennsylvania, had requested his government to send me back.

At this the official started forward, and Parker, thinking that "he was intending to seize me," prepared to knock him down. But the white man came forward holding forth his hand, his "genial, sympathetic manner" convincing the fugitive that "he meant well." "Is this William Parker?" asked the Canadian.

> I took his hand and assured him I was the man. . . .
> He made me sit down, and said,—"Yes, they want you back again. Will you go?"
> "I will not be taken back alive," said I. "I ran away from my master to be free,—I have run from the United States to be free. I am now going to stop running."
> "Are you a fugitive from labor?" he asked.
> I told him I was.
> "Why," he answered, "they say you are a fugitive from justice."

The official questioned Parker further about his life as a slave, the county in which his master lived, his master's name, the name of his master's farm, the nearby towns, river—Parker answered all satisfactorily.

> "How does it happen," he then asked, "that you lived in Pennsylvania so long, and no person knew you were a fugitive from labor?"
> "I do not get other people to keep my secrets, sir," I replied. "My brother and family only knew that I had been a slave." [5]
> He then assured me that I would not, in his opinion, have to go back.[6]

Parker says no more about the outcome of the extradition request, and the British government apparently refused to honor it.

Parker now had other matters to think about:

> I ate breakfast with the greatest relish, got a letter written to a friend in Chester County for my wife, and set about arrangements to settle at or near Toronto.
> We tried hard to get work, but the task was difficult. I think three weeks elapsed before we got work that could be called work. Sometimes we would secure a small job, worth two or three shillings, and sometimes a smaller one, worth not more than one shilling; and these not oftener than once or twice in a week. We became greatly discouraged; and, to add to my misery, I was constantly hearing some alarming report about my wife and children. Sometimes they had carried her back into slavery,—sometimes the children, and

sometimes the entire party. Then there would come a contradiction. I was soon so completely worn down by my fears for them, that I thought my heart would break. To add to my disquietude, no answer came to my letters, although I went to the office regularly every day.

After the Christiana resistance, says Parker, his wife, Eliza, had been "obliged to secrete herself, leaving the children in care of her mother, and to the charities of our neighbors." In the following days Eliza

> had had a very bad time. Twice they had her in custody; and, a third time, her young master came after her, which obliged her to flee before day, so that the children had to remain behind for the time.[7]

Smedley reports that after the resistance Eliza Parker and her sister, Hannah Pinckney, had been arrested at their mother's home, and taken back to Christiana. Eliza's and Hannah's names are listed in newspaper reports of those detained. Smedley relates that, after the two women's arrest, Hannah Pinckney

> asked permission to return and get her baby to take with her. Her request was granted, and the man having the two women in custody took both of them with him in a dearborn. When arriving opposite the house, which stood across a field, with no lane to it, he allowed the women to go for the child while he remained in the vehicle. As they staid an unusual length of time, his suspicions became aroused. Entering it he saw no one. An empty cradle first greeted his eye. Baby and women had gone, and he was left alone to ponder over the "vicissitude of earthly things." [8]

Smedley also reports that "about 7 o'clock on the morning" a day or so after the Christiana "riot," two black women, one carrying a child, called at the door of the Fultons' in Sadsbury Township, Chester County. Joseph Fulton's daughter, Mary Ann, and Julia, a young fugitive employed by the family, were apparently the only ones home. The women at the door were

> much excited and in great distress, and asked if "something could not be done for them; they didn't know what to do,

nor where to go to." On being asked who they were, they replied they were the wives of Parker and Pinckney: that they had got away from their masters the afternoon before, and were endeavoring to escape to some place of safety. As soon as it was dark in the evening they started out, but getting bewildered they had wandered about all night, while the home they left was but five miles distant. They were asked why they came there, and replied that on the road they inquired who lived at that house, and when told, they thought they would have friends there who would do something for them. Mary Ann, with a woman's sympathy and that inspiration and impulse that come in the hour of need, took the case into her own hands at once, and ordered "Julia" to run out the carriage while she went to the field to ask her brother for one of their fleetest young horses.

"What for?" he asked.

She told him. He remonstrated with her against such a dangerous adventure, and refused her the horse, saying she would have all their property confiscated. But she persisted, and would not be put off. He told her then she might take "old blind Nance," thinking possibly she would not risk going with her. But she did. And when ready to start, the question arose in her mind, Where shall I take them? She thought of some person near Caln Friends' Meeting-house who were wanting help, and went there, thinking she could secure places for them until the officers had left their neighborhood. But all in vain. Every one she called upon refused to take them. Evening now came on; and as they drove through a wood, the darkness of approaching night, with their want of success thus far, began to bring a shade of gloom over their spirits, and they halted to consider what they should do next. While thus deliberating in silence, they saw a little colored woman coming toward them, carrying a tub on her head. Mary Ann asked her some questions and then began to explain their situation, when the colored woman interrupted her by saying, "You need not tell me. I knows, I knows all about it. I've helped in many a scrape as this. Just drive down the hill there,

you'll see my house. Just go in an' set them down; I'll be
back in a little bit." They did as she directed. What this
little colored woman did with them, we have not been able
to find out. The last account received of them was, that
they had got to Edwin H. Coates, who took them to
Thomas Hopkins, and he conveyed them to Norristown on
the eve of the Governor's election. They were then placed
on board the cars at Bridgeport, in care of Benjamin
Johnson, colored, who accompanied them to Canada. . . .[9]

In Toronto, after a long period of silence, William Parker finally
received word of his family: "At last I got a letter with the glad
news that my wife and children were safe, and would be sent to
Canada." Parker, then illiterate,

told the person reading for me to stop, and tell them to
send her "right now,"—I could not wait to hear the rest of
the letter.

On November 24, 1851, Eliza Ann Elizabeth Parker joined her
husband in Canada:

Two months from the day I landed in Toronto, my wife
arrived, but without the children.

The youngsters had been left in the care of friends, and Parker
admits he was "so glad" to see his wife "that I forgot about the
children."
"The day my wife came," says Parker,

I had nothing but the clothes on my back, and was in debt
for my board, without any work to depend upon. My
situation was truly distressing.

Parker resolved to look again for employment

and went to a store where I made known my circumstances
to the proprietor, offering to work for him to pay for some
necessaries. He readily consented, and I supplied myself
with bedding, meal, and flour. As I had selected a place
before, we went that evening two miles into the country,
and settled ourselves for the winter.[10]

The Canadian Anti-Slavery Society gave the Parkers and their companions from Christiana some aid during the winter. Then, in warmer weather, the Society supplied some money to convey them partway to Buxton, the Elgin Association settlement, on the southwestern edge of Lake Erie, fifty miles from Detroit.[11]

Soon after landing in Canada, Parker had been told of the Buxton settlement and its agents, the Reverends Dr. Willis and Mr. King. The Presbyterian minister William King had only a few years before founded the Buxton Mission and Elgin Association as a colony for black immigrants. Through the Canadian government the Association had been granted nine thousand acres of "wild lands," of which fifty-acre plots were made available at $2.50 an acre exclusively to black settlers.

The Reverend Dr. Michael Willis, as one of the first vice-presidents of the Buxton settlement, aided his fellow Presbyterian William King by acting as the settlement's Toronto agent. The energetic, earnest Willis had come to Canada from Scotland in the 1840s. Willis's early interest in the plight of the poor had led to a concern for the victims of slavery, and Willis became, by the 1850s, a leading Canadian abolitionist. Just eight months before Parker's arrival, Willis had been elected President of the newly formed Anti-Slavery Society of Canada.[12]

William Parker's Canadian informant, after "stating all the particulars" about the Buxton colony,

induced me to think it was a desirable place; and having quite a little sum of money due to me in the States, I wrote for it, and waited until May. It not being sent, I called upon Dr. Willis, who treated me kindly. I proposed to settle in Elgin, if he would loan means for the first instalment. He said he would see about it, and I should call again. On my second visit, he agreed to assist me, and proposed that I should get another man to go on a lot with me.

Abraham Johnson and I arranged to settle together, and, with Dr. Willis's letter to Mr. King on our behalf, I embarked with my family on a schooner for the West. After five days' sailing we reached Windsor. Not having the means to take us to Chatham, I called upon Henry Bibb, and laid my case before him.[13]

Henry Bibb. (Wm. L. Katz Collection)

Henry Bibb, a fugitive slave from Kentucky, had, after making his own escape, returned south to rescue his wife. Bibb had been captured,—and again escaped, making his way to Detroit. By the late 1840s Bibb had become one of the best known black anti-slavery orators then making lecture tours from Michigan to Massachusetts. After the passage of the 1850 fugitive law Bibb had settled opposite Detroit, at Windsor, Canada, where he edited and published an anti-slavery newspaper, the *Voice of the Fugitive*.[14]

Arriving in Windsor at the end of May or early June, 1852, William Parker brought with him to Henry Bibb a letter of introduction from the Reverend Hiram Wilson, a dedicated minister to the fugitive community in St. Catharines, Canada. The Reverend Mr. Wilson's letter read:

> Dear Brother Bibb,—It gives me pleasure to introduce to you the bearer, Bro. Wm. Parker, who was the hero of the

Christiana battle for freedom and protection against the hellish slave hunters. He is bound for the Elgin Settlement with his family, and in company with quite a number of others, who are destined to the same place.

As they are short of means, please have the kindness to favor them when they arrive at Windsor, with such advice and encouragement as may be in your power to render.

I have favored them what I could: they deserve our sympathy and ought to have assistance.

> Yours truly,
> Hiram Wilson.[15]

Bibb published Wilson's letter in the *Voice of the Fugitive* on June 3, 1852, with an editorial headed "The Christiana Hero is in Canada." William Parker, declared Bibb, was

said to have carried out the sublime idea, that "resistance to tyrants is obedience to God." Suppose he is guilty of the charge, under the circumstances of the case, will any patriotic philanthropist blame him? We say no. If we had thousands of such colored men scattered over the nominally free States, the Fugitive Slave Bill would soon become a dead letter. This man in our estimation deserves the admiration of a Hannibal, a Toussaint L'Ouverture, or a George Washington. A nobler defense was never made in behalf of liberty on the plains of Lexington, Concord or Bunker Hill than was put forth by William Parker at Christiana. We bid him, with his family, and all others, from that hypocritical Republic welcome to this our gracious land of adoption, where no slavehunter dare to step his feet in search of a slave.

Upon arriving in Windsor, says Parker, Henry Bibb

took us in, treated us with great politeness, and afterwards took me with him to Detroit, where, after an introduction to some friends, a purse of five dollars was made up. I divided the money among my companions, and started them for Chatham, but was obliged to stay at Windsor and Detroit two days longer.

While stopping at Windsor, I went again to Detroit, with

two or three friends, when, at one of the steamboats just landed, some officers arrested three fugitives, on pretence of being horse thieves. I was satisfied they were slaves, and said so, when Henry Bibb went to the telegraph office and learned through a message that they were.

Parker and Bibb evidently followed the prisoners to the jail, where an angry group of blacks soon gathered:

In the crowd and excitement, the sheriff threatened to imprison me for my interference. I felt indignant, and told him to do so, whereupon he opened the door. About this time there was more excitement, and then a man slipped into the jail, unseen by the officers, opened the gate, and the three prisoners went out, and made their escape to Windsor.

Here was Parker, himself a "fugitive from justice," only ten months after the Christiana resistance, re-entering the United States and jumping immediately to the defense of his brethren, in an affray which threatened to place him directly into the hands of the law. For Parker's participation in this event there is only his own word. One might justifiably doubt this event had ever occurred if several contemporary newspapers did not document the arrest and escape of three fugitives from Detroit at the time, and in much the same way as Parker describes, without, however, mentioning his anonymous participation.[16]

On June 3, 1852, the night of the three fugitives' escape, William Parker remained in Detroit,

and started the next day for Chatham, where I found my family snugly provided for at a boarding-house kept by Mr. Younge.

Chatham was a thriving town at that time, and the genuine liberty enjoyed by its numerous colored residents pleased me greatly; but our destination was Buxton, and thither we went on the following day. We arrived there in the evening, and I called immediately upon Mr. King, and presented Dr. Willis's letter. He received me very politely, and said that, after I should feel rested, I could go out and select a lot. He also kindly offered to give me meal and pork for my family, until I could get work.[17]

The Reverend William King was a most unlikely mixture of social ingredients, a Scotch-Irish missionary and Louisiana slave owner turned Canadian abolitionist. King had been born in Ulster, North Ireland, studied for the Presbyterian ministry in Scotland, immigrated to America, and married into a slave-owning Louisiana family. His wife had died, and King, having inherited her property, found himself a slave owner. Since both he and his church were opposed to slavery, King secretly arranged to emancipate his fifteen slaves, and after several years of planning, in 1849 moved with them to Canada. There, with the support of the Presbyterian church, and Lord Elgin's government, King founded the Buxton Mission and Elgin Association colony.

The Reverend Mr. King's petition for lands for a black colony at first provoked the strong opposition of an organized, racist, white minority in nearby Chatham. This group was highly displeased with the possibility of blacks' moving into their neighborhood, and were concerned about falling property values. Although white Canadians were generally opposed to slavery, they were by no means free of anti-black feelings. Competition of blacks and whites for jobs and land made this British territory no utopia for dark-skinned settlers or active white allies such as King.

In August, 1849, when William King came to Chatham, threats were made on his life, and a group of armed black men made their own arrangements to be the Reverend's constant bodyguard. When a gang of armed Chatham whites threatened to prevent King and his party from surveying Elgin Association lands, a large group of armed Chatham blacks went hunting in the area. Only the sickness of one of King's party resulted in canceling the surveying for that day—and prevented an armed confrontation. Had he gone out, says King in his autobiography, "there probably would have been bloodshed." He adds: "The coloured people were determined to fight if I should be attacked." King felt, however, that a "collision" with the area's whites at that time "would in all probability have proved fatal to our cause," and he counseled the blacks "to be patient and suffer rather than fight." This advice was accepted politely, but when King's party was ready to go out surveying, the blacks went out hunting again. The Association's boundaries were laid out, and its land divided into fifty-acre "concessions." [18]

Starting with a nucleus of his own ex-slaves King founded a colony designed to attract black pioneers, as the Association's charter stated, "of approved moral character." One hundred and thirty families settled in Buxton within the first three years, many of them fugitive American slaves. A school, church, minister's home, store, hotel, pearl ash factory, and blacksmith shop were among the colony's first buildings. Buxton soon became the most successful of the black Canadian settlements.

Although King's organizational ability was important in Buxton's success, and his advice was apparently asked for and respected by the black settlers, the day-to-day operation of the colony gradually gravitated into the hands of its black residents. At a "town meeting" called by King early in 1850, the white minister proposed the establishment of an elected board to settle the colony's internal disputes and to decide all secular matters. A five-member, all-black Court of Arbitration was immediately elected. Although King had disqualified himself from election to the Court, he seems to have dominated its operation for the first few years. But as King took on more duties as Buxton's liaison with the white community, the black Court of Arbitration gradually began to consider an increasing number of problems, until it became the community's controlling body.[19]

When Frederick Douglass visited Buxton in August, 1854, he cited it as "one of the most striking, convincing, and gratifying" proofs that the black man

> can live, and live well, without a master, and can be industrious without the presence of the blood-letting lash to urge him on to toil.

Douglass reminded his readers that "four years and few months" earlier the forest had been the only "dwelling" in the Buxton area. "How different now," Douglass remarked. There were now "SEVEN HUNDRED SOULS" in the settlement, who had "built themselves snug cottages."

> Rich fields of corn, of grass, and grain, are springing up—and the country presents an appearance of advance-

ment, equal to parts of our Western States settled a dozen years ago. In one direction you may see the colored farmer behind his plough—in another leveling the forest—in another erecting his cottage—in another making brick— and in another threshing out his grain. . . . The people have thrown off the bowed down look of slaves, and menials. They bear themselves like free men and women.

Douglass mentions the Reverend William King's "superinten- dence" of the settlement, and calls King "a most sensible, industrious, enterprising and competent gentleman, thoroughly devoted to the interests of the people under his charge." King, said Douglass, "shared the love and respect of all around him." [20]

In 1856, Benjamin Drew visited Buxton and reported the philosophy of its founder:

Mr. King having full faith in the natural powers, capacity and capabilities of the African race, is practically working out his belief by placing the refugees in circumstances where they may learn self-reliance, and maintain a perfect independence of aid: trusting, under God, on their own right arm.

Drew noted that "the settlers at Buxton are characterized by a manly, independent air and manner." [21] King's enlightened pater- nalism evidently permitted the growth and development of the settlement's members.

The Reverend Mr. King seems to have barely known of William Parker or Abraham Johnson. King's autobiography contains only a vague and inaccurate reference to Parker or Johnson. The Christiana resisters, says King, "made their escape and one of them who fired the fatal shot, made his way to me in Canada with his family, entered one of the lots, and became a peaceful, sober and industrious settler." [22]

"In due time" after their arrival in Buxton, says William Parker, he and Abraham Johnson "each chose a fifty-acre lot." In Toronto, Parker and Johnson had agreed with Dr. Willis to take one lot between them, and the doctor had loaned them the down payment. But "when we saw the land," says Parker

we thought we could pay for two lots. I got the money in a little time, and paid the Doctor back. I built a house, and we moved into it that same fall. . . .[23]

A "Register of Lands," found recently in the Public Archives of Canada, shows that on October 28, 1852, Abraham Johnson signed for a section of "Lot 10," and on November 20, 1852, William Parker registered for part of "Lot 12." Parker's section of "Concession 12," and Johnson's of "Concession 13" apparently made the two Christiana refugees neighbors.[24]

A MEMORIAL, to be Registered, pursuant to the Statute in that case made and provided, of an Indenture of Lease, in the words and figures following, that is to say:

THIS INDENTURE, made the *Twenty-Sixth* day of *September* A. D., 186 5, in pursuance of the Act respecting Short Forms of Leases, BETWEEN *William Parker*

of the Township of *Raleigh, in the County of Kent, C. W.* Yeoman, of the First Part, and *Edward H. Jones Gentleman of Bothwell C. W.*

of the Second Part, WITNESSETH, That in consideration of the rents, covenants and agreements, hereinafter reserved and

Part, on non-performance of the covenant for commencing operations, and those subsequent to it. And the party of the First Part covenants with the part of the Second Part, for quiet enjoyment, without disturbance or interruption by any persons whomsoever.

(Signed) *William Parker* [LS]

A deed apparently signed by William Parker, September 26, 1865. (Kent County Registry Office, Chatham, Ontario, Canada)

Soon after arriving in Buxton, William Parker probably attended night classes for adults in the settlement's fine school. The colony required all heads of families to read and write and by 1864 illiteracy was reported eliminated in Buxton. William King's idea of education differed from many other abolitionists in his insistence on classical, not merely vocational, studies for blacks. Classes in Greek and Latin were begun in 1851. By 1856 five black students from the Buxton school were in Knox and Trinity Colleges in Toronto.[25]

Before William Parker's arrival the Buxton school had seen stormy days. When on the first Sunday in April, 1850, William King announced the school would begin enrolling pupils of all colors the following day, Chatham whites had threatened to prevent the opening and gangs had roamed the nearby woods. Early the next morning, unknown to King, Chatham blacks again decided to go hunting. With a group of armed blacks ringing the new log school in the forest, fourteen black children and two whites enrolled without incident.

The Buxton school soon became famous for its excellence. Although education in Canada was generally segregated, and color prejudice strong, even white people began to transfer their children to the black colony's school. The regular district school was soon forced to close down for lack of pupils. As time went on the fame of the Buxton school spread, and applications for admission came from all over Canada West, and even the United States.

Despite the prejudice he had first encountered in Canada, Parker was optimistic about the change in attitudes he saw taking place during his years of residence in that country. "When I first settled in Buxton," says Parker,

> the white settlers in the vicinity were much opposed to colored people. Their prejudices were very strong; but the spread of intelligence and religion in the community has wrought a great change in them. Prejudice is fast being uprooted; indeed, they do not appear like the same people that they were. In a short time I hope that foul spirit will depart entirely.[26]

Parker also continued to grow and change. It was only after "a struggle of many years," he says, "and, indeed, since I have settled upon British soil, that I have realized fully the grandeur of my position as a free man." [27]

19 Epilogue

THREE YEARS after the Christiana resistance, on January 19, 1854, fugitive slave John Henry Hill wrote an untutored but earnest letter from Toronto to black Philadelphian William Still:

> I have notice several articles in the freeman one of the Canada weaklys concerning the Christiana prisoners respecting Castnor Hanway. . . . if I had one hundred dollars to day I would give them five each, however I hope that I may be able to subscribe something for their Relefe.

The young, six-foot John Henry Hill no doubt felt a kinship with the Christiana rebels. An armed battle with his master had preceded Hill's own escape from Richmond, Virginia, and the fugitive had provided himself with a "Brace of Pistels" for his journey north. Hill's kinship with the Christiana resisters is also indicated in another letter: hearing of a southern slave insurrection, Hill wrote that, while he still believed in praying,

> I do believe that the fire and sword would affect more good in this case. . . . The world are being turned upside down, and I think we might as well take an active part in it as not.[1]

In 1856, five years after Parker's escape to Canada, an editorial

John Henry Hill. (Still)

in *The Provincial Freeman*, the black-owned and -edited newspaper published in Chatham by I. D. Shadd and Mary Ann Shadd Cary, compared the leader of the Christiana resistance to the Haitian revolutionary Dessalines:

A NOBLE FELLOW

We had the pleasure on last Saturday, of taking by the hand, Mr. Wm. Parker, the hero of Christiana. The memory of that conflict of *five* noble bondmen, unarmed in protection of their wives and children, against an armed gang of thirty wretches in the employment of the United States, with the hireling *Kline* of Philadelphia, and old Gorsuch or Gorsooch, and son slaveholders of Maryland at the head, will never be effaced.

Mr. Parker is a slender man, rather tall, mild and forgiving in expression and character, but as decisive as death, as determined as a hurricane, and as brave as a Dessalines. A hundred such villains as Kline of Pennsylvania, would be made to tremble and quake before the masterly eye of such a man as Mr. Parker. Grant, that his manly arm could have reached the cowardly breasts of the whole thirty who assailed him at the time, instead of only two! His ever faithful wife, suffered many privations till she reached him; but they are now happy in their own domestic abode, under the protection of the British Lion.[2]

By 1857, northern black Americans were pointedly *not* celebrating the July 4 "Independence Day" which, they felt, was made a mockery of by American slavery and prejudice. Northern blacks had begun to hold their own annual celebration commemorating the emancipation of slaves in the British West Indies on August 1, 1834.

Frederick Douglass addressed one such West India Emancipation celebration on August 4, 1857, at Canadaigua, New York. Always anxious to prod his people into action, Douglass criticized the "stolid contentment, the listless indifference" with which American blacks were facing their oppression. Douglass praised those who fought for their liberty when they had "the means of doing so,"—those the world over who "were standing up for their own rights against an arrogant and powerful enemy."

Douglass especially commended those battles "in which colored men take a leading part. . . . This struggle may be a moral one, or it may be a physical one, . . ." said the black leader,

> but it must be a struggle. Power concedes nothing without a demand. It never did and it never will.

"Injustice and wrong," said Douglass, must be "resisted with either words or blows, or with both."

Douglass cited the Jerry rescue in Syracuse, the Shadrach rescue in Boston, and the battle at Christiana as examples of successful black resistance, declaring: "Parker and his noble band of fifteen,"

> who defended themselves from the kidnapper with prayers and pistols, are entitled to the honor of making the first successful resistance to the Fugitive Slave Bill. But for that resistance, and the rescue of Jerry and Shadrack, the man-hunters would have hunted our hills and valleys here with the same freedom with which they now hunt their own dismal swamps.[3]

The following year, 1858, the black leader William Wells Brown wrote to William Lloyd Garrison of attending "the West India Emancipation celebration at Christiana." Brown reported:

> The place was fitly chosen, and the meeting was got up by the colored people, many of whom had been slaves themselves. Not less than 2000 were present. Wm. Wells Brown was the only speaker advertised. He spoke an hour

and a half in the forenoon and an hour in the latter part of the day. Mr. Thomas Whitson made a few remarks in the afternoon. A band of music was in attendance, and dinner was served up at 3 o'clock. It was the largest meeting of colored persons I ever met at one time, and it was a pleasure to see so many together, and all peaceable and quiet, not a drunken person on the grounds. All appeared to be deeply interested in the meeting, and to feel the importance of the occasion. There are many colored men in the neighborhood of Christiana, who own fine farms, and are tilling them on their own account; and, although the laws of the State disfranchise its colored citizens, and shut its schools against them, they, nevertheless, seem to be making rapid progress in their own elevation. . . .

The house where Mr. Gorsuch found the fugitive, and the spot where he stood when killed, were pointed out to me, and there is an impression in Christiana that a slaveholder will never come there again in pursuit of fugitive slaves.[4]

On May 8 and 10, 1858, John Brown held a major organizational meeting in Chatham, Canada. Brown was seeking black recruits for his planned guerrilla attack on the slave system. Although Chatham was only ten miles from William Parker's new home, Parker's name is not among those of the thirty-three black men who signed John Brown's Chatham Constitution. It seems probable, however, that Parker would have known of and approved Brown's enterprise.[5]

The following year, 1859, John Brown, Jr., was in Canada on a last recruiting mission for his father's proposed rebel bands. Together with the black leader James W. Loguen, John Brown, Jr. visited the fugitive slave communities at Hamilton, St. Catharines, London, Windsor, Chatham, and Buxton. In a letter dated August 27, 1859, to John Henry Kagi, his father's comrade in arms, John Brown, Jr. tells of forming "associations" whose officers were "to hunt up good workmen and raise the means among themselves to send them forward. . . ." One of these "associations" was formed in Buxton, where John Brown, Jr. met a local leader to whom Kagi had previously referred him. Without mentioning any name John Brown, Jr. wrote:

At ("B-n") I found *the* man, the *leading spirit* in that "affair," which you, Henrie, *refered* to. On Thursday night last, I went with him on foot 12 miles; much of the way through new paths, and sought out in "the bush" some of the *choicest*. Had a meeting after 1 o'clock at night at his home. He has a wife and 5 children; all small, and they are living very poorly indeed, "roughing it in the bush," but his wife is a heroine, and *he will be on hand* as soon as his family can be provided for. He owes about $30; says that a hundred additional would enable him to leave them comfortable for a good while.

After viewing him in all points which I am capable of, I have to say that I think him worth *in our market* as much as *two or three hundred average men,* and even at this rate I should rate him too low. For *physical capacity,* for *practical judgement,* for courage and moral tone, for *energy and force and will*, for *experience* that would not only enable him to *meet* difficulty, but give *confidence* to overcome it, I should have to go a long way to find his equal, and in my judgement, [he] would be a cheap acquisition at almost any price.

I shall *individually* make a strenuous effort to raise the means to send him on.[6]

John Brown, Jr., to be prudent, does not name the Buxton

John Brown, Jr. (Villard)

leader who so impressed him, but it seems very probable this man was William Parker. Parker had been "the leading spirit" in a previous *"affair,"*—"an *experience* that would not only enable him to *meet* difficulty, but give *confidence* to overcome it." Parker's wife, Eliza, had before been accurately termed a "heroine," and they are reported to have had six children in all, one more than Brown, Jr., reports in 1859 when Eliza was twenty-nine. In that year Parker still owed something on his land, not paying for it in full until 1867. Brown, Jr.'s description of the Buxton leader sounds like other descriptions of Parker, and it would be completely in character for William Parker to have been planning to join John Brown. There is no additional evidence of this, although a number of anonymous black men were said to be on their way to join Brown when the Harper's Ferry raid was launched ahead of schedule.

In January, 1859, ten months before the Harper's Ferry raid, a new black publication, *The Anglo-African Magazine*, carried an introductory editorial by its publisher, Thomas Hamilton of Brooklyn. Hamilton declared that those who try to write off "the negro as something less than a man" are beset by "an unaccountable consciousness, an aching dread" that black people are "somehow endowed with forces" which may, in "some grim revel," "shake the pillars of the commonweal." Blacks were "a force," said Hamilton, that could not yet be estimated.

The black publisher pointed to the small resistance against English oppression then being made by Irish rebels. "Compare these," said Hamilton,

> with Sam [Ringold] Ward, Frederick Douglass, or those who fought in Christiana, or the man who suffered himself to be scourged to death in Tennessee rather than betray his associate insurrectionists.

These black individuals had already suggested the potential power of their people.[7]

The following month's *Anglo-African* included an article by the black intellectual Dr. James M'Cune Smith. In a tribute to black resisters, both known and anonymous, Smith declared:

> We live in the heroic age of our country, and the negro is

the hero. We live in the Romance times, and the negro is again the hero. . . .

Smith cited the black heroes of Christiana and Wilkes-Barre, Pennsylvania, where a fugitive, who had thrown himself into the river to avoid capture, had been shot at and left for dead. There were black heroes, said Smith, not only at Christiana and Wilkes-Barre,

> but in ten thousand unknown spots consecrated to Liberty by her sable children, suffering hunger and thirst, and bruises and wounds, and cruel separation, more bitter than death, in the highways, and in the rapid rivers and in the pathless woods.[8]

At a Boston meeting, December 3, 1860, commemorating the first anniversary of John Brown's execution, ruffians hired by the city's commercial classes tried to break up the proceedings. Attacked by this mob, Frederick Douglass "fought like a trained pugilist," but was thrown "down the staircase to the floor of the hall." [9] Later that same day, Douglass addressed the meeting. Douglass approved, he said, "all methods of proceeding against slavery," political and moral, warlike and peaceful. But since the moral abolitionists had won larger audiences in the last twenty-five years, Douglass would devote his speech that day to "advocating John Brown's way . . ."

Moral appeals to the conscience of the nation and to slaveholders had failed, said Douglass:

> We must . . . as John Brown, Jr., has taught us this evening, reach the slaveholder's conscience through his fear of personal danger. We must make him feel that there is death in the air about him. . . . The negroes of the South must do this. . . .

"We do not need a general insurrection to bring about this result," declared Douglass, only a thousand armed, anti-slavery fighters, scattered in the mountains from Pennsylvania to Alabama. These guerrilla warriors could lead blacks to freedom, and destroy the slave system.

Less violent, moral appeals were ineffective, said Douglass, describing "moral suasion people" looking on indignantly while slave catchers shot at fugitive John Thomas in the Wilkes-Barre river. There the abolitionists' "cries of indignation and shame" had not been heeded, and "no hand was lifted" to strike down the slave hunters. What was wanted at that time, said Douglass, was

> a few resolute men, determined to be free, and to free others, resolved, when men were being shot, to shoot again. Had a few balls there whistled, as at Christiana, about the heads of the slave-catchers, it would have been the end of this slave-catching business. . . . The only way to make the Fugitive Slave Law a dead letter is to make a few dead slave-catchers. [Laughter and applause.] There is no need to kill them either—shoot them in the legs, and send them to the South living epistles of the free gospel preached here at the North. [Renewed laughter.] [10]

In 1861 the Civil War began. Peter Woods, a black resident of Christiana who enlisted in the Union Army and served for nearly three years in the 3rd Regiment of the U.S. Colored Infantry, reported meeting William Parker's comrade-in-arms Alexander Pinckney in Charleston, South Carolina, during the war. It was rumored in the Lancaster County area that William Parker had also returned to fight in the Union Army, but attempts to verify this have failed.[11] It is still rumored in the area that when Lee invaded Pennsylvania, at the time of the battle of Gettysburg, the rebel general inquired for Christiana, and wanted to burn it, in retaliation for the "riot" years before. Fortunately, Lee's army did not reach the town.[12]

In February and March, 1866, not long after the Civil War, William Parker's narrative appeared in the *Atlantic Monthly*. The narrative's title, "The Freedman's Story," connected Parker with the recently freed black people of the south. Reconstruction was beginning and the right of southern blacks to vote was still in question. Parker's story was published by the editors of the liberal, Boston-based *Atlantic* as evidence of its author's and his people's "manhood"—a humanity which still had to be proved to many whites.[13]

Recent research reveals that work on Parker's narrative had begun in Chatham, Canada, at least eight years before its publication. An old ledger, originally belonging to the black Chatham resident Abraham D. Shadd contains two diary entries by his son, Israel D. Shadd, referring to the progress of work on Parker's story. I. D. Shadd was the co-editor and publisher of *The Provincial Freeman*, and Shadd's diary notations suggest that Parker's narrative was composed with the aid of four black men at the *Freeman*'s Chatham office.

Shadd's diary entry of "Monday, March 1," 1858, reads:

> Augusta took first manuscript of Parker's life to work upon. Johnson came in from Buxton to see about it.

The entry of "Tues., March 16th" says:

> Joseph and Anderson working in office on Parker's life.

In the first entry "Johnson" is clearly Abraham Johnson, William Parker's fellow resister. "Augusta" is probably Alexander T. Augusta, later a doctor, lieutenant-colonel, and one of the highest ranking black men in the Union Army during the Civil War. In the second entry "Anderson" is probably Anderson Abbot, a bright, young college student whose father was among the first black leaders of the Buxton settlement. Since the second entry seems to use first names the "Anderson" mentioned is probably *not* Osborn Perry Anderson, a "printers devil" in the *Freeman* office, and later the only black member of John Brown's band to escape capture and death for participating in the Harper's Ferry raid. "Joseph" is probably I. D. Shadd's brother. Although published by the *Atlantic* as the autobiographical composition of its single narrator, William Parker, with no other authors mentioned, the article was evidently a group effort.[14]

While there is no direct proof of William Parker's actually writing or dictating the narrative, it is clear from internal evidence that Parker was intimately involved in its creation. One evidence of Parker's involvement is the narrative's wealth of personal and historical detail, significant items of which are verified by external sources. The careful notation of names, dates, and other details indicates both Parker's participation and an intention to record his history with completeness and accuracy. This attention to detail gives the piece a sense of authenticity, suggesting it is the product of careful thought and research.

A number of the Christiana resisters had made their way to Canada, and some of these were apparently consulted, and their testimony used in the composition of the piece. The narrative also mentions the records of both Castner Hanway's and Samuel Williams's trials; these and other printed documents were no doubt studied for the reconstruction of the confrontation, and events leading to it.[15] It should be noted, however, that the narrative does not borrow directly from these or other printed sources.

Although there are some discrepancies between Parker's narrative and other sources, what is remarkable is the great number of details for which external evidence has been found. The genealogy of the Brogden family, for instance, confirms Parker's recollection of several details; the origin of David Brogden's nickname "Mack," as reported by Parker, only becomes clear when the genealogy reveals Brogden's middle name to have been "McCulloch." A contemporary newspaper suggests that Parker did arrive in Rochester after the resistance on the date given by Parker. The fugitive escape in Detroit did take place in the manner and at the time Parker indicates. These and other details indicate that William Parker's story may be safely accepted as the authentic narrative of an early militant black leader.

When Parker's narrative appeared in the *Atlantic* each installment of "The Freedman's Story" was introduced by an editor who signed himself only "E. K." Recent research reveals these initials stood for "Edmund Kirke," the pen name of James Gilmore, a contributor to the magazine.[16] Gilmore was a popular and prolific writer, who during the Civil War once went south on a secret mission for Lincoln, to sound out rebel leaders on the prospects for peace.

In his introduction to "The Freedman's Story" Gilmore emphasizes that the article is the original work of its black narrator, William Parker. "The Freedman's Story" manuscript, says Gilmore, had been handed to him to "revise it for publication, or weave its facts into a story which would show the fitness of the Southern black for the exercise of the right of suffrage." But, says Gilmore, the manuscript is correctly spelled, and clearly written:

> Therefore it needs no revision. On reading it over carefully,
> I also discover that it is in itself a stronger argument for the

manhood of the negro than any which could be adduced by one not himself a freedman; for it is the argument of facts. . . . Therefore, if I were to imbed these facts in the mud of fiction, I should simply oblige the reader to dredge for the oyster, which in this narrative he has without the trouble of dredging, fresh and juicy as it came from the hand of Nature,—or rather, from the hand of one of Nature's noblemen,—and who, until he was thirty years of age, had never put two letters together.

The narrative, Gilmore continues,

has about it the verisimilitude which belongs to truth, and to truth only when told by one who has been a doer of the deeds and an actor in the scenes which he describes. It has the further rare merit of being written by one of the "despised race"; for none but a negro can fully and correctly depict negro life and character.

Possibly with Harriet Beecher Stowe's *Uncle Tom's Cabin* in mind, Gilmore adds:

Every man and woman who has essayed to depict the slave character has miserably failed, unless inoculated with the genuine spirit of the negro; and even those who have succeeded best have done only moderately well, because they have not had the negro nature. It is reserved to some black Shakespeare or Dickens to lay open the wonderful humor, pathos, poetry, and power which slumbers in the negro's soul, and which now and then flash out like the fire from a thunder-cloud.

I do not mean to say that this black prophet has come in this narrative. He has not. This man is a doer, not a writer. . . . The prophet is still to come; and he *will* come. God never gives great events without great historians; and for all the patience and valor and heroic fortitude and self-sacrifice and long-suffering of the black man in this war, there will come a singer—and a black singer—who shall set his deeds to a music that will thrill the nations.

Gilmore re-emphasizes: "The author of this narrative—of every line in it—is William Parker," whom Gilmore identifies as the "principal actor in the Christiana riot," an event which

> aroused the North to the danger of the Fugitive-Slave Law, and, more than any other event, except the raid of John Brown, helped to precipitate the two sections into the mighty conflict which has just been decided on the battle-field.
>
> Surely the man who aided towards such results must be a man, even if his complexion be that of the ace of spades; and what he says in relation to the events in which he was an actor, even if it have no romantic interest,—which, however, it has to an eminent degree,—must be an important contribution to the history of the time.
>
> With these few remarks, I submit the evidence which he gives of the manhood of his race to that impartial grand-jury, the American people.[17]

Despite Gilmore's explicit disclaimer of any rewriting or editing, and his emphatic attribution of authorship to Parker—despite the internal and external evidence indicating Parker's intimate involvement, if not actual authorship—four later scholars have questioned the authenticity of "The Freedman's Story." It is not their skepticism itself which today seems suspect, but the content of these scholars' arguments, and their particular conclusions.

M. G. McDougall in 1891 and W. H. Siebert in 1899 both casually credit the white minister Thomas Wentworth Higginson as the author or co-author of the narrative.[18] The basis for this is not revealed by either historian, although it presumably derives from the fact that the militant Higginson was a frequent contributor to the *Atlantic* on anti-slavery themes, and that many "autobiographies" of ex-slaves were actually written by whites. Later evidence, however, suggests that Higginson was *not* connected with the writing of "The Freedman's Story." In 1899 T. W. Higginson wrote to W. U. Hensel specifically about the Christiana case, recalling its details vaguely and even incorrectly. Most significantly, Higginson fails to mention any personal connection with the *Atlantic* narrative, as he would have been likely to do if he had indeed been among its authors.[19]

In 1911, W. U. Hensel, in his book *The Christiana Riot*, . . . emphasizes "E. K.'s" statement that he had been asked to revise "The Freedman's Story" manuscript, "or weave its facts into a story which should show the fitness of the Southern black for . . . the right of suffrage." [20] Despite Gilmore's emphatic disclaimer of any rewriting Hensel declares:

> The editor evades the natural inquiry whether the text is wholly Parker's or partially his own. . . .

Hensel concludes that the literary style of the narrative "leaves little room for doubt" that Parker's manuscript "was edited by some one with a purpose other than strictly historical." Hensel suggests that this manuscript, which did originate with Parker, has been edited with the propagandist aim of exalting the freed women and men of 1866.

It is the narrative's very wealth of detail which suggests to Hensel serious doubts about its historical exactness:

> That he [Parker] could remember its details so exactly as to verbally reproduce the many conversations in the *Atlantic* fifteen years later, is more than doubtful—it is impossible; and his pretense to do so discounts the attempt.

Although a definite note of boastfulness and exaggeration *is* found throughout Parker's comments, the events in which he acted were certainly, in themselves, extraordinary. As for Parker's quotation of his conversation with Gorsuch, if the words are not exact, the tone and content of the slave owner's language does perfectly coincide with the eyewitness reports of Gorsuch's own posse members and family. Many details of conversation and action mentioned by Parker are confirmed by these reports, especially Gorsuch's repeated references to his "property." Parker's version of the confrontation is at least as accurate as those versions testified to by Gorsuch posse members soon after the battle.

Hensel himself admits that "in many respects" Parker's "narration accords with the testimony of other eyewitnesses. . . ." He admits that when Parker's version of the resistance was published he had "nothing to gain or lose from telling the truth." Hensel's doubts about the accuracy of Parker's story are qualified by his conclusion "that in the main it is true and it certainly throws more illumination on the actual occurrences than the testimony of any other single witness."

As late as 1961, Roderick W. Nash, writing in *The Journal of Negro History*, declares with a tone of great authority: "Since Parker could neither read nor write this article was written for him." [21] In his narrative Parker himself admits that at the time of the 1850 resistance he could not read or write.[22] It is strange, to say the least, that historian Nash assumes from this admitted early illiteracy that Parker could not have written a narrative published fifteen years later. Even without the historian's knowing anything about the fine Buxton school, or the black colony's literacy requirements, it is odd to assume that Parker could not have learned to read and write in such a length of time.

Nash, like Hensel, emphasizes "E. K.'s" statement that he had been asked to "revise" "The Freedman's Story" manuscript, implying that the work has been edited, simply ignoring "E. K.'s" disclaimer to the contrary. There seems, however, no particular reason to question the sincerity of "E. K.'s" statements; Gilmore clearly indicates where his own introductions end, and Parker's narrative begins.[23]

The readiness of four historians to deny the authenticity of Parker's narrative is, to put it charitably, unfortunate. The notations in the Shadd diary confirm that Parker did have collaborators, but that all of these were black. This possibility, that the narrative is an authentic black creation, seems to have simply been dismissed. It is just this creative ability of black people to "do for themselves" that is so often denied.

In the summer of 1872, seven years after the Civil War, and almost a quarter of a century after the Christiana resistance, William Parker returned to Pennsylvania, visited old friends and the site of the "battle for liberty." Two recently discovered short newspaper items document and date Parker's presence in the area. On June 26, 1872, the *Oxford* [Pennsylvania] *Press* reports:

> William Parker (colored), the hero of the Christiana riot, and the slayer of Gorsuch the slave-hunter, has recently visited his old home and acquaintances. He was present at the Commencement of Lincoln University on Wednesday last [June 19]. He has been residing in Canada for about

twenty-one years, to which place he fled for safety at the time of the Christiana tragedy.[24]

Parker's attending the commencement at Lincoln University, a black secondary school and college, was particularly appropriate. The Christiana resistance had been one of the events leading to the Reverend John Miller Dickey's interest in the plight of Pennsylvania blacks, and to his founding of Lincoln University, in 1854. Thaddeus Stevens had given a political assist, helping to secure passage of the school's charter in the Pennsylvania Senate.[25]

Another item discovered in the Lancaster *Examiner and Herald* documents Parker's presence in Christiana two months later, on August 30, 1872. Also present was Parker's fellow Buxtonite William Howard Day, described by the Lancaster paper as "the distinguished colored orator, . . . editor of 'Our National Progress . . .' " [26]

The Presidential campaign of 1872 was in progress. Republican Ulysses S. Grant was running for re-election against Democrat/ Liberal-Republican Horace Greeley. Frederick Douglass was campaigning vigorously for Grant, viewing this candidate's re-election as the best guarantee of his people's protection—a protection desperately needed in the post-Civil-War south.[27]

The Lancaster *Examiner and Herald* reports a political meeting of Chester and Lancaster county black voters who, like Douglass, were supporting Grant in his race against Greeley. The crowd met in the woods of J. D. Pownall, near Christiana. The paper reports:

> There was a large crowd of all colors present, and the meeting was one of the best held in the country for a long time past.

The crowd having been called to order,

> a colored gentleman . . . was placed in the chair, surrounded by a number of vice-presidents, none of whom we knew except our old friend Wm. Clegget, of Columbia, and Mr. Parker, at whose house the battle of Christiana took place in 1851.

Parker's presence at this political meeting suggests his continuing concern for his people's protection.

Years later, Christiana resident Peter Woods told W. U. Hensel that after William Parker's 1872 visit "he took back with him to Canada the widow of Henry Simms—one of the defendants in the treason case. . . ." Hensel presumes that Parker was "then a widower and Mrs. Simms became his second wife." [28] After this, all documentary records of William Parker's life cease, and history fades into speculation.

On Sunday, August 13, 1911, as citizens of Christiana were preparing to commemorate the sixtieth anniversary of the 1851 "riot," a black man named Zachariah Walker was lynched in Coatesville, twenty-five miles away.

Tensions had been building as Coatesville's 6000 Anglo-Saxons and 3000 eastern European immigrants competed for jobs with the mill town's 2000 blacks. On Saturday night, August 12, Zach Walker had drunk too much and fallen into a dispute with Edgar Rice, a steel company policeman. The black man had shot Rice to death, Walker later claimed in self-defense, after Rice had attacked him.

Posses headed by the local police chief searched for the missing black man most of Saturday night, but Sunday came without his capture. When finally found Walker had tried, unsuccessfully, to kill himself. He was taken to the Coatesville hospital where a bullet was removed from his jaw, he was strapped to an iron bed, his right leg chained to a bedpost. That Sunday, as evening church services ended, their congregations joined the large and frenzied crowd of thousands at the Coatesville hospital, where shouts rang out: "Lynch him! Lynch him! Lynch him!"

The hospital's spinster superintendant, her assistants, and a local policeman barricaded the doors. The chants grew louder as a group of about fifteen men, some wearing masks, broke through the barricade, entered the hospital, and dragged Zach Walker outside. In the open countryside, on the outskirts of Coatesville, the Pennsylvania mob burnt Zach Walker to death.

Although the danger of a lynching had been evident for a night and a day before it occurred, state troopers were finally rushed in on the evening of the day *after* it had taken place due to fears of black rioting. Twelve men, including the police chief and the officer who had been guarding Walker, were eventually indicted for his murder. But the district attorney was said to be in league

(above) Unidentified black men posing before the ruins of the Parkers' home. (*Lancaster County Historical Society Papers*, Vol. 10, No. 10 [1906])

(below) The Parkers' Home, 1897. In 1898, says Forbes, the "last vestige" of the Parkers' home "has been removed by the owners of the property . . ." (p. 154). (Forbes; The Library Company of Philadelphia Collection)

with the lynchers, the prosecutions were halfhearted, and towns-people refused to identify the ringleaders. The first seven cases were acquitted, the remaining prosecutions dropped, and no one was ever found guilty of burning a black man alive.[29]

A letter to W. U. Hensel is inadvertently ironic in speaking of the recent "Coatesville Affair" and the preparations for the commemoration of the "Christiana Riot":

> Christiana, Pa., Aug. 26, 1911
> Just to advise you what is being done. The essay contest was won by Miss Anna Young. I delivered the $10 gold piece and will send essay to the Local News . . . Foundation for monument is about ready. Rev. Wright the colored preacher informed us at the last meeting that his people have all got cold feet since the Coatesville affair and will not take part. . . . will have the three words Law-Liberty-Peace in laurel letters across front of stand. . . .[30]

Before the 1911 commemoration David S. Cincose, a black minister of Philadelphia, wrote to the Lancaster County Historical Society that he was sorry to have to miss such a "timely anniversary." The "Christiana Riot" was in his opinion "a great chapter in American History," and he added, "I never sleep when I passes through Christiana nor Lancaster—that glorious scene arises before my vision like a mid-day Dreame. . . ."[31]

The Sixtieth Anniversary Commemoration of the Christiana "riot" took place on September 9, 1911, despite a heavy rain. The crowd in attendance was much smaller than that which had enjoyed the more popular recent lynching, but the commemoration perhaps attracted more local dignitaries. The invocation was read by the Reverend R. F. Wright, "the colored preacher." The Christiana Cornet Band played "America the Beautiful," "The Star-Spangled Banner," "Dixie," and "My Old Kentucky Home." The presentation of memorial medals to the granddaughter of Edward Gorsuch was followed by a band rendition of "Maryland, My Maryland." The presentation of a memorial medal to the black man Peter Woods, the sole known survivor of the treason trials, was followed by a rendition of "Old Black Joe." A vocal chorus of "Swanee River" closed the ceremony.[32]

(above) Peter Woods, front center, his wife to his left, with other members of the Woods family. (Courtesy the late Walter Miller, Christiana)

(left) Memorial monument erected in Christiana, Pennsylvania, 1911; inscribed to Edward Gorsuch, who "died for law," to Castner Hanway, who "suffered for freedom," and including the date of the "riot" and names of those accused of treason. (Hensel, *Christiana*)

In 1927, in a story on Christiana, a Pennsylvania newspaper reports

> A building near the scene of the riot, where fugitive slaves were harbored, was razed some years ago, although the colored people of the town had made an effort to preserve it as a memorial to the emancipation of the negro.[33]

The 100th anniversary of the Christiana "riot" was observed on Sunday, September 9, 1951. That day 800 whites and blacks assembled on the lawn of a farmhouse overlooking the "riot" site. A large American flag marked the place of battle. The Reverend Gordon Jones prayed:

> Father, we come to this historic spot today, not with hearts filled with pride, but with humiliation as we realize the errors of Thy children in their efforts to obtain freedom. . . .

The music on this occasion included "My Old Kentucky Home," "Carry Me Back to Old Virginy," "Old Black Joe," and "The Star-Spangled Banner."[34]

Toward the close of the ceremony a black man, the president of Lincoln University, Dr. Horace Mann Bond, addressed the crowd, an occasion he would recall years later with much fondness. Dr. Bond's theme that day was "Freedom Precedes Peace," a proposition whose militant tone must have caused the Reverend Mr. Jones and others to shift nervously in anticipation.

"We are celebrating today the centennial of an American tragedy," said Dr. Bond, "the tragedy" of humanity in a world without love, where violence and bloodshed appear the only alternative to suffering the lack of human equality. Dr. Bond noted, with what must have been some bitterness, the recent case of a Winnebago Indian war hero, refused burial in an Iowa cemetery "because the blood he shed for his country had not been 'Caucasian. . . .'" Dr. Bond was grateful that "two generations after the inarticulate enslaved generation," whom Thaddeus Stevens had defended in the Christiana treason case, he, Bond, had now been "given voice and words" to honor Stevens's belief in "the equality of man before his creator."

"But I wish to speak principally," said Dr. Bond,

(above) The Christiana "Riot" Centennial, September 9, 1951; descendants of Peter Woods, Samuel Hopkins, and the Gorsuch family. (Robert I. McCollough, Quarryville, Pa.)

(below) Dr. Horace Mann Bond, fourth from left, with participants in the 1951 Centennial. (Robert I. McCollough, Quarryville, Pa.)

of the man who . . . seems to me to be the symbol—the
distilled essence—of the meaning of the Christiana Riot; to
be, indeed, the symbol of all violence and bloodletting, and
alternate hope and despair, in the world then, and
now. . . .
    His name was William Parker.

Parker, declared Dr. Bond,

is the tragic symbol of our Centennial, of the troubles of his
generation, and of our own. This is the Centennial of the
violence engendered by great passions and forces, but also
by one man. It is the story of A Man Without A Country;
it is the tragedy of William Parker; it is the tragedy of
mankind everywhere who would be free, but must resort to
violence to obtain their freedom.

William Parker, said Dr. Bond, was "a man who loved Freedom
passionately, and who used violence to get it for himself and for
others." Bond paraphrased historian R. C. Smedley:

Sarah Pownall had a conversation with William Parker the
night before the riot, and urged him, if slaveholders should
come, not to lead the colored people to resist the Fugitive
Slave Law by force of arms, but to escape to Canada. He
replied that if the laws protected colored men as they did
white men, he too would be non-resistant and not fight; but
would appeal to the laws. "But," said Parker, "the laws for
personal protection are not made for us, and we are not
bound to obey them. If a fight occurs I want the whites to
keep away. They have a country and may obey the laws.
But we have no country."

In closing his 1951 address Dr. Bond implored:

Give men freedom in this world, and equality before their
Creator, in life, and in death; give men the equal protection
of all of the laws of all of the townships and cities and
counties and commonwealths and nations and the United
Nations—everywhere in the world . . . [and] we shall have
peace . . . brotherhood . . . love . . . and no Christiana
Riots nor its multiplication in war's violence.[35]

The Parkers' home was on the light-colored ground, right foreground; site of the Christiana resistance, 1969. (Jonathan Katz)

20 Speculations

As a slave owner Edward Gorsuch was at home. His "homestead" was his castle, he was lord of the manor owned by his family for two hundred years. He wanted no change in the little society he controlled, in the way of life he knew. He wanted nothing to disturb the languid drift of southern life, or of his own existence; he was deeply conservative. All disruptive forces must be kept in check on the margins of his society, in the back of his mind. For two years the theft and escape of his four slaves rankled. They had defied his authority, questioned his proprietorship. To ease his mind he sought their return.

The very same slaves promised their freedom had run away. Gorsuch was at once mystified, hurt, insulted, angry, and patronizing. His "boys" had taken their freedom and would "not come home and behave themselves" when their good master promised leniency. His fugitives, he thought, must have been incited to flight by a free black; Gorsuch denied any real conflict between masters and slaves. Conflict came from without; basically his slaves were content. Needing to believe that all was well the slave owner invented the fantasy of an idyllic order, the myth of a romantic, chivalrous south. Looking northward critically he compared the cold relation of capitalist to wage worker with that of master and slave. Northward he saw relations of cash payment replacing all

300

more intimate contacts. Slavery's patriarchal, familial relations seemed vastly superior.

If they would repent, the benevolent Gorsuch could quite easily forgive his fugitives' theft and flight. Indeed, he would not allow them blame, or responsibility; he would deny them both their guilt and their glory. They were his erring "boys," he would be their forgiving father; the relation of parent to child would be maintained, the very act of forgiving would confirm Gorsuch's paternal rule and power. His philanthropy would reaffirm his goodness.

His benevolence paid psychic dividends. The loss of a slave by emancipation brought psychological profit, the emancipator confirmed his own enlightenment. Giving a slave his freedom Gorsuch remained, in one real sense, the master. That he even contemplated an occasional emancipation is a clue to its essential fraudulence—it would be a formal change, no more. In essence, nothing would be changed at all. A few slaves would be free in name, but still bondsmen in fact.

Emancipating themselves, Gorsuch's fugitives had denied his mastership; that it was no longer his to bestow freedom or forgive a theft Gorsuch could not accept. To the extent that he defined himself as a slave owner, to that extent he ceased to exist without his slaves. Slave owning was a state of having, and of being. His secret thought was, "I possess, therefore I am." Dispossession was a death; ceasing to have he ceased to be. Slave owning was not a function, not an act; what managerial functions he might perform were inessential to his identity as slave owner. Ceasing to act, he did not cease to own. Others, his inferiors, were defined by their acts; labor, performed by slaves, was looked down upon. As a slave owner he was essentially a possessor, and nothing but—a parasite, psychically and economically. His existence depended on others. Built into his very real power was this essential dependency. The labor of his slaves provided his food, clothes, housing, wealth, leisure, culture, freedom. He took his own power from others, living off their energy, their work. The all powerful master owed his slaves his very life.

The slave owner fed on his slaves like a vampire, a leech, a tick. This bloodsucker had an appetite for possession, a taste for ownership, an insatiable hunger, a great emptiness. As much as he gorged he was never filled. In him was a void, an absence, a lack; he was a man without qualities—a man of property, a man without properties. Having no value in himself he took his identity from his possessions, his objects lent him their value. He lived a borrowed life. Like a commodity he realized his value only in exchange. Apart from this relation he had no self, he was no one.

As he had no inner sense of self he could not know the inner life of others, he saw them only through his desperate need for them as objects to be used for his own self-aggrandizement. With no real independence he could not conceive of his slaves' independence. As he did not exist for himself apart from them, so apart from him, he imagined, they could not exist.

To himself he was quite unknown. He perceived himself through others. His sense of self came from outside himself; he was always looking outward, fearfully in anticipation of judgment, longingly for recognition. Desperately he looked around him for confirmation of his very being. He searched for his reflection in the humble eyes of his slaves. These averted eyes, those downcast glances, that slavish look revealed to him his mastership; his slaves must look up to him, he must look down on them. He needed his inferiors to feel like himself. He looked to his slaves to see his whiteness contrasted with their blackness, for by their color did he judge them, and keep them in their place. By this sign, by his mystical concept of race, he permanently endowed them with their character as slaves, and guaranteed his own eternal character as master.

As a slave William Parker was not at home. Seeing those he knew auctioned off to the highest bidder he felt homeless, helpless, uncared for. His life controlled by others, he felt an essential discomfort; his clothes chafed, his very breath seemed constrained by "some supernatural power." Comparing his unfree state to the liberty of the poor whites he felt the injustice of his own condition. Early he learned to fight for himself. He moved from battling other slaves for a warm place near the fire, to fighting another man's slave for his master's sport, to finally fighting his master to justify escape.

Parker early conceived of escape; the very idea helped protect him. To the extent that his enslavement remained a state from which he could run away, to that extent it remained an external situation, separate and alien from himself. Early aware of slavery as an imposed, unjust condition, he kept it from becoming a fully internalized part of his own psyche—he began to develop a sense of independence.

Finally, when he had reached manhood, the time came to run away; not to overturn the system, but to escape it was his goal. He escaped his master's preachers, his patrols, his whips, his dogs, his eyes. He embraced the rebel in himself. To submit to slavery meant a psychic death; he chose to live. To gain his freedom Parker had literally to steal himself. He stole away. Quite literally he became a thief. But the very fight and flight which made him a criminal in the eyes of his master helped him break those psychic ties which bound him within the master-slave morality.

He ran from, and he ran to. His act was both a refusal and an affirmation. He asserted his self-possession, he declared his independence. With great courage he moved from the known into the unknown, he broke with a world he knew for a freedom which, until actualized, could be little more than an abstraction, an idea, a vague hope, a utopian dream. He acted on faith—in himself, in the possibility of a freedom he could not yet have fully experienced. With no assurance of success he gave himself to an undetermined future.

Crossing from Maryland to Pennsylvania, Parker literally moved out of one social-economic system, out of the master-slave relation into another; he literally stepped from slavery into capitalism, from the class of slaves into the class of free rural wage workers. In changing his geographic location he radically altered his place in the social universe. Changing his situation he moved from one state of mind toward another.

In Pennsylvania his labor was his own to sell, his leisure was his own to enjoy; he experienced new feelings and thoughts, the new consciousness of a rural wage worker who had been a slave. He contrasted his past with his new present, and felt his own freedom as only one could who had known slavery. He overturned his psychic state.

Through his activity Parker came to know himself anew. Through his labor as free man he began to feel his own power. Through his action on the world he began to see himself as a creator, as a force with whom to be reckoned. He and the other ex-slaves with whom he settled plowed the fields and planted corn, they took trees and turned them into floors, they took stones and made them into houses. Those who labored learned that those who owned were quite unnecessary. Those who had been taught only their market price created a new sense of their own value.

Parker organized with other blacks for that protection he had lacked as a child, and which he and others still needed to defend their stolen freedom. Through these self-defense activities and their work, these ex-slaves created their new identities. When Parker's was attacked their means of work became their tools of war. Blacks ran across the fields carrying axes and hunting rifles, they waved corn-cutters and scythes above their heads like flags. Dark figures gathered like the clouds before a storm. Grim faces confronted the Gorsuch posse, dark faces, black and burning.

A white Quaker advised the blacks to flee. But those who had once run from slavery had now stopped running, they stayed to meet the master face to face. By their resistance they asserted their hard-won self-respect; they would not flee again without a fight. The slave owner was warned.

William Parker, born a slave, had reinvented himself as a free man, he had turned himself inside out. Thus he learned that human beings make themselves and their own history. He learned that what human beings have made they can unmake, and remake. He learned that the world can be turned upside down, that things as they are are not settled forever. He took his life into his own hands, he was no longer in the grip of fate. Who was he? One who had produced himself by his acts, an individual, impatient, critical, dissatisfied, who looked to the future, judging what was by what could be. Who was he? A disturber of the peace, an agitator, one who would be useful in the liberation battle, one who would be free.

Facing Parker, Gorsuch looked to the past, judging the present by what had been, preaching humility and resignation. Confronting Parker, Gorsuch's proprietary sense of self made him rigid, his narrow pride paralyzed him. He would maintain his mastership at any cost. Uncompromising, unyielding, he hung on to his property for all he was worth.

The marshal called a retreat; posse members started from the scene. Taking a few steps away from the blacks Gorsuch felt an overwhelming sense of loss and his own hollowness. Then his face changed, he looked "calm and stern," he said, "My property is here and I will have it or perish in the attempt." He would risk his death for a few possessions. He would not permit his slaves to liberate themselves—for the very life of him. At the last moment the slave owner was hard as rock, unfeeling as the stones, unmoved as the mountain.

After all the warnings Gorsuch turned back. Without these slaves nothing was left of him, the pillar of society was without foundation, the man of substance was quite unsubstantial. The solid citizen vanished in the smoke which rose above the corn.

It was an extraordinary moment. The ex-slave and the slave owner faced each other on the field of battle. The sun came up. It was a new day, a day on which the master would be mastered, the possessor dispossessed, a day on which the humble servants were humble no longer, and the property disowned its owner.

Gorsuch's ex-slave "struck him the first and second blows. . . . *The women put an end to him.*"

Much of ourselves, of our own society, may be found in that classic conflict.

Acknowledgments

THIS BOOK COULD NOT HAVE BEEN COMPLETED without all the help, encouragement, and interest I received during the long years of work on it.

My late father, Bernard Katz, devoted much time and energy to a careful reading of the manuscript and a detailed critique. Both he and my mother, Phyllis Katz, were extremely helpful with editorial advice. I also learned much from my brother, William Loren Katz, who showed real concern and continued interest.

A grant from the Louis M. Rabinowitz Foundation was encouraging and important at an early stage in my research; Karl H. Niebyl is to be thanked for his recommendation; Michael Folsom and Alphonse Pinkney are to be thanked for their recommendations and for continued help. Angus Cameron was also encouraging at an early and crucial point in this project.

I especially wish to credit the late Walter R. Miller, of Christiana, whose kindness and invaluable assistance will always be remembered.

Vivian Robbins Chavis is to be thanked for the important references contained in the Shadd ledger and other information. I wish to thank Victor Ullman for many long letters and important leads, and Sara D. Jackson for answering repeated requests for information. LaVerne D. Rettew, of Christiana, provided several wonderful old photographs. Seymour Kleinberg is to be thanked for reading the manuscript and for his interest. My editor, Nick Ellison, was always most pleasant and helpful.

I am grateful for the help of Thelma Keyser, formerly of the Lancaster newspaper office; Laura Lundgren, Lancaster County Historical Society; Dorothy B. Lapp, Chester County Historical Society; Lillian Tonkin, The Library Company of Philadelphia; John D. Kilbourne, Historical Society of Pennsylvania; Helen W. M. Johnson, Historical Society of Montgomery County; Cora B.

ACKNOWLEDGMENTS 307

Decker, Bucks County Historical Society; John W. Heisey, Historical Society of York County; Carol Straub, Norristown Public Library; Charles Blockson, Norristown; Edwin B. Bronner, Library, Haverford College; Sophy H. Cornwell, Library, Lincoln University; Philip S. Foner, Lincoln University; Robert E. Scudder, Free Library of Philadelphia; Roberta Wilkey, Moore Memorial Library, Christiana; Janet L. Hargett, Edward E. Hill, M. M. Johnson, Elmer O. Parker, National Archives; the late Horace Mann Bond; Benjamin Quarles, Morgan State College; Eleanora M. Lynn, Enoch Pratt Free Library, Baltimore; Lois Ann Green, The Public Library, Annapolis; Hester Rich, Maryland Historical Society; Gregory Wilson, Harvard University Archives; Blake McKelvey, Office of the City Historian, Rochester, N.Y.; John Lovell, Jr., Howard University; Jane H. and William H. Pease, University of Maine; Arthur Detmers, Buffalo and Erie County Historical Society; Charles M. Snyder, State University College, Oswego; Harriet C. Jameson and Robert Carr, Library, University of Michigan.

I am also grateful to the following Canadians: William H. Cooper, Department of Public Records, Toronto; Edith G. Firth, Metropolitan Toronto Central Library; C. Backhaus, Kingston Public Library; Sherman Brown, Administrator, Kent County, Chatham; J. Atherton, Claude Le Moine, and Bernard Weilbrenner, Public Archives of Canada, Ottawa; Robin Johnston, South Buxton; Frank Parker and Dorothy Shadd Shreve, North Buxton; Victor Lauriston, Chatham; E. Spicer, The Library and Museum, London; John K. A. Farrell, University of Windsor; V. Blake, Windsor Public Library; and the late Fred Landon, London.

For their encouragment and support through thick and thin I would like to thank Becky Johnston, Carol and Robert Joyce, Jacqueline Katz, David Roggensack, Albert Wolsky, Constance Zoff, Faye and Gil Burgos, and most especially Herbert Freudenberger.

The responsibility for this book's contents is, of course, my own.

Jonathan Katz

A Note on the Research

IN 1967 THE VIOLENT RAGE and fiery assertiveness of many American blacks were first becoming visible to many stunned, confused, and often hostile whites. These whites were being forced into a new and uneasy awareness of the depth and pervasiveness of black discontent. Many blacks were no longer appealing primarily for civil rights, but were aggressively demanding power and control of some important institutions affecting their lives. A black liberation movement was underway. Something new was in the smoke-filled air.

In that year my interest in black history and documentary theater combined to suggest the 1851 fugitive slave resistance at Christiana as an appropriate subject for a documentary play relevant to the new black militancy and current white reaction. A $1500 grant from the Louis M. Rabinowitz Foundation made possible one summer's research, and the writing of the play *Inquest at Christiana*, based on the documents of the Christiana resistance, subsequently performed on WBAI-FM, New York.

By the end of that first summer's research I had become fascinated by the Christiana resistance and dedicated to tracking down all clues and evidence relating to it and its participants. In following years investigation continued in preparation for the present documented history. Original research trips were undertaken to Christiana, Lancaster, Philadelphia, Baltimore, Boston, Detroit, Toronto, Chatham, and Buxton, Canada. Research also continued in the Schomburg Center for Research in Black Culture in New York, in the main research division of the New York Public Library—and through correspondence with persons as far west as Toledo, Ohio, and as far south as Atlanta, Georgia. Study of the major books on black history and black resistance helped set the Christiana battle in general perspective, as did many invaluable discussions with

308

my brother, William Loren Katz, author of *Eyewitness: The Negro in American History,* and other books on black history.

One of the most exciting moments in my research occurred in September 1969, when I drove down a dirt road in North Buxton, Canada, to the home of Frank Parker, William Parker's grandson. Seeing an old man in the yard, supervising the delivery of a new refrigerator, I introduced myself, saying I had come from New York City to do some research about a black man who had settled in Buxton in 1852, William Parker. "That's my grandpa," said the old man, smiling, "he came with a man named Johnson." The seventy-eight-year-old Frank Parker, born on November 27, 1891, to William Parker's son Frank, recalled nothing about his grandfather. But he did remember Eliza Parker: "Oh, I remember my grandmother. She was a big woman, dark. I remember her walking along the road carrying a pail of water on her head, and a pail of water in each hand. I remember her walking along carrying a box of eggs on her head, and knitting as she walked. Why the top of her head was as flat as the top of that old stove there."

Frank Parker took me to see Mrs. Lorne Chase, widow of William Parker's grandson Lorne, son of Cynthia, Parker's daughter. Lorne had told of staying with his "Grandma Parker" when he was four or five, and recalled going with her to collect hickory nuts. Eliza Parker and young Lorne had gone searching for the hickory trees in which the squirrels were busily at work. Telling Lorne to be very quiet, Eliza Parker and her grandson watched the squirrels work, then went to gather up the nuts that they had knocked to the ground. "Lorne liked his grandmother," said Mrs. Chase, "Oh yes, he thought an awful lot of his Grandma Parker." Frank Parker and Mrs. Chase had only the vaguest recollection of any story about slave catchers. Mrs. Chase recalled a neighbor having a book, *The Underground Railroad,* which was supposed to tell about William Parker and the slave catchers. She had always intended to read it, but never had. Mrs. Chase gave me an old family photo of Lorne, with his mother, Cynthia, whom she said looked just like her own mother, Eliza Parker. I was very moved to have come this much closer to the subjects of my history.

My attempt here has been to tell the history of the resistance as often as possible in the words of its participants and witnesses. My interest has been both in accuracy and in evoking through this contemporary testimony an immediate sense of this historic event. Of major importance among the documents quoted is the narrative of William Parker, published as "The Freedman's Story," in the *Atlantic Monthly,* in 1866. This document has not received the recognition it deserves as an authentic account of an early, militant black leader. While my Canadian research has revealed that Parker had several black collaborators, both the internal and external evidence confirms the narrative's general accuracy. (For a detailed discussion of this question, see chapter 19.)

The testimony of the major white participants in the Christiana conflict is quoted here as it was recorded in the reports of several preliminary hearings, and in Robbins's official, book-length, verbatim transcript of the trial that followed the resistance. Robert C. Smedley's *History of the Underground Railroad,* . . . published in 1883, is another important source of information especially on

William Parker's escape. The major previous history of *The Christiana Riot* . . . by W. U. Hensel, published in 1911, although a useful work, is incomplete, and decidedly dated in its author's moral equation of the slave owner's desire for his slave property with the Christiana blacks' desire for freedom.

My research has revealed a surprisingly large number of forgotten documents and information on the Christiana resistance and its black leader, William Parker. Among these are the manuscript of Christiana resident George Steele; the I. D. Shadd diary referring to the date and authorship of Parker's narrative; two newspaper reports verifying Parker's 1872 return to Pennsylvania; a black Canadian newspaper's editorial on a meeting with Parker; Frederick Douglass's editorial on the Christiana resistance; the editorial of black Canadian newspaperman Henry Bibb, welcoming Parker to Canada; and the genealogy of Parker's master's family.

It should encourage future researchers in the history of black resistance that so much documentary material was found on this one case. There is, in fact, more source material available now than there was in the years immediately following the Christiana battle. Certain incriminating facts were disclosed only after the Civil War, when the possibility of prosecution no longer existed. Even the known documents (e.g., William Still's *The Underground Railroad*), upon close reading, are found to shed new light on important aspects of the case. Interested historians should be encouraged: there are other important cases of black resistance whose stories have not been researched, documented, and presented in detail.

The sources mentioned, among others, have made possible a fairly complete and reliable reconstruction of the Christiana resistance, in a documentary form intended to make this history accessible and interesting to the general reader. I will be pleased to have made this history as exciting to read as it was to research. Hopefully, this story will convey some insights into our present troubled society.

New York City
October, 1973

Notes

Bibliographic Abbreviations

Brasher: Thomas L. Brasher, ed., *Walt Whitman: The Early Poems and the Fiction* (New York, 1963).

Brent: Robert James Brent, "Report of the Attorney General . . . ," Maryland General Assembly Documents (Annapolis, 1852).

Brown: David Paul Brown, *The Forum; or Forty Years Full Practice at the Philadelphia Bar,* 2 vols., (Philadelphia, 1856).

Douglass, "Freedom's Battle . . .": Frederick Douglass, "Freedom's Battle at Christiana," *Frederick Douglass' Paper,* September 25, 1851.

Douglass, *Life*: Frederick Douglass, *Life and Times of Frederick Douglass Written by Himself* (1892: reprint, New York, 1962).

1850 Census, Sadsbury Township: 1850 United States Census, Sadsbury Township, Lancaster County, Pennsylvania. Copies in the National Archives, Washington, D.C.; the Lancaster County Historical Society, Lancaster, Pennsylvania; the collection of Walter Miller, Christiana, Pennsylvania.

Foner: Phillip S. Foner, *The Life and Writings of Frederick Douglass,* 4 vols. (New York, 1950).

Forbes: David R. Forbes, *A True Story of the Christiana Riot* (Quarryville, Pennsylvania, 1898).

Gara: Larry Gara, *The Liberty Line: The Legend of the Underground Railroad* (Lexington, Kentucky, 1967).

Gorsuch, J. S., letter of September "17," 1851: John S. Gorsuch, letter dated Christiana, September 17, 1851 (in Lancaster *Intelligencer,* September 17, 1851). The date of this letter was later corrected by Gorsuch to September

311

16 (in Lancaster *Intelligencer,* October 14, 1851). The letter of September "17" was widely reprinted.

Hanson: George A. Hanson, *Old Kent: The Eastern Shore of Maryland . . .* (Baltimore, 1876).

Hensel, "Aftermath": W. U. Hensel, "Aftermath Supplementary to Christiana Riot, 1851," *Lancaster County Historical Society Papers,* vol. 16, no. 5 (1912).

Hensel, *Christiana*: W. U. Hensel, *The Christiana Riot and the Treason Trials of 1851: An Historical Sketch,* second and revised edition (Lancaster, Pennsylvania, 1911).

Hurst: James Willard Hurst, *The Law of Treason in the United States* (Westport, Connecticut, 1971).

Jackson: [W. A. Jackson,] *History of the Trial of Castner Hanway and Others for Treason . . .* (Philadelphia, 1852).

King: William King, MS autobiography, Public Archives, Ottawa, Canada. Typescript, made from photocopies of the original MS, in the Buxton Museum, Buxton, Ontario, Canada.

McClure, *Old Time Notes*: Alexander K. McClure, *Old Time Notes of Pennsylvania* (Philadelphia, 1905).

McClure, *Recollections*: Alexander K. McClure, *Recollections of Half a Century* (Salem, Massachusetts, 1902).

Nash: Roderick W. Nash, "The Christiana Riot: An Evaluation of Its National Significance," *Journal of the Lancaster County Historical Society,* vol. 6, no. 2 (Spring, 1961).

Parker: William Parker, "The Freedman's Story," *The Atlantic Monthly,* vol. 17 (Part I, February, Part II, March, 1866).

Pease: William H. and Jane H. Pease, *Black Utopia: Negro Communal Experiments in America* (Madison, Wisconsin, 1963).

Report: A Full and Correct Report of the Christiana Tragedy . . . (Lancaster, Pennsylvania, 1851).

Robbins: James R. Robbins, *Report of the Trial of Castner Hanway for Treason . . .* (Philadelphia, 1852).

Siebert: Wilbur H. Siebert, *The Underground Railroad from Slavery to Freedom* (New York, 1899).

Simmons: Rev. William J. Simmons, D.D., *Men of Mark: Eminent, Progressive and Rising* (New York, 1968).

Smedley: Robert C. Smedley, *History of the Underground Railroad in Chester and the Neighboring Counties of Pennsylvania* (Lancaster, Pennsylvania, 1883).

Steele: [George Steele,] "Description of the Christiana Riot . . . written . . . by George Steele, uncle of Samuel Pownall . . . by the request of the Lancaster County Historical Society, September 11, 1911." Typescript in collection of the late Walter Miller, Christiana, Pennsylvania.

Still: William Still, *The Underground Railroad* (Philadelphia, 1872).

Ullman: Victor Ullman, *Look to the North Star: A Life of William King* (Boston, 1969).

Villard: Oswald Garrison Villard, *John Brown, 1800–1859, A Biography Fifty Years After* (Boston, 1910).

Whitson, "Abolitionists": Thomas Whitson, "Early Abolitionists of Lancaster County," *Lancaster County Historical Society Papers,* vol. 15 (1911).

Whitson, "Hero": Thomas Whitson, "The Hero of the Christiana Riot," *Lancaster County Historical Society Papers,* vol. 1 (1896).

Winks: Robin W. Winks: " 'A Sacred Animosity': Abolitionism in Canada," in Martin Duberman, ed., *The Antislavery Vanguard* . . . (Princeton, 1965).

Notes

1. Parker (pages 6–21)

1 William Parker, "The Freedman's Story," *The Atlantic Monthly*, vol. 17 (Part I, February 1866; Part II, March 1866). The authorship and history of this narrative are discussed in chapter 19.

2 Parker, pp. 153–154.

3 "Description of the Christiana Riot . . . written . . . by George Steele, uncle of Samuel Pownall . . . by the request of the Lancaster Historical Society, September 11, 1911," p. 1. Typescript in collection of Walter Miller, Christiana, Pennsylvania. Steele's claim that Parker told him he was a fugitive slave is contradicted by Parker's statement (Parker, p. 291) that in Pennsylvania only his own family knew he had been a slave.

4 J. T. Scharf, *History of Baltimore City and County* (Philadelphia, 1881), pp. 848–849; *The Maryland Horse*, vol. 8, no. 6 (June 1943), p. 14; "Autumn meeting press brochure," Maryland Jockey Club (October 30–November 13, 1941), pp. 62–64.

5 Parker, p. 153; Brogden genealogy: George A. Hanson, *Old Kent: The Eastern Shore of Maryland* . . . (Baltimore, 1876), pp. 88–89. Hanson spells the name of the Brogden estate as "Roe Down." Parker, in his narrative, misspells "Row Down" for "Roe Down," and "Brogdon" for "Brogden," understandable errors since at the time he heard these words he could not read or write. The 1850 U.S. Census for Sadsbury Township, Lancaster County, Pennsylvania, taken August 26, lists William Parker's age as twenty-eight. This would make Parker's year of birth 1822. Other references to Parker's age suggest the accuracy of this date: (1) Parker says in his narrative (p. 153) that his first master, Major William Brogden, "died when I was very young." Hanson (p. 88) says Brogden died in

314

1824, when the census figures indicate Parker was two. (2) The introduction to Parker's narrative (p. 152) suggests that he did not learn to read or write "until he was thirty years of age." That Parker was illiterate in 1850 is verified by that year's Census. If Parker was born in 1822, as the Census suggests, he would have been thirty in 1852, the year after he escaped to Canada, the year in which he probably learned to read and write (see chapter 18). All my calculations of Parker's age, and of the years in which various events occurred, are based on Parker's year of birth being 1822.

6 Parker, p. 157.

7 *Narrative of the Life of Frederick Douglass* (Boston, 1845), p. 1. Besides Parker's few references (pp. 160, 290, 293) there is no other information on his acquaintance with Douglass in Maryland.

8 *My Bondage, My Freedom* (New York, 1855), pp. 34–35. All three versions of Douglass's autobiography state his regret at not knowing his age. Late in life Douglass also wrote: "It has always been a source of dissatisfaction to the writer that he neither knows exactly when nor exactly where he was born." [Phillip S. Foner, *The Life and Writings of Frederick Douglass* (New York, 1950), vol. I, no. 1, p. 423.]

9 Parker, pp. 153–155.

10 Parker, p. 153. Parker does not explain the origin of David Brogden's nickname, "Master Mack," which only becomes clear when the Brogden genealogy reveals David Brogden's middle name to have been McCulloch. This is one of the little details in Parker's narrative confirmed or explained by external evidence and substantiating its authenticity and Parker's intimate involvement in its authorship. The roll call *Records of the Maryland Senate and House of Representatives* (at the Enoch Pratt Free Library, Baltimore), 1820–1840, do not mention any David Brogden.

11 Joshua Dorsey Warfield, *The Founders of Anne Arundel and Howard Counties, Maryland* (Baltimore, 1905), pp. 199–200.

12 Parker, p. 154. Parker does not use Margaret Brogden's first name; it is in Hanson, p. 89.

13 Parker, pp. 154–155.

14 Eugene D. Genovese, *The Political Economy of Slavery* (New York, 1967), pp. 27, 99, 130, 137, 140, 143, 152.

15 Parker, pp. 155–156.

16 Parker, pp. 156–158.

17 Frederick Douglass, *Life and Times of Frederick Douglass Written by Himself* (1892; reprinted, New York, 1962), p. 145.

18 Parker, p. 158. *Gammon*, meaning "nonsense, humbug" (and *chap* [for "boy"] in Parker, p. 153) are Englishisms indicating the Canadian-English influence on the style of Parker's narrative.

19 Parker, pp. 157–158.

20 Parker, pp. 157–158. Parker says he was about seventeen at the time of his June escape. If he was born in 1822 as the 1850 Census indicates, he was seventeen in 1839.

21 Douglass, *Life and Times*, p. 143.

22 Parker, p. 158.

23 If Parker's information, and calculations of the date of his escape are correct, in the June 1839 issue of some Maryland or Pennsylvania newspaper, among the advertisements for fugitive slaves, there may exist one ad giving exact physical descriptions of Parker and his brother. As existing descriptions of Parker's appearance are few and unreliable (see chapter 2, n. 14) this ad would be an important find. Unfortunately, my own attempts to find this ad have so far proven unsuccessful. Interested researchers might look for the names William and Charles "Thomas" (as well as Parker) as there are several hints that "Thomas" was Parker's family name before his escape from slavery: (1) Parker's grandson Frank, living in Buxton, Canada, in 1969, reported that Parker's "real name" was "Thomas" (letter, Vivian Robbins Chavis to J. K., September 28, 1969). (2) A "William Thomas" is among those Christiana resisters indicted for treason. No arrest of such an individual seems to have been reported. This name appears at the bottom of the list of those indicted, along with the names of several of Edward Gorsuch's fugitives, as if it was added at the same time by someone associated with the Maryland posse. (3) During his escape to Canada, Parker (in his narrative, p. 289) mentions asking at a post office (as a ruse to get information) for a letter addressed to "John Thomas." Parker (p. 157) mentions a brother named John. One of Parker's sons is listed on the 1850 Census as "John T."

24 Parker, pp. 158–159.

25 William Whipper to William Still, New Brunswick, New Jersey, December 4, 1871; in William Still, *The Underground Railroad* (Philadelphia, 1872), pp. 735–736.

26 Parker, pp. 156–160. Robert Loney's activities as an underground railroad conductor are reported by Robert C. Smedley, *History of the Underground Railroad* . . . (Lancaster, Pennsylvania, 1883), pp. 49, 51, 77.

2. "An Organization for Mutual Protection" (pages 22–34)

1 Parker, p. 160.

2 Leon F. Litwack, *North of Slavery: The Negro in the Free States, 1790–1860* (Chicago, 1961), pp. 75, 86–87, 100–102, 114, 121, 158, 162, 165–166, 169.

3 Parker, p. 160. Parker refers to "Dr. Dengy." Hensel identifies Parker's employer as Dr. Obadiah Dingee, father of Charles Dingee "of West Grove nursery and rose culture fame" [W. U. Hensel, *The Christiana Riot* . . . (second and revised edition, Lancaster, Pennsylvania, 1911) p. 28.]

4 Parker (p. 160) indicates that Garrison and Douglass "came into the neighborhood" while he was living at Dr. Dingee's (according to my calculations sometime between the early fall of 1839 and early fall of 1840). Parker's recollection of the time period in which he heard Garrison and Douglass seems to be mistaken. Douglass only began to speak at anti-slavery meetings (in New England) in the summer of 1841. He apparently did not appear in Pennsylvania until the winter of 1843, when he spoke, without Garrison, on November 25, in

West Chester, and in Philadelphia during the first week in December, at a meeting celebrating the tenth anniversary of the American Anti-Slavery Society [Foner, vol. I, pp. 22, 26, 57–58; Benjamin Quarles, *Frederick Douglass* (New York, 1968), p. 33; *Anti-Slavery Standard*, December 14, 1843, clippings file: Chester Co. Hist. Soc.] Parker might have heard Douglass and Garrison speak together in Philadelphia, Norristown, or Harrisburg in August, 1847 (Quarles, *Douglass*, pp. 60–61). Douglass escaped from slavery in Maryland on September 3, 1838, about one year before Parker. The first version of Douglass's autobiography was published in 1845 (Foner, vol. 4, pp. 557–558).

5 Parker, p. 160.

6 W. U. Hensel, *The Christiana Riot* . . . (second and revised edition, Lancaster, Pennsylvania, 1911), p. 15, n. A p. 135. Hensel notes that there were, of course, exceptions, some of these whites were "outspoken" abolitionists. In the Quarryville area, whose white population was both German and Scotch-Irish, there was even some intermarriage between the races. The Pennsylvania Germans' hostility was common despite a Mennonite anti-slavery proclamation of 1688 which preceded similar declarations by the Quakers.

7 Hensel, *Christiana*, pp. 14–15. Hensel distinguishes between the "placid aspect of the Quakers of Fulton and Drumore Townships" and the Hicksite branch of Friends inhabiting the eastern end of Drumore, Colerain, and Little Britain, who "were more aggressive in their hostility to slavery."

8 Hensel, *Christiana*, p. 15, n. A p. 135; Parker, p. 162.

9 The Unitied States Constitution's fugitive clause and 1793 fugitive act: Wilbur H. Siebert, *The Underground Railroad from Slavery to Freedom* (New York, 1898), pp. 359–361; Edward Raymond Turner, *The Negro in Pennsylvania* (Washington, D.C., 1912), pp. 117–118, 230–233.

10 Hensel, *Christiana*, pp. 14–18, n. J p. 138. Contemporary references to this gang are found in James R. Robbins, *Report of the Trial of Castner Hanway* . . . (Philadelphia, 1852), Pennington testimony: pp. 114–116; Rhay testimony: pp. 117–118; Cuyler statement: p. 109; Stevens statement: p. 112. At a pre-trial hearing Thaddeus Stevens declared that Bill Baer and Perry Marsh "were known to be in the neighborhood" when the attack on Parker's occurred [David R. Forbes, *A True Story of the Christiana Riot* (Quarryville, Pennsylvania, 1898), p. 37]. A letter from informer William Padgett to slave owner E. Gorsuch mentions as meeting places "Benjamin Clay's tavern" at the Gap and Kinzey's Hotel (Hensel, *Christiana*, p. 24). Christiana resident George Steele ("Description . . . ," p. 3) speaks of "a gang of horse thieves and counterfeiters who had their headquarters at [Amos] Clemson's Tavern near Mount Vernon. They were in the business of slave capturing." Steele associates Wm. Padgett with this gang. Important secondary sources referring to this gang are Hensel, *Christiana*, pp. 15–17, n. J p. 138; Smedley, pp. 91, 98, 107–108; Marianna G. Brubaker, "The Underground Railroad," *Lanc. Co. Hist. Soc. Papers*, vol. 15, no. 4 (1911), p. 117.

11 Parker, pp. 161–162. Parker says this self-defense organization was formed while he was living at Dr. Dingee's, during his first year and a half of freedom. In the chronology of events as Parker presents them his hearing the anti-slavery speeches of Garrison and Douglass precedes the organization for self-defense. It

is not clear whether, in actuality, the speeches preceded, and thus perhaps helped to inspire, the organization. Hensel (*Christiana*, p. 28) thinks Parker was inspired to organize by hearing Garrison and Douglass. See n. 4, this chapter. Parker (pp. 164–166) mentions from five to seven active members of the self-defense organization.

12 Only one local historian (Smedley, p. 108) suggests any direct white participation in the formation of the organization (not its armed activities!). As Smedley describes it, the black people of the area, exasperated by slave hunters, "held meetings, assisted by their white friends, to consider and adopt means for self-protection." Parker never mentions any white participation, nor do other reliable sources. Joseph Townsend was the white man who loaded his gun and gave it to the black, John Roberts (Robbins, p. 102). Although George Steele does not speak of any white participation in the self-defense organization, Steele thinks it certain that when Parker's was attacked in 1851, whites told the blacks to "go and take your gun." Perhaps one or two whites encouraged the blacks' armed resistance, but general white support of this kind was highly unlikely, and in any case unnecessary. At the trial which followed the September 1851 resistance the prosecution charged that the blacks had been led and incited by whites; the defense said that the area's whites had tried to pacify and discourage the armed blacks. The defense position seems to be accurate, although the prosecution's claim seems to be a major origin of the myth of white incitement.

13 "Freedom's Battle at Christiana," Editorial, *Frederick Douglass' Paper*, September 25, 1851.

14 The four sources referring to Parker's appearance are (1) the 1850 U.S. Census of Sadsbury Township; (2) Marshal Kline's testimony, *A Full And Correct Report of the Christiana Tragedy* . . . (Lancaster, Pennsylvania, 1851), p. 4 (hereafter cited as *Report*); (3) Thomas Whitson, "The Hero of the Christiana Riot," *Lanc. Co. Hist. Soc. Papers*, vol. 1 (June 1896), p. 33; (4) "A Noble Fellow," Editorial, *Provincial Freeman*, March 22, 1856.

15 For Woods: Hensel, *Christiana*, p. 23; for Hopkins: pp. 28–29. Hopkins says this party occurred the night before the Christiana resistance of September 11, 1851.

16 Parker, pp. 160, 163, 165. Frank Parker recalled his grandmother Eliza as "dark" (interviewed by J. K., North Buxton, Canada, September 6, 1969). The 1850 U.S. Census lists the Parker family.

17 All in all, Parker accounts for eight years and five months of his life in Pennsylvania, apparently omitting only the length of time he lived in the stone house near Christiana, rented from Levi Pownall.

18 Parker, pp. 163–164. The Pinckney family is listed on the 1850 Census as living with the Parkers, and gives their ages, also indicating that the Pinckneys had been married within the last year.

19 Smedley, pp. 77–78. Smedley says that Abraham Johnson worked for Jeremiah Moore for five and a half years: "The mother lived with Lindley Coates, and the sister with Thomas Bonsal for a while, when she removed to Reading and married."

20 W. U. Hensel, "Aftermath Supplementary to Christiana Riot, 1851," *Lanc.*

Co. Hist. Soc. Papers, vol. 16, no. 5 (1912), pp. 138–139. The 1850 Census lists "Alex Johnson," a twenty-five-year-old black, born in Maryland, as living with the Joseph D. Pownall family. Despite the difference in first names this is probably Parker's friend Abraham Johnson. If, as Sarah M. McFadden says, Johnson was eighteen when he came to her family's, and lived with them for six years, he would have been twenty-four when he left. This fits with the 1850 Census listing Johnson's age as twenty-five at the time he was living with the Pownall family. The quote from Johnson is in Parker (p. 286).

21 Smedley, pp. 108, 113.

22 Smedley, pp. 99, 113. Lindley Coates's barn burning is reported in the Lancaster *Examiner and Herald*, July 30, 1851. Whittier's description: Thomas Whitson, "The Early Abolitionists of Lancaster County," *Lanc. Co. Hist. Soc. Papers*, vol. 15 (1911), p. 71. Coates's comment on Parker: Smedley, p. 113.

23 Whitson, "The Hero of the Christiana Riot," p. 33.

3. Kidnappers (pages 35–47)

1 Parker (pp. 161–166) mentions eleven incidents involving kidnappers or their agents. The self-defense organization took action in eight of these cases. Two of these eight actions involve the organization's reprisals against black informers in league with slave catchers. The following is a chronological list of local conflicts between "kidnappers" and blacks, similar or identical to incidents described by Parker, and for which there is contemporary documentation:

a) June 2, 1847: Blacks in Carlisle, Pennsylvania, try to rescue several fugitives; slave owner James H. Kennedy fatally injured; two slaves rescued, one remanded (Lancaster *Examiner and Herald*, June 9, 1847). See chapter 4, pp. 50–51.

b) April 18, 1848: Kidnapping of slave from home of Zebulon Thomas, near Downingtown, Chester County (Lancaster *Examiner and Herald*, May 3, 1848). See n. 15, this chapter.

c) September 1850: Henry Williams kidnapped (Cuyler testimony: Robbins, p. 109; Hensel, *Christiana*, n. J, p. 138). See n. 11, this chapter.

d) September 1850: Lancaster County area said to be patrolled by "armed bands of negroes," after a report that slaveholders had come up for slaves. These "armed bands" are said to have gone "from house to house in the neighborhood," swearing vengeance "against the slave catchers," and expressing a desire to kill them (G. L. Ashmead statement: Robbins, pp. 147, 159–162). See chapter 14, p. 207.

e) November 1, 1850: Black resistance about this date at hotel near West Chester (Lancaster *Examiner and Herald*, Jan. 1, 1851). See n. 10, this chapter.

f) December 1850: Fugitive slave resistance, Coatesville (same source as above).

g) January 1, 1851: Lancaster *Examiner and Herald* reports: "for several weeks, there has been an organization among the blacks to prevent the arrest of fugitive slaves."

h) January 13?, 1851: Kidnapping of John Williams from home of Wm.

Marsh Chamberlain, near Parker's, in Sadsbury Township (Robbins, pp. 115–117). See chapter 13, p. 199.

i) January 24, 1851: Letter of this date describes arrest of fugitive slave Stephen Bennett, and resistance, especially by black women, Columbia, Pennsylvania (Lancaster *Intelligencer*, January 28, 1851). See chapter 4, p. 62.

j) March(?) 1851: Joel Henry Thompson kidnapped from Lancaster County by G. F. Alberti and J. Frisbie Price (*Pennsylvania Freeman*, March 6, 1851).

k) March 16, 1851: Kidnapping of Thomas Hall from Sandy Hill in West Caln Township, Chester County (Lancaster *Examiner and Herald*, April 30, 1851; J. M. McKim to G. Thompson: in Still, p. 581).

l) April 1851: Maryland slave owner Samuel Worthington goes to get his fugitive, Jacob Berry, at home of family named Haines in Christiana area; is resisted by armed force (G. L. Ashmead: Robbins, pp. 147, 162–163). See chapter 14, pp. 208–209.

2 Parker, p. 161.

3 Parker, pp. 161–162. A William Dorsey is mentioned by Peter Woods as being present in the Christiana area in September 1851 (Forbes, p. 31). Smedley (pp. 113–114) contains a version of this case, apparently based on Parker, but omitting the victim's name. Robert Purvis describes a case involving fugitives William, Basil, Thomas, and Charles Dorsey, but this appears to be an entirely different incident (Smedley, pp. 356–361). The Doylestown rescue of Basil Dorsey, as R. Purvis reportedly recounted it is in Edward H. Magill, "When Men Were Sold," *Bucks Co. Hist. Soc. Proceedings*, vol. 2 (1909), pp. 511–516. William Whipper describes still another Dorsey case (Still, pp. 738–739). Several fugitive rescues similar but not identical to the Dorsey rescue described by Parker are reported in chapter 4 of this book.

4 Parker, p. 162.

5 Parker, pp. 162–163; Smedley, pp. 96–97. A somewhat similar case of the abduction of a young black woman is reported in the Lancaster *Examiner and Herald*, May 3, 1848: On April 18, 1848, early in the morning, a party of slave catchers entered the kitchen of Zebulon Thomas, in Downingtown, Chester County. Taking a candle from a terrified black boy who was kindling the fire, they proceeded upstairs to the garret, forced the bolted door, seized a teen-aged black female, and placed a gag in her mouth. When Zebulon Thomas, awakened by the commotion, threatened to rescue the young woman, the ruffians placed a pistol at his head and threatened to blow out his brains. Another black woman in the house, said to be the mother of the younger woman, concealed herself and escaped capture. The young woman was carried quickly to Maryland where, according to Smedley, she was eventually rescued from the slave traders and, with her mother, helped to Canada. Smedley (pp. 299–300) also describes the above case.

6 A James G. Henderson is listed on the 1850 tax records of Sadsbury Township as owning 137 acres ("Owners of Real Property, List No. 1; Lanc. Co. Hist. Soc.). James G. Henderson testified for the defense at the trial of the Christiana resisters (Robbins, p. 131). Parker identifies the other "respectable citizen" as "Dr. Duffield." A Dr. Samuel Duffield was chairman of a local Whig

meeting at which J. G. Henderson was appointed vice-president (Lancaster *Examiner and Herald*, Oct. 3, 1849). A Dr. Duffield is mentioned as the tutor of J. M. McKim (Still, p. 655).

7 An abolitionist, Dr. F. J. Lemoyne, was nominated Liberty Party candidate for Governor of Pennsylvania in 1844 (Smedley, pp. 45, 60).

8 Parker, pp. 162–163; Smedley, pp. 96–97.

9 Joseph Moore is listed on the 1850 Census and on that year's Tax List No. 1 as owning 225 acres.

10 Parker, p. 164. A somewhat similar case is described in the Lancaster *Examiner and Herald*, Jan. 1, 1851: The paper mentions a violent altercation in Parkesburg between a black man and white, the white having called the black a fugitive slave, and threatened to inform on him. The paper then reports "the fact that for several weeks, there has been an organisation among the blacks to prevent the arrest of fugitive slaves. Armed gangs have patrolled the neighborhood during the night and guarded particular persons that were supposed to be in danger from slave hunters. About the 1st of November three or four men were in the township from an adjoining state in pursuit of slaves. The hotel at which they put úp for the night was surrounded by thirty or forty armed negroes.—The landlord being somewhat alarmed for the safety of his lodgers who had retired, notified them of the danger. They rose from their beds, and hastily arranged upon a variety of fire-arms, knives, &c., and then returned to their beds, telling the landlord that he should give himself no trouble on their account. No violence, however, was committed on either side" (West Chester *Village Record*, n.d., Chester Co. Hist. Soc.).

The same paper reports another case, in late December 1850, of slave catchers, authorized by Commissioner Edward Ingraham, going to Coatesville, in Chester County, to arrest a fugitive: "They arrived at the house where the fugitive was supposed to be secreted, and knocked at the door." They were let in by a black woman, "and were proceeding up stairs [when] they were met by two colored men and two colored women. The women and one of the men were armed with axes, and the other man had a gun. The Marshal told them that they were in search of a fugitive slave; but they [the blacks] refused to let him or any of his men enter the room. The gun was taken from the [black] man, and the [marshal's] party endeavored to disarm the man with the axe. A pistol was fired at him [the black with the axe], the ball of which must have entered his breast, but he still maintained his resistance. The fight continued until the Southern gentleman, who was with the party, advised the Marshal to withdraw, remarking that he would not have one of them killed for all the negroes in Pennsylvania. Several shots were fired, and more than one colored person is supposed to have been shot. One was seen to fall as the officers were leaving. None of the Marshal's party were injured."

11 The 1850 Census lists Allen Williams, fifty years old, a black laborer, place of birth unknown, living with his wife, Lydia, fifty, black, place of birth unknown. No Henry Williams is listed on this Census. Lawyer Theodore Cuyler relates that a gang of "professional kidnappers" who resided on the border of Lancaster County, in September, 1850, "entered the house of Henry Williams,

and at his very fire side, seized and carried into perpetual slavery, without right and without process of law of any kind, an innocent hired man in his employ" (Robbins, p. 109). Despite the confusion of names, this appears to be the same case related by Parker. Hensel mentions the kidnapping of Henry Williams in 1850: he says that "memoranda in pencil preserved in the Pownall family," prepared by one of its members, indicates "that the night Henry Williams was kidnapped he was knocked down, tied with a bed cord, carried off in a dearborn belonging to Bill Baer, drawn by a gray and sorrel horse, and the route taken by his captors was via Nickel Mines and the Green Tree" (Hensel, *Christiana*, p. 16, n. J p. 138).

12 Parker, pp. 164–165.

13 Parker, p. 166.

14 There is some disagreement about the date of this kidnapping. T. Pennington says it was in January (1851), "some say it was the 13th" (Robbins, pp. 114, 116); M. Pennington says it occurred on January 13, 1851 (Robbins, p. 118); Henry Rhay says it occurred on a Monday evening in February 1851 (Robbins, p. 117); an 1851 letter from James Miller McKim to George Thompson mentions an article in the *Pennsylvania Freeman* of January 2, 1851, which describes a successful kidnapping attempt in Chester County. McKim adds: "A week or two after this occurred, and not far from the same place," another kidnapping took place whose details (in McKim's description) match those of the Chamberlain case (Still, p. 580). In a Lancaster County court case apparently having some connection with this kidnapping "Oliver Perry Marshe" was indicted for "assault and battery upon Capt. John Rea, at the Gap, in this county, on the 13 of January last. Plea not guilty. Verdict guilty. Def't ordered to pay $50 fine and costs" (Lancaster *Examiner and Herald*, April 30, 1851). See n. 17, this chapter.

15 The 1850 Census lists John Williams, a black, thirty-five years old, place of birth, Maryland, as living with the Chamberlain family; T. Pennington's testimony indicates that the black man worked on Chamberlain's farm (Robbins, p. 116); Smedley, pp. 97–98.

16 Robbins, p. 117. The 1850 Census lists the "Henry Rhey" family.

17 T. Pennington says that "a few minutes" after the men went away "neighbor James Ray came running to the house, and told my son-in-law [William M. Chamberlain], [that] his brother John [Ray, or Rhey, or Rhea] had been out from home, and had fell down dead as he entered the door of his own house. This created a great deal of alarm in the family, and my son-in-law went immediately to the house to see as to what James came for him to do" (Robbins, p. 115). The death of John "Ray" would seem to have some connection with the assault and battery apparently committed on him by Perry Marsh on January 13, 1851 (see n. 14, this chapter). The 1850 Census lists "John Rhea," age fifty-six, a laborer, and "James Rhea," age sixty-two, a farmer.

18 For Pennington: Robbins, pp. 114–117; for R. Chamberlain: Robbins, pp. 117–118. Pennington says Perry Marsh "resided in the neighborhood of the Gap, and there he kept an oyster house" (Robbins, p. 115).

19 Parker, pp. 165–166. Parker's statement indicates that Alexander Pinckney

and Samuel Thompson were members of the self-defense organization. Parker elsewhere identifies Samuel Thompson as one of E. Gorsuch's fugitive slaves (Parker, p. 184). The 1850 Census lists Samuel Thompson, age twenty-two, a "mulatto," a laborer, born in Pennsylvania, as living with the Joseph Moore family. A "Dr. Savington," a mean, hard-drinking, old slave owner of Harford County, Maryland, is mentioned by Still, p. 417; Smedley, p. 99.
  20 Smedley, pp. 98–99.

4. 1851 (pages 48–65)

  1 Thomas L. Brasher, ed., *Walt Whitman: The Early Poems and the Fiction* (New York, 1963), pp. 38–39.
  2 Hensel, *Christiana*, pp. 9–10, 57. Edward Raymond Turner, *The Negro in Pennsylvania* . . . (Washington, D.C., 1911), pp. 118, 236–238.
  3 Quoted: Lancaster *Examiner and Herald*, June 9, 1847. Eleven black men originally sentenced on a misdemeanor charge to three years in the Eastern Penitentiary were released on a technicality in June 1848, after serving about a year in prison (Lancaster *Examiner and Herald*, June 14, 1848). Lancaster County lawyer W. U. Hensel reports that when the first rescue attempt occurred in the courtroom, "The judge seized a club and attempted to defend Mr. Kennedy, but the latter was mortally wounded. This riot was almost exclusively among the negroes. Of the white people who gathered few took part. After Kennedy's death there was a public meeting in Carlisle in which the action of the mob was denounced as a disgrace and Mr. Kennedy was extolled as a citizen 'whose whole life was an ornament and whose character was a valuable example of a good man' " (Hensel, *Christiana*, nn. I and M pp. 138–139).
  4 Siebert, pp. 361–366.
  5 Brasher, pp. 36–37, 47–48.
  6 Distance of Georgetown from Parker's: Hensel, *Christiana*, p. 18. Lancaster *Examiner and Herald*, October 23, 1850. Public opinion in the area was by no means unanimous, however. Another public meeting in Georgetown, on February 12, 1851, proposed four resolutions in *favor* of the fugitive slave law (Lancaster *Examiner and Herald*, February 19, 1850).
  7 Datelined West Chester, October 15: Lancaster *Examiner and Herald*, October 23, 1850.
  8 Douglass, *Life*, pp. 273–275. W. E. B. Du Bois, *John Brown* (New York, 1962), pp. 105–108.
  9 Oswald Garrison Villard, *John Brown* . . . (Boston, 1910), pp. 50–53.
  10 For Delany: William Loren Katz, *Eyewitness: The Negro in American History* (New York, 1967), p. 189. J. W. Loguen, *The Rev. J. W. Loguen, As A Slave And As A Freeman* (Syracuse, 1859), pp. 392–393.
  11 The information on black resistance in the following section is found throughout Benjamin Quarles, *Black Abolitionists* (New York, 1969).
  12 Letter dated Columbia, Pennsylvania, January 24 in Lancaster *Intelligencer*, January 28, 1851; also see another letter from Columbia, same paper, February 11, 1851.

13 Lancaster *Examiner and Herald,* January 29, 1851.

14 Robert F. Lucid, ed., *The Journal of Richard Henry Dana* (Cambridge, Massachusetts, 1968), vol. 2, pp. 410–412.

15 "Diseases and peculiarities of the negro race," *De Bow's Review,* vol. 11 (September 1851), pp. 331–334.

16 *Uncle Tom's Cabin* (1881; reprint, New York, 1967), p. 83.

5 Fugitives (pages 66–80)

1 W. U. Hensel, "Aftermath Supplementary to Christiana Riot, 1851," *Lanc. Co. Hist. Soc. Papers,* vol. 16, no. 5 (1912), pp. 136–137. This "Abraham Johnston," "Johnson," or "Jonson"—the legal documents are not particular about the spelling of his name—was evidently not the "Abraham Johnson" who resided at William Parker's in 1851. Sarah M. McFadden's testimony suggests that Parker's "Johnson" lived in the Christiana area before Gorsuch's "Johnston" escaped from Maryland. Hensel accepts McFadden's statement ("Aftermath," pp. 138–139); Smedley (p. 77) also corroborates it. Parker (p. 284) says that, during the confrontation with Gorsuch, "Johnson" was called to the window to confront the slave owner, which suggests that this "Johnson" had no fear that Gorsuch might recognize him. On the other hand, the Reverend J. S. Gorsuch says that the "Johnson" charged with stealing his father's wheat *was* among the Christiana resisters at Parker's (letter dated Christiana, September "17," 1851: Lancaster *Intelligencer,* September 17, 1851. The date of this letter was later corrected by Gorsuch to September 16: Lancaster *Intelligencer,* October 14, 1851. The letter of September "17" was widely reprinted). See also chapter 2, n. 20.

2 Hensel, "Aftermath," pp. 135–136.

3 Hensel, *Christiana,* p. 22.

4 Hensel, "Aftermath," pp. 135–136; Hensel, *Christiana,* p. 22.

5 The vertical file in the Enoch Pratt Free Library, Baltimore, lists genealogical information about the Gorsuch family.

6 *Along This Way* (1933, reprinted ed., New York, 1968), p. 28.

7 Myles Jackson, producer, Dr. Florence Jackson, associate producer, "Two Man War At Christiana, 1851" (recording), *Viewpoints on American Abolition* (Random House, 1971). This is a marvelous presentation of the Christiana resistance and its present-day implications based on taped interviews with Gorsuch family members, black and white citizens of the Christiana area, teachers, students.

8 Governor of Maryland E. Louis Lowe, "Annual Message of the Executive, . . ." Maryland State Documents (Annapolis, 1852), p. 36; Hensel, *Christiana,* p. 20. In 1828 Edward Gorsuch arranged for the future emancipation, twenty-seven years later (on February 12, 1855) of his then four-year-old slave Giles Wallis. The slave was to become a free man at the age of thirty-one. Edward Gorsuch did not live to see Wallis get his freedom (Hensel, "Aftermath," pp. 133–134).

9 Reverend J. S. Gorsuch letter of September "17," 1851. The Reverend Mr. Gorsuch says his father's four fugitive slaves were "between the ages of nineteen and twenty-two" when they escaped in 1849. Hensel ("Aftermath," p. 133) disagrees with the Reverend Mr. Gorsuch about the manumission age being twenty-eight. Hensel concludes from the 1828 manumission arrangements for the four-year-old Giles Wallis twenty-seven years later, that "the age of thirty-one was the period of freedom." Hensel (*Christiana*, p. 20) reports that the term of servitude of Gorsuch's two older slaves, Noah Buley and Joshua Hammond, had almost expired when they escaped. The two younger slaves, Nelson Ford and George Hammond, who were about twenty-one years old (in 1849?), are said to have had about six or seven years to serve before being freed.

10 Hensel, *Christiana*, pp. 20, 22; Myles Jackson, producer, "Two Man War" (recording, Random House, 1971), side 1.

11 Hensel, *Christiana*, pp. 20–23. No Alexander Scott is listed on the 1850 Census for Sadsbury Township.

12 Hensel, "Aftermath," pp. 135–137. The Governor of Maryland had previously declined to honor the Governor of Pennsylvania's requisition for a slave owner found guilty of kidnapping in 1845 (Hensel, *Christiana*, p. 8).

13 Hensel, "Aftermath," p. 138.

14 Letter quoted from Hartford *Republican*, n.d.; *Liberator*, October 3, 1851. See also *Liberator*, November 1, 1851 and Forbes, p. 11. With this letter were found "several memoranda . . . written in pencil probably by the slaveholder himself" of the railroad schedule, names of persons in the area "with whom it was supposed colored men resided," together with the following:

"Robert M. Lee
John Agan   Henry H. Cline
Depatised
Marshal Kline
Lawyer Lee
and Benit
Commissioner
Ingraham
O. Riley's Telegraph
avoid Halzel
Councilman
Cpt Shutt
J.R. Henson"

Hensel (*Christiana*, p. 35), in reference to the above, says, "The significance of these entries will be recognised." For a non-local, later generation the implications of these notations are unfortunately mostly lost.

15 Pennsylvanian Alexander K. McClure also says that Padgett was ostensibly a traveling clock mender; McClure says Padgett communicated with the owners of fugitive slaves "through Henry H. Kline, who was then conspicuous as a slave-catching constable from Philadelphia, and who acted under the direction of Commissioner Ingraham . . ." [McClure, *Recollections of Half a Century*

(Salem, Massachusetts, 1902), pp. 19–20]. McClure is the only source who directly connects Padgett, fugitive slave commissioner Ingraham and U.S. Marshal Kline.

16 Thomas Whitson, "Early Abolitionists of Lancaster County," *Lanc. Co. Hist. Soc. Papers*, vol. 15 (1911), p. 83. On October 3, 1851, *The Liberator* ran a letter about William Padgett headlined "Spy and Informer" (reprinted from the Hartford *Republican*, n.d.).

17 Smedley, p. 129.

18 Smedley, p. 123.

19 Hensel, *Christiana*, pp. 24–25. A stranger from lower Lancaster County is said to have earlier arrived in Dr. Pearce's area, claiming to be able to locate a missing slave of Pearce's and a number of fugitives from Baltimore County.

20 McClure, *Recollections*, p. 20. Lancaster *Examiner and Herald*, January 1, 1850. In another case in February, 1851, a black woman named "Mahala," or Tamor Williams, the mother of six, had also been legally remanded to her owner by Commissioner Ingraham. The reversal of Ingraham's decision on a technicality, and the freeing of Tamor Williams by Judge Kane caused great happiness among Philadelphia blacks who placed the woman in a carriage and "hauled her, amid a rejoicing crowd, to her home" (Lancaster *Examiner and Herald*, February 12, 1851). A long, detailed description of this case, condensed from the *Pennsylvania Freeman*, January 13, 1857, is found in Still, pp. 566–576. Another fugitive case in which Ingraham issued warrants is reported in the Lancaster *Examiner and Herald*, January 1, 1851. In another case, when Ingraham remanded a fugitive named Stephan Bennett, $700 was collected in Bennett's hometown, Columbia, Pennsylvania, to buy his freedom (Lancaster *Examiner and Herald*, January 29, 1851). Ingraham remanded fugitive Daniel Hawkins in July 1851 (Lancaster *Examiner and Herald*, July 23, July 30, 1851).

21 Kline's appearance: Robbins, pp. 64, 94; his notoriety: Still, p. 350; Kline testimony: Robbins, p 57; Hensel, *Christiana*, p. 25.

22 Still, p. 349.

23 Kline testimony: Robbins, p. 57; Lancaster *Examiner and Herald*, September 24, 1851.

24 Testimony reported in Forbes, pp. 32, 34. A white Quaker, Joseph Scarlett, was also said to have returned from a business trip to Philadelphia early in the week, bringing back a warning of the impending fugitive slave hunt (Hensel, *Christiana*, p. 25).

25 For Kline: Robbins, p. 57; for the Reverend J. S. Gorsuch, September "17" letter.

26 Later Kline himself went off to find Agan and Tully, in case Gorsuch had missed them. The two officers were still intending to go back to Philadelphia, but promised Kline to return (Kline testimony: Robbins, p. 57).

27 For Kline: Robbins, pp. 57–58. Padgett was never specifically identified as the guide by any posse members; his name was apparently not mentioned at the treason trial, or at any preliminary hearings.

28 Kline: Robbins, pp. 58, 69.

29 For N. Nelson: Robbins, p. 87; other testimony in Robbins referring to

this first horn, Pearce: p. 74; J. M. Gorsuch: pp. 80–81; D. Gorsuch: p. 83; Hutchings: p. 85; Nelson: p. 86. Miller "Nott," who lived nearby, heard no horns blow that morning (Robbins, p. 89). The posse's testimony about horns served the prosecution's theory, at the later trial, of a local conspiracy to resist the fugitive slave law; the defense emphasized other reasons why horns might be blown: Lewis Cooper says, "At that season of the year it is the custom of all farmers to call their hands to breakfast by blowing horns . . . awhile before sunrise. . . ." Cooper heard no unusual horns that morning (Robbins, pp. 141–142). John Houston described a horn being blown to call local railroad workers to their jobs (Robbins, p. 143).
    30 Robbins, pp. 58, 64.

6. Prelude (pages 81–91)

    1 Parker, pp. 281, 283.
    2 Young testimony: *Report*, p. 19; Cooper testimony: *Report*, p. 18. Parker (p. 293) identifies George Williams as "one of our men, and the very one who had the letters brought up from Philadelphia by Samuel Williams." George Williams was later one of those arrested and charged with treason.
    3 Parker, p. 283; Douglass, "Freedom's Battle, . . ." *Douglass' Paper*, September 25, 1851. Gorsuch had warrants out for four slaves: Noah Buley, Joshua Hammond, George Hammond, and Nelson Ford. There is much confusion over their aliases. Peter Woods told Hensel in 1911 that the names used by Gorsuch's slaves were John Beard, Thomas Wilson, Alexander Scott, and Edward Thompson; Hensel also reports that a written "brief" by a member of the Pownall family identifies John Beard as Nelson Ford (*Christiana*, pp. 20, 23, 138). "John Beer" is said by John "Nott" to be known as one of Gorsuch's fugitives (Robbins, p. 92). Parker (pp. 283–284) identifies those Gorsuch slaves present in his house as Joshua Kite and Samuel Thompson.
    4 Smedley, p. 115.
    5 Kline's testimony (quotation marks added): Forbes, p. 24. See also J. M. Gorsuch testimony: Robbins, p. 81; N. Hutchings testimony: Robbins, p. 85. There is much disagreement about the identity of the one (or two) slaves who were chased to the house.
    6 The Rev. J. S. Gorsuch letter of Sept. "17," 1851.
    7 Hutchings testimony ("Pierce" in original corrected to Pearce): Robbins, p. 85; Pearce testimony: Robbins, pp. 74–75; J. M. Gorsuch testimony: Robbins, p. 81. See also N. Nelson testimony: Robbins, p. 86. Pearce and Dickinson Gorsuch went to stand guard in back of the house (Robbins, p. 83).
    8 Kline's testimony: Robbins, p. 63.
    9 Hensel (*Christiana*, p. 30) identifies the fish "gig." Parker (p. 283) says that E. Gorsuch started up the stairs first; Kline says he started upstairs, with E. Gorsuch in back of him (Robbins, p. 58).
    10 Parker, pp. 283–284; Douglass, "Freedom's Battle, . . ." *Douglass' Paper*, September 25, 1851.

11 The marshal's threat to burn the house is mentioned by Parker, but not in Kline's or any other testimony. This threat is mentioned in [W. A. Jackson's] *History of the Trial* . . . (Philadelphia, 1852), p. 34.

12 Parker, p. 284. Kline reports hearing one horn blown from the house, and others in the neighborhood: Robbins, pp. 63–64. Pearce, J. M. Gorsuch, Dickinson Gorsuch, Hutchings, and Nelson heard horns sound from the house: Robbins, pp. 77, 82, 84–85, 87. The tone and wording of the posse's testimony about these horns from the house suggests that Parker's version is exaggerated.

13 Parker, p. 284. Jackson (p. 35) also claims that Kline's shot at Parker was the first fired.

14 Kline's testimony: Robbins, pp. 58, 61. Kline's testimony that the blacks fired first (at E. Gorsuch) is corroborated by Pearce, D. Gorsuch, J. M. Gorsuch, Hutchings, and Nelson: Robbins, pp. 75, 81, 85–86.

15 For J. M. Gorsuch: Robbins, p. 81; for Pearce: Robbins, p. 74.

16 Parker, p. 284.

17 Abraham Johnson's age is based on the assumption that he is the "Alex Johnson," age twenty-five, listed on the 1850 Census of Sadsbury Township. Gorsuch's date of birth, April 17, 1795, would make him fifty-six in September 1851.

18 Parker, pp. 284–285; Dr. John Lovell to J. K., May 13, 1970. This refrain is sung by slaves in chapter 4 of *Uncle Tom's Cabin* (New York, 1963), p. 83.

19 Parker, p. 285. Kline says he bluffingly told one of his men "to go to the sheriff and fetch over a hundred men. I thought that would intimidate them [the blacks]" (Robbins, p. 58). See also Pearce and J. M. Gorsuch testimony: Robbins, pp. 77, 83.

20 Parker, p. 286. The presence of other whites at Parker's is suggested by a number of sources: As Dr. Pearce ran from the scene when the battle started he saw six or seven white men running across the fields (Robbins, pp. 76–77). J. M. Gorsuch noticed "some whites" at the scene, "but didn't notice who" (Robbins, p. 81). Reporting on the event soon after its occurrence, C. M. Burleigh declares that during the confrontation "the slave holders told the blacks that resistance would be useless as they had a party of thirty men in the woods near by" (*Pennsylvania Freeman*, n.d.; Still, p. 350). At a pre-trial hearing Thaddeus Stevens says that William Baer and Perry Marsh, two notorious local kidnappers, "were known to be in the neighborhood when the affair [at Parker's] occurred" (Forbes, p. 37). Frederick Douglass, probably repeating the story as it had been told to him by Parker just nine days after the event, says that fifteen men were in the posse when it first appeared ("Freedom's Battle, . . ." *Douglass' Paper*, September 25, 1851). Jackson (p. 34) reports that after the first confrontation "the number of besiegers seems to have been increased, and as many as fifteen are said to have been near the house." George Steele (p. 3) believes that kidnappers had planned to abduct Parker "as he had interfered with the business of the Clemson gang." Smedley (p. 118) says, "About twenty or more white men came out of the woods close by, whom Parker supposed to be members of the Gap gang in collusion with the slaveholders. . . ." Their object was to kidnap Parker and Pinckney. "These men were immediately enrolled by Kline as

'Special Constables.' " Hensel (*Christiana*, p. 31) says, "Other white men came trooping along, who in Parker's imagination were Gap gangsters, . . . but there is no satisfactory proof that these were anybody but residents of the vicinage attracted to the place by the commotion." Informer Padgett in his letter to Gorsuch mentions a Gap tavern as a place of rendezvous with the slave owner's posse. Kline preceded the rest of the posse to the area by a day, possibly to make arrangements with local kidnappers. Kline's travels about the Gap, and the posse's starting out for Parker's from a Gap tavern, all suggest some collusion with local kidnappers.

21 Kline's testimony: Robbins, p. 58; Dickinson Gorsuch: Robbins, p. 83.

7. "Freedom's Battle" (pages 92–103)

1 1850 Census, Sadsbury Township; Jackson, p. 36; Parker, p. 286; Lewis's testimony: Robbins, p. 120. Isaiah Clarkson had probably been warned of the kidnappers by Joseph Scarlett, as Clarkson came up to Lewis's from the direction of Scarlett's (Robbins, pp. 122, 124). A boy named John Bodely (or Bodily) with "a white slouch hat on" apparently accompanied Lewis to Parker's: Nelson testimony (Robbins, p. 87); for Kline: Robbins, p. 65. See also Bodely testimony, *Report*, p. 16.

2 Cuyler statement: Robbins, p. 108. According to lawyer Cuyler, in his opening for the defense at the trial which followed the resistance, Hanway had been born in Delaware; at the age of five he moved with his father to Chester County, Pennsylvania, and after living there for several years moved, first to Maryland, and then to one of the western states. About three years previously he had returned to Chester County, married, and in the spring of 1851, settled as a miller in the Chester Valley, Lancaster County, near Parker's. "Burt" testimony: Robbins, p. 125; Lewis testimony: Robbins, p. 120.

3 Pearce testimony: Robbins, p. 75; Hutchings testimony: Robbins, p. 86; Nelson testimony: Robbins, p. 86; D. Gorsuch testimony: Robbins, p. 83; J. M. Gorsuch testimony: Robbins, p. 83. Marshal Kline says he did not notice any change in the blacks in Parker's when Hanway rode up (Robbins, p. 63). See also Jackson, pp. 75, 86. Pearce (Robbins, p. 77) says he asked Hanway what his object was in coming there, "whether he did not suppose his presence inspired" the blacks. Hanway, says Pearce, "gave me a very decided answer at that time which struck me," but which Pearce could not later recall.

4 The posse members' testimony emphasizing the blacks' elation at Hanway's arrival served the (false) prosecution argument that Hanway had led and incited the black resisters. But the posse members' testimony on this point has a quality of veracity. I do not think the testimony was contrived simply to support the prosecution's argument. The posse's testimony seems to express accurately the actual (though false) perceptions of these white men. See chapter 12.

5 Parker, p. 286; Hutchings testimony: Lancaster *Examiner and Herald*, September 24, 1851. Dickinson Gorsuch saw the blacks in the house "looking out of the windows, and they said there was some person at the bars [fence] on a

330   NOTES

horse, and they shouted" (Robbins, p. 84); Hensel, *Christiana*, p. 21. Other witnesses also saw Noah Buley at the scene: Pearce testimony: Robbins, pp. 77–78; N. Nelson testimony: Robbins, p. 86. Testimony about the appearance of armed blacks immediately after Hanway—Kline: p. 59; Pearce: p. 74; J. M. Gorsuch: p. 81; D. Gorsuch: p. 85; Hutchings: p. 85; Nelson: p. 86, all in Robbins.

6 Roberts testimony: Robbins, pp. 101–102. Roberts first went to notify a black man who worked for Joseph Moore, but no one was home. The 1850 Census lists Samuel Thompson as living at Joseph Moore's on September 17 of that year. Parker (p. 284) identifies Sam. Thompson as one of Gorsuch's slaves. Because of giving Roberts his loaded gun Jacob Townsend was one of the five whites later indicted for treason.

7 For those blacks who came to the scene of battle and were probably active in the resistance, see n. 28, chapter 11. Estimates of the total number of blacks present are many and various, ranging from Jackson's estimate (pp. 36–37) of "about" 25, to N. Hutchings's of 150 "or more" (Robbins, p. 85). "How many [blacks] there were on the ground during the affray it is now impossible to determine," says Jackson. "It is known," he says, that there were not 200 blacks within eight miles of Parker's, nor 100 within four miles, "and it would have been almost impossible to get together even thirty at an hour's notice. It is probable that there were about twenty-five, all told, at or near the house from the beginning of the affray until all was quiet again." Jackson suggests that fear magnified the estimates of those witnesses who testified to seeing much larger numbers.

8 *Report*, p. 4.

9 Kline testimony: Robbins, pp. 58–59, 109; Forbes, p. 29.

10 Lewis testimony: Robbins, p. 120; Pearce testimony: Robbins, p. 74; *Report*, p. 11.

11 Parker, p. 286.

12 Robbins, p. 66.

13 Robbins, pp. 120–121.

14 Robbins, p. 59.

15 Robbins, pp. 83–84; the Reverend J. S. Gorsuch letter of Sept. "17," 1851.

16 Robbins, p. 81 (punctuation edited for clarity).

17 Pearce testimony: Robbins, pp. 74–75, 79; Lewis Cooper testimony: Robbins, pp. 130, 141 (quotation marks added); J. C. Dickinson testimony: Robbins, pp. 129–130 (this is the section added in brackets).

18 Pearce testimony: Robbins, pp. 75–77; Lancaster *Examiner and Herald*, September 24, 1851.

19 Parker, pp. 286–287. Frederick Douglass, probably repeating a version of the conflict told to him by Parker, also says the battle started with Dickinson firing on Parker ("Freedom's Battle, . . ." *Douglass' Paper*, September 25, 1851). C. M. Burleigh was told soon after the battle that a black had started out of Parker's house and was ordered back by Edward Gorsuch: "The colored man replied, 'You had better go away if you don't want to get hurt,' and at the same time pushed him aside and passed out. Maddened at this, and stimulated by the

question of his nephew, whether he would 'take such an insult from a d----d nigger,' Gorsuch fired at the colored man and was followed by his son and nephew, who both fired their revolvers. The fire was returned by the blacks. . . ." (Still, p. 351).

20 Parker, p. 287; *Report*, pp. 22–23.

21 Parker, pp. 287–288. The armaments of the Gorsuch posse are a matter of dispute. Parker (pp. 286–287) says E. Gorsuch had two guns. Kline did not think E. Gorsuch had any weapons, and claimed there were only four revolvers among the seven posse members (Robbins, p. 73). The Reverend J. S. Gorsuch (letter of Sept. "17," 1851) says that four men, Edward, Dickinson, J. M. Gorsuch, and Dr. Pearce, were armed. The Gorsuch family told Hensel about 1911 that they did not think it would have been in character for E. Gorsuch to have had any arms (Hensel, *Christiana*, p. 35). Frederick Douglass says in his autobiography that Parker gave him E. Gorsuch's gun as a memento (*Life*, p. 282). A visitor to the Christiana fugitives when they passed through Douglass's Rochester home on their way to Canada after the battle confirms that they had Gorsuch's pistol with them (*Syracuse League*, n.d.: *Liberator*, October 3, 1851).

8. Inquest at Christiana (pages 104–119)

1 Lewis Cooper testimony; p. 141; Pearce testimony: pp. 75, 79; Kline testimony: p. 75; J. M. Gorsuch testimony: p. 81, all in Robbins.

2 Rogers's testimony: Lancaster *Examiner and Herald,* October 1, 1851 ("Pierce" corrected to "Pearce"); Robbins, p. 128; *Report,* p. 17.

3 Parker, p. 287.

4 Robbins, pp. 75, 79–80.

5 Parker, p. 287.

6 J. M. Gorsuch testimony: Robbins, pp. 81, 83: Kline testimony: Robbins, p. 60.

7 Lancaster *Examiner and Herald,* Oct. 1, 1851. Dr. Pearce's further itinerary is reported by the Reverend J. S. Gorsuch, a few days after the battle: "At a distance of half a mile from the negroes' house, he reached a dwelling, and bolted in asking two ladies who were then the only persons whom he saw in the house to protect him. They expressed fear lest the negroes might come and find him there, and kill them for concealing him. He told them he would not expose them to danger then, and turned to go out, when they consented to conceal him. Soon his infuriated pursuers came to the house and asked if he was not there.—They were told that someone had gone past, and they kept on to the woods, which they searched and guarded until late at night, to find and to butcher their desired victim" (letter of Sept. "17," 1851).

8 Smedley, pp. 124–125.

9 Parker, p. 287; Kline testimony: Robbins, p. 66.

10 Lewis testimony: Robbins, p. 121.

11 Robbins, pp. 59–60, 73.

12 Burt (or Birt) testimony: Robbins, pp. 125–126. Squire Joseph D. Pownall

rode up "in his shirtsleeves"; Kline asked Pownall the whereabouts of a doctor and started off (Robbins, p. 60).

13 Kline testimony: Robbins, p. 60.

14 M. Knott testimony: Robbins, pp. 88, 90; J. Knott: Robbins, pp. 91–92. There are variant versions of how Dickinson Gorsuch was saved: The Reverend J. S. Gorsuch reports that "some of the fiends" followed Dickinson away from the scene, "and would have most cruelly murdered him but an old negro, who had been in [the] affray, threw himself over his body, and called upon them for God's sake to assist him for he would soon die anyhow" (letter of Sept. "17," 1851). A day or so after the battle, C. M. Burleigh was "told that Parker himself protected the wounded man from his excited companions, and brought water and a bed from his house for the invalid . . ." (*Pennsylvania Freeman*, n.d.: Still, p. 351). Smedley (pp. 119, 216) reports that Joseph Scarlett, "arriving at the place where Dickinson Gorsuch lay wounded, and seeing some of the colored men who were frenzied by the fight pressing forward with vengeful spirit to kill him, he placed himself between them and Gorsuch, and advised them against taking his life. Having great respect for Scarlett and a warm attachment to him as their friend, they yielded to his monitions and left their enemy in his protection." Compare Knott's statement about the blacks saying "they would as soon die then as live" with Hutchings's report: "The colored people in the house stated they felt like dying," both meaning the blacks were inspired to new resistance (Robbins, p. 83).

15 M. Knott testimony: *Report,* p. 15; Robbins, p. 99.

16 D. Gorsuch testimony: Robbins, pp. 76, 84; Pearce testimony: Robbins, p. 75; *Report,* p. 10; J. M. Gorsuch testimony: Robbins, p. 82; Dr. Cain's testimony: Robbins, p. 100.

17 Parker, pp. 287–288 ("Pownell" corrected to "Pownall").

18 D. Gorsuch testimony: Robbins, p. 84; Smedley, pp. 119, 216.

19 Cooper testimony: Robbins, pp. 140–141; Pearce testimony: Robbins, pp. 76, 78; Hensel, *Christiana,* pp. 35–36. Hensel says D. Gorsuch died August 2, 1882.

20 Steele, p. 2.

21 Smedley, pp. 120–121.

22 Cain testimony: Robbins, pp. 126–127. Cain's testimony, incidentally, corroborates Smedley. John Long is identified on the 1850 Census. Brubaker, pp. 105–106.

23 Hensel, *Christiana,* pp. 41–42. Interviewed about 1911, Woods added, "I guess I am the last man living of our party."

24 Steele, p. 1; Joseph Hutchinson Smith, "Some Aspects of the Underground Railway, . . ." *Bulletin of the Montgomery Co. Hist. Soc.,* vol. 3, no. 7 (October 1941), pp. 13–14.

25 Kline testimony: Robbins, p. 60; Smith testimony: Robbins, p. 99. For more testimony about the missing money see J. Knott in: Forbes, pp. 21–22; for Tamsey Brown: Forbes, p. 2; Hensel, *Christiana,* p. 34. Gorsuch was no doubt carrying this money to pay off his mercenary assistants after recapturing his slaves.

26 Lewis Cooper testimony: Robbins, pp. 140, 142. Postmortem: Lancaster *Examiner and Herald*, September 17, 1851; Hensel, *Christiana*, pp. 35, 38; Kline testimony: Robbins p. 60. The extent of the violence done to E. Gorsuch's body is unclear. Parker's description of the attack on the slave owner indicates its fierceness, but southerners especially emphasized and probably exaggerated the violence done to Gorsuch.

27 The jury of inquest consisted of Geoorge Whitson, John Rowland, E. Osborne Dare, Hiram Kinard, Samuel Miller, Lewis Cooper, George Firth, Wm. Knott, John Hillis, Wm. H. Millhouse, Joseph Richwane, and Miller Knott (Hensel, *Christiana*, p. 37). For John Beard's identity see n. 3, chapter 6.

28 Lancaster *Examiner and Herald*, September 17, 1851; for Kline testimony: Robbins, p. 60; for Brent: Robbins, p. 204.

29 Hensel, *Christiana*, pp. 53–54.

9. Arrests (pages 120–136)

1 Jackson, p. 67.

2 Reigart testimony: Robbins, pp. 93–95; Proudfoot testimony: Robbins, pp. 95–96.

3 Robbins, p. 93.

4 John Bacon testimony: Robbins, p. 165. Another witness, William Hopkins (p. 139), reports that Kline also had a "fight" or "a scuffle with a man by the name of Alberti." Alberti was the last name of a notorious slave catcher; this testimony seems to indicate his presence at Christiana, following the battle.

5 Robbins, p. 60.

6 Hensel, *Christiana*, pp. 40–41; Jackson, p. 43. Hensel mentions a dispute between Lancaster County District Attorney Thompson and U.S. Attorney Ashmead about whether the prisoners should be held for murder in Lancaster or treason in Philadelphia. Each party made their own arrests.

7 Still, p. 349.

8 Lancaster *Intelligencer*, September 16, 1851.

9 New York *Tribune*, n.d.: *Liberator*, October 3, 1851.

10 *Anti-Slavery Standard*, n.d.: *Liberator*, October 3, 1851.

11 Hensel, Christiana, p. 41.

12 Forbes, p. 36.

13 Hensel, *Christiana*, pp. 136–137; Reigart testimony: Robbins, pp. 93–95.

14 Hensel, *Christiana*, p. 137.

15 Hensel, "Aftermath," p. 140. R. M. Armstrong, who was a boy at the time of the resistance, and lived about five miles from Parker's, recalled many years later how "the United States Marshalls [sic] came into our locality and arrested every Blackman [sic] in that section taking from our farm four (4) men that did not have any thing to do with the killing. They were taken to Philadelphia and kept there for some months, . . ." and finally released (to Robert B. Risk, Council Grove, Kansas, September 11, 1911: Lanc. Co. Hist. Soc.).

16 Kline testimony: Lancaster *Examiner and Herald*, September 24, 1851; Jordan and Hines testimony: New York *Daily Times*, September 24, 1851.

17 Hensel, *Christiana*, pp. 42–43 (the last three lines of Wood's statement are transposed from an earlier section; a "t" has been added to "Scarlett").

18 *Liberator*, October 17, 1851; Smedley, pp. 125–126. The 1850 Census lists a "Catherine Warner," age fifty, "black," place of birth "Unknown." She was married to Isaac Warner, age seventy, "black," a laborer, place of birth "Unknown." The Census also lists "Catherine" as William and Eliza Parker's youngest daughter. Eliza Parker's will mentions a daughter named Cassandra (Book 28, No. 12879, Kent Co. Registry Office, Chatham, Ontario, Canada). William Parker's grandson Frank Parker listed "Cassie" as the name of one of his grandfather's children (interviewed by J. K., September 6, 1969).

19 New York *Tribune*, September 17, September 18, September 30, 1851. The first issue of the New York *Daily Times*, September 18, 1851, reports the arrest, near Christiana, of a fugitive slave named Abraham Hall. For Alberti see n. 4, this chapter. Smedley, p. 127.

20 Parker, pp. 293–294; Thomas Whitson, "The Early Abolitionists of Lanc. Co.," *Lanc. Co. Hist. Soc. Papers*, vol. 15 (1911), pp. 72–73.

21 Steele, pp. 1–2.

22 Smedley, p. 70.

23 A detailed, day-by-day enumeration of those arrested, the dates, charges, and outcome is found in Jackson (pp. 42–46). A transcript of the Christiana hearings of September 13–15, apparently copied from a newspaper, is found in Forbes (pp. 20–35).

24 Scott testimony: Forbes, pp. 22–23, 26–27; Lancaster *Examiner and Herald*, September 17, 1851.

25 Forbes, pp. 29, 35; Jackson, pp. 43–44.

26 Thomas Whitson, "The Hero of the Christiana Riot," *Lanc. Co. Hist. Soc. Papers*, vol. 1 (1896–1897), p. 31; Steele, p. 3 (Bill "Blair" corrected to "Baer").

27 Kline testimony: Forbes, p. 29; Steele, pp. 1, 3.

28 On the illness of Collister Wilson and James Moore: Robbins, pp. 70, 90; Jackson, p. 47; Steele, p. 3. Smedley (pp. 128–129) reports one version of a story widely circulated at the time: "One of the colored prisoners, a pious man, who was arrested and put in Moyamensing jail, was heard by Anthony E. Roberts, United States Marshal, praying to the Lord to 'shake Kline over Hell,' but in the fullness of his charity he ejaculated, 'but Lord, don't drop him in.' " Steele (p. 3) tells the same story, attributing the praying to Daniel Caulsberry.

29 New York *Daily Times*, n.d.: Lancaster *Examiner and Herald*, November 12, 1851; Jackson, p. 58.

30 Still, pp. 615–616.

31 Hensel, *Christiana*, p. 142.

10. Reaction (pages 137–155)

1 There are two studies of the press reaction to the Christiana "riot," Albert K. Hostetter, "The Newspapers and the Christiana Riot," *Lanc. Co. Hist. Soc. Papers*, vol. 15, no. 10 (December 1, 1911), pp. 296–308; Roderick W. Nash,

"The Christiana Riot: An Evaluation of Its National Significance," *Journal of the Lanc. Co. Hist. Soc.*, vol. 65, no. 2 (Spring 1961), pp. 65–91. The shorter excerpts from newspapers mentioned below are from Nash.

2 Fairfield (South Carolina) *Herald*, n.d.: *Liberator*, November 21, 1851.

3 Baltimore *Clipper*, September 20, 1851.

4 Washington, D.C. *Republic*, September 15, 1851.

5 New Orleans *Picayune*, September 17, 1851.

6 Raleigh (North Carolina) *Standard*, November 13, 1851; Jacksonville *Floridian and Journal*, September 18, 1851.

7 Boston *Journal*, September 16, 1851.

8 Philadelphia *Pennsylvania Inquirer*, September 17, 1851; New York *Courier and Enquirer*, September 17, 1851.

9 Boston *Journal*, September 16, 1851; New York *Express*, September 22, 1851; Lancaster *Examiner and Herald*, September 17, 1851.

10 September 29, 1851.

11 Rochester *Advertiser*, n.d.: *Douglass' Paper*, October 23, 1851.

12 September 20, 1851.

13 October 9, 1851.

14 September 15, 1851.

15 September 19, October 10, 1851.

16 *Pennsylvania Freeman*, n.d.: Forbes, p. 9.

17 September 25, 1851.

18 *Impartial Citizen*, n.d.: *Liberator*, October 3, 1851 [quoted in Herbert Aptheker, *A Documentary History of The Negro People in the United States* (New York, 1965) vol. 1, p. 324].

19 *Liberator*, October 24, 1851.

20 Lancaster *Examiner and Herald*, November 12, 1851.

21 Lancaster *Intelligencer*, November 11, 1851.

22 *Liberator*, November 1, 1851.

23 October 2, 1851.

24 "Letter No. XV," *Douglass' Paper*, October 9, 1851. This letter is unsigned, but the next letter in the series is signed "J.G."

25 Foner, vol. 2, pp. 50–54.

26 "The fight at Christiana," Douglass began, "continues to excite general discussion." The nation's reaction to the Gorsuch posse's fate was no less strong than its earlier reaction to the recent southern-sponsored, U.S.-based, ill-fated Cuban invasion: "The sensation produced by the death of the kidnappers is not surpassed by that which occurred throughout the country on the hearing of the fate of the Cuban invaders. The failure of these two patriotic expeditions, undertaken so nobly by our *law-abiding* citizens must long be regarded as among the most memorable events of this eventful year."

27 Frederick Douglass, "Freedom's Battle, . . ." On October 2, 1851, *Douglass' Paper* reports its editor had delivered "an able lecture," mentioning "in glowing terms, the noble and successful stand recently made by the colored men at Christiana . . ."

28 November 27, 1851; *Liberator*, November 14, 1851. At the same Rhode

Island meeting a Mr. Wheeler "criticized" the Reverend Theodore Parker's statement honoring armed black resistance. Mr. Wheeler "depreciated" the Reverend Mr. Parker's "approval of violent resistance to the Fugitive Slave Law." Douglass replied "that Mr. Parker was both consistent and right." *Frederick Douglass' Paper* reports: "The discussion was very interesting on both sides. . . ."

29 *Frederick Douglass' Paper*, October 16, 1851. Speakers at other New York City meetings in support of the Christiana resisters included a white man, Lewis W. Paine, who had spent six years in a Georgia prison for helping a runaway.

30 *Frederick Douglass' Paper*, November 13, 1851.

31 *Frederick Douglass' Paper,* January 8, 1852.

32 *Frederick Douglass' Paper*, November 13, 1851; *Pennsylvania Freeman*, February 12, 1852.

33 *Voice of the Fugitive*, December 3, 1851.

34 *Voice of the Fugitive*, January 15, 1852.

35 *Voice of the Fugitive*, February 12, 1852.

36 Samuel Ringold Ward, *Autobiography of a Fugitive Negro* . . . (Toronto, 1855), pp. 116–117.

11. Treason (pages 156–173)

1 Lancaster *Examiner and Herald*, September 24, 1851.

2 Baltimore *Weekly Sun*, September 20, 1851; Hensel, *Christiana*, pp. 38–39.

3 Hensel, *Christiana*, p. 39. A letter from Z. Collins Lee, a U.S. District Attorney of Baltimore, and a speaker at the meeting, to President Fillmore (September 26, 1851: Buffalo and Erie Co. Hist. Soc.) says the crowd numbered 10,000.

4 Philadelphia *Pennsylvanian*, September 20, 1851; Hensel, *Christiana*, pp. 39, 145; Richard Grau, "The Christiana Riot of 1851: A Reappraisal," *Journal of the Lanc. Co. Hist. Soc.*, vol. 68, no. 4 (1964), pp. 164, n.1; 172–173.

5 A. McClure, *Old Time Notes of Pennsylvania* (Philadelphia, 1905), pp. 188–189.

6 George E. Reed, ed. *Papers of the Governors, 1845–1858*, Pennsylvania Archives, 4th Series, vol. 7 (Harrisburg, 1900), p. 280.

7 A. McClure, *Old Time Notes*, pp. 188–189; Hensel, *Christiana*, pp. 51–53.

8 Hensel, *Christiana*, pp. 145–146.

9 Hensel, *Christiana*, pp. 146–147.

10 Hensel, *Christiana*, pp. 49–50; the Reverend J. S. Gorsuch to Pennsylvania Attorney General Thomas E. Franklin, Washington, D.C., October 6, 1851: Lancaster *Examiner and Herald*, October 14, 1851.

11 Hensel, *Christiana*, pp. 148–150.

12 Lancaster *Intelligencer*, September 18, 1851.

13 Lancaster *Examiner and Herald*, October 1, 1851.

14 To Attorney General Franklin, Washington, D.C., October 6, 1851.

15 Hensel, *Christiana*, pp. 51–53.

16 Hensel, *Christiana*, pp. 150–151.

17 H. G. Ashmead to W. U. Hensel, August 20, 1911 (original in Lanc. Co. Hist. Soc.). "Critendon" corrected to "Crittenden" throughout. Hensel (*Christiana*, p. 62) includes a slightly different quote, probably received verbally from H. G. Ashmead. Hensel says the final decision to prosecute for treason was made by Webster and Crittenden who "felt that even if a conviction were not obtained, the effect of the trial would be salutary in checking Northern opposition to the Fugitive Slave Act" (see chapter 16, n. 16).

18 James Willard Hurst, *The Law of Treason in the United States* (Westport, Connecticut, 1971), p. 199.

19 Hurst, pp. 260–261.

20 Hensel, *Christiana*, p. 43; J. S. Gorsuch to Pennsylvania Attorney General Franklin, Washington, D.C., October 6, 1851: Lancaster *Examiner and Herald*, October 14, 1851.

21 Also present for the defense were George M. Kline, George Ford, and O. J. Dickey (Jackson, p. 45).

22 According to Jackson (p. 45) the prosecution lawyers were Thomas E. Franklin, Pennsylvania Attorney General; John L. Thompson, Lancaster County District Attorney; John W. Ashmead, U.S. District Attorney for the Eastern District of Pennsylvania; R. J. Brent, Attorney General of Maryland. Hensel (*Christiana*, p. 44) adds Col. William B. Fordney.

23 Lancaster *Examiner and Herald*, October 1, 1851; *Report*, pp. 18–20; Z. C. Lee letter in Buffalo Hist. Soc.; Lee identified in Jackson, pp. 54–55, 57.

24 Kane charge of September 29, 1851: Robbins, pp. 268–269.

25 Kane charge of November 18, 1851, and background on Kane: Hensel, *Christiana*, pp. 57–78. Judge Kane's two abolitionist sons, Thomas L. and Robert P., mentioned: Still, pp. 366–367.

26 Robbins, pp. 268–269; Hensel, *Christiana*, p. 58.

27 "District Court United States, No. 229, August Sessions, 1851. The United States of America vs. . . . True Bill . . . November 13, 1851" (Gen. Archives Division, National Archives, Washington, D.C.). This bill of indictments, submitted to the Circuit Court on December 1, 1851, is recorded in Robbins, pp. 89–90. Nash, "Christiana," n. 25, p. 87.

28 Of those charged, eight—William Parker, Joshua Hammond, Nelson Ford, Noah Buley, Ezekiel Thompson, Isaiah Clarkson, George Thompson, and Daniel Caulsberry—were probably all active in the battle. In addition, William Howard, James Dorsey, John Long, and Henry C. Hopkins were probably active, although not charged. S. Williams was charged and had brought warning. Reports vary of the number of blacks imprisoned; Hensel (*Christiana*, pp. 83–85), quoting from an unidentified newspaper, says twenty-four; in another place Hensel (*Christiana*, p. 97), quoting from the *Pennsylvania Freeman*, December 4, 1851), says twenty-seven. Still (p. 357) mentions twenty-seven blacks being imprisoned.

29 Still, p. 362; Hensel, *Christiana*, p. 43.

30 John Roberts testimony: Robbins, pp. 101–102; Whitson, "Hero," p. 31; Smedley, p. 216.

31 Enoch Harlan testimony: Robbins, p. 145; Hensel, *Christiana*, pp. 80, 129.
32 Jackson, pp. 47–48; Robbins, p. 99. Hensel (*Christiana*, p. 60) says the escape took place on November 15.
33 Robert James Brent, "Report of the Attorney General . . . ," Maryland General Assembly Documents (Annapolis, 1852), pp. 4–5; Hensel, *Christiana*, p. 47; Jackson, p. 48; Smedley, p. 127.
34 Still, p. 357.

12. Prosecution (pages 177–195)

1 Jackson, p. 52; David Paul Brown, *The Forum* . . . (Philadelphia, 1856), vol. 2, p. 98.
2 Jackson, pp. 50–53; Jean Jacques Antoine Ampère, *Promenade en Amerique* (Paris, 1855), vol. 1, pp. 408–410.
3 Jackson, pp. 54–55, 57.
4 Robbins, p. 91; Louis E. Lowe, "Annual Message . . ." Maryland General Assembly Documents (Annapolis, 1852), pp. 37–38.
5 Jackson (pp. 49–50) says Brent managed the prosecution, but this is apparently false.
6 Jackson, pp. 49–50.
7 Hensel, *Christiana*, pp. 11, 46; Thomas Frederick Woodley, *Thaddeus Stevens* (Harrisburg, 1934), p. 140; J. A. Woodburn, *The Life of Thaddeus Stevens* (Indianapolis, 1913), p. 124; Jackson, p. 74.
8 McClure, *Recollections*, p. 22; Hensel, *Christiana*, pp. 63–64.
9 Brown, pp. 100–101; John William Wallace, *Cases in the Circuit Court of the United States* . . . (Philadelphia, 1854), vol. 2, p. 135.
10 Robbins, pp. 11–12.
11 Jackson, p. 53; Robbins, pp. 12–13, 44–45.
12 Robbins, p. 39.
13 Robbins, pp. 12, 178.
14 For Brent: Robbins, pp. 199–200; for Jackson, p. 73.
15 Robbins, pp. 18–19, 46–47, 243–244.
16 Robbins, p. 19.
17 Jackson, p. 47; Brent, pp. 4–5; Hensel, *Christiana*, p. 73.
18 Jackson, p. 55.
19 Robbins, pp. 26–27, 39, 41, 273–274. The prisoner, Hanway, entitled to thirty-four challenges, actually challenged twenty-four potential jurors. The prosecution set aside thirty-six jurors (Robbins, p. 107).
20 Hensel, *Christiana*, pp. 65–74.
21 Hensel, *Christiana*, pp. 96–97. Jackson (p. 70) identifies this story as coming from the *Pennsylvania Freeman*, December 4, 1851.
22 Brent, p. 4.
23 Still, p. 366.
24 Hensel, *Christiana*, p. 97.
25 Jackson, p. 56; Robbins, p. 45.

26 Robbins, pp. 46, 49.
27 Robbins, pp. 50, 53–54.
28 Robbins, p. 94; Hensel, *Christiana*, p. 76.
29 Kline testimony: Robbins, pp. 56–58.
30 Robbins, pp. 55–56.
31 Robbins, p. 59.
32 Robbins, pp. 58–59, 68.
33 Brent, p. 5.
34 Robbins, pp. 68, 70–72; Jackson, pp. 58–59.
35 Robbins, pp. 74–75, 79.
36 Robbins, p. 83.
37 Robbins, pp. 75, 83, 86. See chapter 7, pp. 92–93.
38 Knott testimony: Robbins, pp. 88–91; Reigart testimony: Robbins, pp. 93–94; Proudfoot testimony: Robbins, p. 95; Smith testimony: pp. 97–98.
39 Robbins, pp. 99–101 ("Scarlet" corrected to "Scarlett," "Pownell" corrected to "Pownall," punctuation edited for clarity).
40 Robbins, pp. 101–102.
41 For Samuel Hanson: Robbins, pp. 102–103; for Samuel Thompson: Robbins, pp. 102–105. Parker (pp. 165, 284) identifies a "Samuel Thompson" as one of his men, and a Gorsuch fugitive active in the battle. There is no indication that the "Samuel Thompson" who testified as a prosecution witness was a Gorsuch slave. The 1850 Census lists a Samuel Thompson as living with the Joseph Moore family. For Jacob Woods: Robbins, p. 105.
42 Robbins, p. 105; Jackson, p. 61.

13. Defense (pages 196–205)

1 Robbins, p. 107.
2 Robbins, p. 109.
3 For Stevens: Robbins, p. 112; for Grier: Robbins, p. 114.
4 Robbins, pp. 115–117.
5 Robbins, p. 117.
6 Robbins, pp. 117–118; Jackson, p. 62.
7 Robbins, pp. 120–125.
8 Robbins, p. 125.
9 Robbins, p. 127.
10 Robbins, p. 128.
11 Robbins, pp. 129–131.
12 For Patterson and Henderson: Robbins, p. 131.
13 Robbins, pp. 141–142.
14 Robbins, p. 143.
15 Robbins, pp. 131–132, 134–135.
16 Robbins, pp. 144–146.
17 For Harlan: Robbins, pp. 144–145; for defense closing: Robbins, p. 146.

14. Rebuttal (pages 206–216)

1 For Ashmead: Robbins, p. 146; for prosecution character witnesses:
Robbins, pp. 149–158.
2 For Keyser: Robbins, pp. 149, 151; Jackson, pp. 65–66.
3 For Ashmead: Robbins, p. 159; for Grier: Robbins, p. 161.
4 Robbins, p. 147 (see also pp. 162–163).
5 Robbins, pp. 59, 65–66.
6 Robbins, pp. 135–138.
7 Robbins, pp. 138–139.
8 Robbins, p. 139.
9 Robbins, p. 166.
10 Robbins, p. 166; Brent, p. 5.
11 Robbins, p. 166; Jackson, p. 48.
12 Robbins, p. 166.
13 Robbins, pp. 167–168.

15. Summations (pages 217–229)

1 For Ludlow: Robbins, pp. 176–177; for Lewis: Robbins, p. 184.
2 Jackson, pp. 69, 76.
3 Hensel, *Christiana*, pp. 83–85 (newspaper not identified).
4 Robbins, pp. 227–228.
5 For Ludlow: Robbins, p. 169; for Brent: Robbins, p. 197.
6 Robbins, pp. 182, 184–185.
7 Robbins, p. 185.
8 Robbins, p. 207.
9 For Ludlow: Robbins, p. 176; for Brent: Robbins, p. 201.
10 Robbins, p. 183.
11 Robbins, pp. 179, 183–185.
12 Robbins, p. 231.
13 Robbins, p. 197.
14 Robbins, pp. 183, 204.
15 Robbins, pp. 213, 216.
16 For Ludlow: Robbins, p. 173; for Brent: Robbins, p. 212; for Read:
Robbins, p. 182.
17 Robbins, p. 173.
18 Robbins, pp. 196–198.
19 Robbins, p. 204.
20 Robbins, p. 202.
21 Robbins, p. 214.
22 Robbins, p. 186.
23 Robbins, pp. 193, 196 (question mark added to last sentence).
24 Robbins, pp. 192–195, 198, 215.
25 Robbins, p. 177.
26 Robbins, p. 239.
27 Robbins, p. 195.

16. Verdict (pages 230–243)

1 Robbins, p. 241.
2 Robbins, pp. 242–243.
3 Robbins, p. 244.
4 Robbins, p. 247.
5 Robbins, p. 248.
6 I am indebted to Hurst (p. 225) for this point.
7 Hensel, *Christiana*, p. 89; Jackson, p. 69; Robbins, pp. 248–249 (punctuation edited for clarity).
8 Robbins, p. 249; Jackson, p. 80.
9 Hensel, *Christiana*, p. 92.
10 Parker, pp. 294–295. A contemporary version of George Williams's escape, by William Still (*Douglass' Paper*, February 19, 1852), generally corroborates Hensel and Parker. Still identifies the lawyer aiding Kline as "Lee," and the tavern stopping place as in Penningtonville. Another source on Williams's escape is a letter to the Philadelphia *Times*, n.d.; West Chester, Pennsylvania, *Daily Local News*, June 5, 1893, (Chester Co. Hist. Soc.).
11 Smedley, pp. 127–128.
12 Parker, p. 295.
13 Hensel, *Christiana*, pp. 98–99; Jackson, p. 83.
14 September 16, 1851; Lancaster *Examiner and Herald*, September 17, 1851.
15 Still, pp. 367–368. Jackson (p. 85) says $50,000; the Toronto *Globe* (tri-weekly ed., May 15, 1851) says $70,000.
16 Hensel, *Christiana*, p. 91; A. H. H. Stuart, Sec'y., Dept. of the Interior, to J. W. Ashmead, November 6, 14, 1851 (Dept. of Interior, Letter Book, Judiciary no. 1, 1849–1853, National Archives, Justice and Executive Branch, Washington, D.C.). There are also another 112 pages of documents concerning Alderman J. Franklin Reigart's demand for payment from the United States Government for expenses incurred by himself, Lancaster District Attorney John L. Thompson, Christiana Constable William Proudfoot, and hotel keeper Frederick Zercher (Attorney General's Papers, Letters received from the President, National Archives, Legislative, Judical and Fiscal Branch, Civil Archives Division, Washington, D.C.).
17 Hensel, *Christiana*, pp. 93–94.
18 Larry Gara, *The Liberty Line* (Lexington, Kentucky, 1967), p. 135.
19 *Pennsylvania Freeman*, n.d.; *Liberator*, January 9, 1852. Hensel (*Christiana*, p. 94) gives the date of a meeting at which Giddings spoke as December 18, a Thursday. But the *Freeman* places the meeting on a Tuesday. *Pennsylvania Anti-Slavery Society, 15th Annual Report* (1852) comments that the Christiana treason prosecutions "made known to the rulers of the country, and to the country itself, a degree and extent of sympathy with abolitionism which before had hardly been suspected. Instead of arresting the progress of our movement, and suppressing all agitation on the subject, they only gave a new impulse to discussion, and aroused the friends of the cause to fresh zeal and activity. The result of the trials was, on the whole, an anti-slavery victory (p. 8)." The 15th

Annual Meeting of the Pennsylvania Anti-Slavery Society took place in West Chester, on October 25, 1852. At this meeting feminist and abolitionist Lucy Stone stated that she "did not agree with Gerrit Smith, that this nation had sinned away its day of grace, and that reform was hopeless . . . ." She believed that anti-slavery work could make this "a nation truly free and just." Abolitionists, said Stone, need courage and firmness, and as at Christiana, should choose prison or to be hung, rather than falter. Quaker Thomas Whitson objected to the 1852 *Annual Report*'s admission that the acts of the Gorsuch posse and the Government's prosecutions "might have done service to our cause. He thought the cause had gone forward in *spite* of such acts, and that it would have gone forward more rapidly had these wicked acts never been performed." Whitson added: "Had the colored men who shot Gorsuch only resisted by moral power, refusing to serve the slave holder, and choosing to die themselves rather than submit to him, or kill him, it would have told more for freedom than it did tell." J. M. McKim remarked that Whitson agreed with the 1852 *Report* in conceding that the actions of the Christiana blacks did *"something"* for the cause of freedom, while maintaining that "moral obligations" forbid us to resort to similar violent actions (*Pennsylvania Anti-Slavery Society, 15th Annual Report*, pp. 40–42).

20 Hensel, *Christiana*, p. 94.
21 Gara, p. 134.
22 Lowe, p. 40.
23 Still, pp. 356–357.
24 Still, pp. 367–368.
25 Douglass, *Life*, p. 282.
26 Hensel, "Aftermath," pp. 140–141.

17. Escape (pages 247–261)

1 I am more confident of the usefulness and general accuracy of these underground railroad reminiscences than some other historians, notably Larry Gara in *The Liberty Line* (Lexington, Kentucky, 1967), p. 174, and Joseph H. Smith, "Some Aspects of the Underground Railway, . . ." *Bulletin of the Montgomery Co. Hist. Soc.*, vol. 3, no. 7 (October, 1941), p. 7. Smith, a Pennsylvanian whose paper was read to the Montgomery County Historical Society, November 21, 1931, concludes: "It is no longer possible to credit any of the local tales which have been told about the flight of William Parker and his friends from Christiana to Canada. . . ." Smith then lists several of these allegedly conflicting accounts, but unfortunately fails to mention where they may be found, thus adding immensely to the historian's difficulty in evaluating them.

I have been able to locate the sources of all but one of these stories: Smith mentions two published accounts by Dr. Hiram Corson; one is a letter in Still (p. 723); the other is an article ["The Abolitionists of Montgomery County, . . ." *Papers of the Montgomery Co. Hist. Soc.*, vol. 2 (1900), pp. 1–76]. Jacob L. Paxson's account (which Smith says is not substantiated by Hiram

Corson) is in Smedley (pp. 223–225). I have not located Isaac Roberts's account, which Smith says contradicts Corson's two accounts. Smith says that William Parker's narrative contradicts all the others. Graceanna Lewis of Chester County, says Smith, never mentioned to "anyone now living" (1931!) the part assigned to her in Parker's escape (in Still, p. 750). Smith himself further adds to the confusion by mysteriously suggesting that there is some "uninvestigated remark" of William Still's which might provide "a clue to the unraveling of this confusion of statements . . ." Although this is not clear, Smith may be referring to Still's revelations about U.S. Marshal A. E. Roberts's aiding in the escape from jail of two black prosecution witnesses in the Christiana case (Still, p. 357). Although these various accounts are not as contradictory as Smith would suggest, they do contain contradictory details. Despite these, the general sense these documents convey of the underground railroad in action seems to me to be fairly trustworthy.

2 Smedley, pp. 30, 81–82. Elijah Lewis's testimony (Robbins, p. 122) confirms William Howard's presence at Parker's at the time of battle. Charles Long's presence at the battle is not documented, but a John Long was wounded in the confrontation (Dr. Cain testimony: Robbins, pp. 100–101). J. Long's injury is mentioned by Smedley (pp. 126–127). John Long, a black, is listed on the 1850 Census. Perhaps the same three men are the unnamed participants in the Christiana "riot" who came to Dr. J. K. Eshelman's, near Downingtown, and "were kept in the barn until next night, and then sent further on" (Smedley, p. 66).

3 Parker, p. 288.

4 J. S. Gorsuch, letter of September "17," 1851; C. M. Burleigh in Still, p. 351; Smedley, p. 120.

5 There are five versions of this incident at the Pownalls': 1) George Steele, p. 2; 2) Elizabeth Price Lewis, "The Story of the Christiana Riot As Told By A Great Niece of Elijah Lewis" (this is the version told to her by George P. Orr, whose great grandfather was Levi Pownall), MS. in Lanc. Co. Hist. Soc.; 3) George P. Orr, "The Christiana Riot," *Tredyffrin Easttown Hist. Club Quarterly*, vol. 5, no. 4 (1943), p. 86, mimeographed pamphlet in Chester Co. Hist. Soc.; 4) Smedley, pp. 121–122; 5) Hensel, *Christiana*, pp. 36, n. J, p. 138. Smedley (pp. 123–124) reports: "A few days after the riot a lawyer came to Pownall's, read a paper to them giving a notice of a suit, and claiming damages for harboring the slaves of Edward Gorsuch. The names of Gorsuch's slaves with alleged aliases were given. Among the aliases were the names of Parker, Pinkney [sic] and Johnson. The date of the escape of Gorsuch's slaves was given correctly, but Parker, Pinkney and Johnson had been in the neighborhood several years before. Sarah Pownall noticed this error, and when the lawyer finished reading, she asked to see the paper. It was given to her. She handed it to a friend who was present, and called his attention to the date. He read it, and testified that Parker had worked for him and for others two years before that time. Seeing the clearness of this error the lawyer took the paper again in his hands. Sarah remarked to him, 'We are witnesses to the date in that paper, and it cannot be changed. It proves that there was no warrant for the arrest of the men living in

our house, but for other men; and *we* have a legal claim for damages against those who entered our house and destroyed property. Thee has no legal claim against us.' Nothing further was ever said about a suit for damages."

6 Robbins, p. 84; Smedley, p. 123; Steele, pp. 2–3.

7 Parker, p. 288.

8 Smedley, pp. 248, 260.

9 Smedley, pp. 251–253.

10 Still, p. 749.

11 Smedley, pp. 251–253.

12 Parker, pp. 288–289. Another version of this incident is contained in an item from the Philadelphia *Times*, n.d., in the West Chester, Pennsylvania, *Daily Local News*, June 5, 1893 (clippings file, Chester Co. Hist. Soc.).

13 Smedley, pp. 223–224 (paragraphing added); description of Paxson: Smith, p. 17.

14 Another version of Parker's Norristown stop is by Dr. Hiram Corson, "The Abolitionists of Montgomery Co. . . . , *Mont. Co. Hist. Soc. Papers*, vol. 2 (1900), pp. 36–37. Dr. H. Corson reports that one of the blacks actively involved in the Christiana resistance and death of Edward Gorsuch (Corson recalled that it was Parker) was, for two or three weeks, "while he was being hunted, . . . concealed in the house of a colored abolitionist, a former slave, in Norristown. . . . His hiding place in Norristown was, of course, at 'Old Dan's,' where more slaves were sheltered than in any other place in our county." The white abolitionists of the area were said to have aided Dan and his wife in this work.

Dr. Corson continues: "I was one evening standing on the pavement in front of [my] brother William's office, when a very light touch on my shoulder caused me to look round and be face to face with Dan. In a low voice he said, 'We want money; Dr. William guv me some. . . . We want to pay for a carriage to take *him* to Bucks County.'

"*Him* meant the fugitive who, though charged with the murder, solemnly declared that it occurred in the struggle to get away from Gorsuch." The fugitive claimed that in this struggle Gorsuch had been accidentally shot with his own gun.

Dr. Corson says: "After giving my contribution to Dan I left for home. At 10 p.m., in that beautiful moonlight night, a few persons were, by appointment, on the common . . . when a carriage drove up to take the fugitive to an underground railroad station. Isaac Roberts, Jacob Hoffman, Larry Corson and, I think, Lloyd Jones were present. Old Dan and the fugitive were too, promptly on hand. As he was parting from them, Larry said to him: 'Now, don't be taken alive.' "

At this, says Corson, the fugitive "drew from some place in his clothes a pistol and merely said, 'that was Gorsuch's.' All felt that enough had been said.

"A moment more and he was in the carriage en route to the designated underground station on his way to Canada. . . .'"

In an earlier account, a letter dated November 1, 1871, Hiram Corson says it was in the Norristown home of a black underground railroad agent Daniel Ross "that the Gorsuch murderer was secreted" (Still, p. 723).

15 Parker, p. 289.

16 Moore's grandson recalls that one of the fugitive slaves who had reached this Quakertown station about 1850 "seemed especially brave, being destitute of fear even in that most trying time. He was . . . known as Bill Budd at home, but on running away from bondage assumed the name of Henry Franklin. . . . This man did not care to be sent to Canada, and was employed as a carter by Richard Moore for several years. During that time he was often engaged in carting coal from the Lehigh River. . . . When slaves were to be sent northward, he would load his wagon with them in the evening, cover them well with straw, and take them up during the night, giving them a start on the lonely journey toward Friendsville; he would then return with a load of coal the next day" [Edward H. Magill, "When Men Were Sold," *Bucks Co. Hist. Soc. Proceedings*, vol. 2 (1909), pp. 501–502].

17 Parker, pp. 289–290.

18 Parker, p. 290; Douglass, *Life*, pp. 281–282.

19 The female visitor mentioned by Parker may have been Douglass's white assistant editor Julia Griffiths, who aided Parker's escape and mentions receiving a letter from a black "Hannible" in Canada ("Letter No. XV," *Douglass' Paper*, November 13, 1851).

20 *Syracuse League*, n.d.: *Liberator*, October 3, 1851; Parker, p. 290.

21 Foner, vol. 2, n. 16, p. 545.

22 Douglass, *Life*, pp. 281–282. I have deleted the section in which Douglass indicates that Parker reached his house "two days and nights" after the Christiana battle. Parker and the Syracuse newspaper indicate that Parker arrived at Douglass's on Saturday, September 20, nine days after the resistance.

23 Parker, p. 290.

18. Canada (pages 262–276)

1 Parker, p. 155.

2 Parker, pp. 290–291.

3 Roman J. Zorn, "Criminal Extradition Menaces the Canadian Haven for Fugitive Slaves, 1841–1861," *Canadian Historical Review*, vol. 38 (December 1957), pp. 284–294. No additional information has been found on the attempt to extradite Parker.

4 The "Government House" was a frame residence located on the corner of King and Simcoe streets (Frank Yeigh, *Ontario's Parliament Buildings* . . . (Toronto, 1893), p. 84.

5 George Steele (p. 1) claims that Parker had told him of being a fugitive slave.

6 Parker (p. 291) adds: "Many coming in at this time on business, I was told to call again at three o'clock, which I did. The person in the office, a clerk, told me to take no further trouble about it, until that day four weeks. 'But you are as free a man as I am,' said he. When I told the news to Pinckney and Johnson, they were greatly relieved in mind."

7 Parker, pp. 288, 291–292.

8 Smedley, p. 125.

9 Smedley, pp. 92–93. "Caln" is the name of a town.

10 Parker, p. 292.

11 On July 5, 1852, T. Hennings, Secretary of the Canadian Anti-Slavery Society, protested to Henry Bibb that the *Voice of the Fugitive* had not reported that William Parker and the other fugitives from Christiana "had been kindly received by the Society in Toronto,—aided by them during the winter, and supplied with money to convey them to the Elgin Settlement, if not to pay a part of their first instalment for their farms" (*Voice of the Fugitive*, July 15, 1852).

12 Fred Landon, "The Buxton Settlement in Canada," *Journal of Negro History*, vol. 3 (October 1918), p. 360; Robin W. Winks, " 'A Sacred Animosity': Abolitionism in Canada," in Martin Duberman, ed., *The Antislavery Vanguard* . . . (Princeton, 1965), pp. 310–311, 318.

13 Parker, p. 292.

14 Benjamin Quarles, *Black Abolitionists* (New York, 1969), pp. 61–62.

15 Letter dated St. Catharines, May 25, 1852.

16 An item in Henry Bibb's *Voice of the Fugitive* (June 17, 1852) reports that on June 3, 1852, "a telegraphic despatch was received in Detroit, from Toledo, ordering the arrest of three colored men, who would arrive in Detroit on board of a steamboat the same afternoon. When the steamer arrived, the Sheriff was on the alert, and arrested the men, and conveyed them to gaol in a carriage, the sight of which created a suspicion, and caused an excitement among the colored population of the city." Bibb reports that the Sheriff, not knowing with what crime the black men were charged, announced he would telegraph Toledo for information. The excited black Detroiters grew quieter as they awaited the reply. The answering telegram from Toledo asked only that the blacks be held until more information could be obtained from Kentucky.

Meanwhile, says Bibb, the Detroit District Attorney called the three black men "into the Hall, to interrogate them in relation to what crime, if any they had committed. The fugitives, seeing an opportunity to escape, took to their heels and cleared the prison; and, although a large number of colored people were keeping watch around the prison, they so little expected such an event, that they did not see the escaping fugitives, else they could have been landed in Canada in 15 minutes. But they wandered alone on the shores of the city, for a chance to cross, for half the night. At last they seized on a boat and crossed over. . . ." Bibb adds that the fugitives' escape might have been "*connived*" at by "prominent" Michigan politicians, who did not relish the embarrassment of a fugitive slave case at a "critical moment of Presidential nominations."

The three fugitives' escape is also reported in the Detroit *Tribune* (n.d., cited in the following), the Detroit *Michigan Christian Herald* (June 10, 1852), and the Detroit *Daily Advertiser* (June 5, 1852).

17 Parker, p. 292.

18 Victor Ullman, *Look to the North Star; A Life of William King* (Boston, 1969), pp. 108, 118–119, 128. Typescript King's autobiography, pp. 77–78, in Buxton Museum, Buxton, Ontario, Canada. This typescript is made from

photocopies of the original manuscript in the Public Archives, Ottawa, Canada. Also see William H. and Jane H. Pease, *Black Utopia: Negro Communal Experiments in America* (Madison, Wisconsin, 1963), chapter 5 on the Elgin (or Buxton) settlement, pp. 84–108.

19 Ullman, pp. 178–180.

20 *Douglass' Paper*, August 25, 1854. Perhaps the relation between King and the black people of Buxton was not so idyllic as Douglass painted it. Present-day members of old Buxton families relate some critical and apparently traditional legends about the founding father.

21 Benjamin Drew, *Northside View of Slavery* (Boston, 1856), p. 297. This book includes a section on the Buxton settlement.

22 King's "Autobiography," pp. 79–80.

23 Parker, pp. 292–293.

24 William King Papers, Manuscript Group 24, J. 14, Public Archives, Ottawa, Canada. Abraham Johnson is said to have paid off $180 for fifty acres of Lot 10 on June 29, 1864 (Victor Ullman to J. K., February 6, 1968). On September 26, 1865, Parker leased some land to Edward H. Jones for oil digging (Book D, Raleigh Folio, 605, Doc. 257, Kent County Registry Office, Chatham, Ontario, Canada). A *Gazeteer and Directory of the Counties of Kent, Lambton and Essex, 1866–67*, lists William Parker (p. 84) as holding two properties in Kent County, the 12th Lot of Concession 12 and the 20th Lot of Concession 8; Abraham Johnson is listed (p. 82) as holding the 10th Lot of Concession 13 (information furnished by the Moore Memorial Library, Christiana, Pennsylvania). On September 25, 1867, William Parker paid off $150 and received a deed to his fifty acres of the west half of the southeast half of Lot 12 in the 12th Concession of Raleigh Township (Book E, p. 413, Doc. 224, Kent County Registry Office). Several other legal documents concerning the Parkers can be found in the same office: William J. Parker, Jr., etc., to Elizabeth A. E. Parker, September 5, 1889, quitclaim to property (Book E, No. 9179 Raleigh); Eliza A. Parker, will, July 18, 1891, probated July 10, 1899 (Book 28, No. 12879 Raleigh); Cynthia A. M. [Parker] Chase to Cassandra [Parker] Goodall, August 31, 1901, quitclaim to property (Folio 799, No. 13571 Raleigh).

Three sources name William and Eliza Parker's children: 1) The 1850 Census of Sadsbury Township lists Mariah L., age four, John "T" or "J," age two, and Catherine, age one, all born in Pennsylvania. 2) Eliza Parker's will lists Francis M., Cassandra (Parker) Goodall, Samuel, Alfred J., Cynthia (Parker) Chase, William J., Mary (Parker) Ellis. 3) Frank Parker (William and Eliza's grandson, interviewed in 1969) listed Frank, Alfred, William, Samuel, Cynthia, Cassie, Mary.

25 The history of the Buxton school is recounted by Winks, pp. 314–316; Pease, pp. 101–103; Ullman, pp. 145–162. Two of the Buxtonites at Trinity won the highest honors in the history of their college up to that time. Among the graduates of the Buxton school were James T. Rapier, later the first black congressman from Alabama, and Thomas W. Stringer, a black leader of the Mississippi Constitutional Convention of 1868.

26 Parker, p. 293.

27 Parker, p. 158. In closing his narrative Parker thanks "Almighty God for the many mercies and favors he has bestowed upon me, and especially for delivering me out of the hands of slaveholders, and placing me in a land of liberty. . . ." This seemingly conflicts with Parker's earlier emphasis on himself as his own liberating agent.

19. Epilogue (pages 277–299)

1 Still, pp. 198, 200. Perhaps Hill had seen a report about Hanway petitioning the United States Government for financial relief. The West Chester, Pennsylvania, *Village Record* (January 18, 1853, May 23, 1854) reports Hanway's attempts to seek repayment for the costs of his trial (Chester Co. Hist. Soc.).

2 *The Provincial Freeman*, March 22, 1856 ("Desoline" corrected to "Dessalines").

3 Foner, vol. 2, pp. 426–439.

4 Letter dated Philadelphia, August 10, 1858, signed "W. W. B.": *Liberator*, August 20, 1858.

5 James Cleland Hamilton, "John Brown in Canada," *The Canadian Magazine*, vol. 4 (December 1894), p. 124.

6 Letter from Sandusky, Ohio: *Calendar of Virginia State Papers*, vol. 2, pp. 315–317; also in Toronto *Weekly Globe*, November 4, 1859; part of this letter is quoted in Landon, "Buxton Settlement," p. 367.

7 *Anglo-African Magazine*, vol. 1, no. 1, p. 2.

8 *Anglo-African Magazine*, vol. 1, no. 2, p. 48.

9 Boston *Evening Transcript*, December 3, 1860, in: Foner, *Douglass*, vol. 2, pp. 571–572.

10 *Douglass' Monthly*, January 1861, in: Foner, vol. 2, pp. 533–538 (brackets in original).

11 Hensel, *Christiana*, pp. 27, 126.

12 Myles Jackson, "Two Man War . . . ," Side 1.

13 Parker, 152–153.

14 The Shadd Ledger is in the Buxton Museum, Buxton, Ontario, Canada. I am indebted to Vivian Robbins Chavis for showing me the ledger and suggesting to whom it refers. The diary entries do not specify the year, but a perpetual calendar indicates that March 1, 1858, was a Monday, and March 16, 1858, a Tuesday. The diary also mentions John Brown's May 8 and 10, 1858, meetings in Chatham. Anderson Abbot is identified in Ullman, pp. 156, 235, 239, 289, 294–299, 326. Alexander T. Augusta is mentioned in James M. McPherson, *The Negro's Civil War* . . . (New York, 1967), pp. 261–262; Ullman, pp. 240, 295–296.

15 Parker, pp. 282, 293. Parker (p. 288) indicates that at the time his narrative was written he was still in touch with Gorsuch's fugitives.

16 Charles W. Morton (associate editor, *Atlantic Monthly*) to Victor Ullman, November 9, 1966. Mr. Ullman has kindly furnished me with a typed copy of this letter.

17 Parker, pp. 152–153.

18 Marian Gleason McDougall, *Fugitive Slaves* (*1619–1865*) (Boston, 1891), p. 128; Siebert, p. 373.

19 Hensel, *Christiana*, n. N, pp. 139–140.

20 Hensel, *Christiana*, pp. 101–103.

21 "William Parker and the Christiana Riot," vol. 46, no. 1 (January 1961), n. 2, p. 23. In the Spring 1961 *Journal of the Lanc. Co. Hist. Soc.*, R. W. Nash repeats that the narrative was "written for the admittedly illiterate Parker by a sympathetic editor" ("Christiana Riot," p. 90).

22 Parker, p. 292.

23 Parker, pp. 153, 280.

24 "Christiana Riot" clippings file, Chester Co. Hist. Soc., West Chester, Pennsylvania.

25 For history of Lincoln University: Thomas Jesse Jones, ed., *Negro Education* . . . , Department of the Interior, Bureau of Education Bulletin No. 38 (Washington, D.C., 1916–1917), pp. 689–691; Horace Mann Bond to J. K., August 20, 1969 [Bond's source is George P. Carr, *John Miller Dickey* . . . (rev. and ed. by William P. Finney, Philadelphia, 1929), pp. 150–153].

26 Lancaster *Examiner and Herald*, September 4, 1872. William H. Day was editor of "Our National Progress," published in Wilmington, Delaware, from 1870 to 1875 [Armistad S. Pride, "A register and history of Negro newspapers in the U.S.: 1827–1950" (Evanston, Illinois, microfilm of typescript, Schomberg Collection, New York), p. 203.] Pride says no copies of this paper exist. If copies could be found for July, August, September, 1872, there would undoubtedly be some interesting reference to William Parker. Did he, for instance, in September 1872, attend a twenty-first anniversary commemoration of the Christiana resistance?

27 Foner, vol. 4, pp. 82–85.

28 Hensel, *Christiana*, n. E, p. 136. ("Sims" corrected to "Simms"). A present-day resident of North Buxton, Dorothy Shadd Shreve, writes in July 1968: "The Grandson of Abraham Johnson has informed me that according to the knowledge of his parents, Mr. William Parker made a return trip to [the] U.S.A. and was not heard of or from, by his wife and family again." Writing after the assassinations of Martin Luther King, Malcolm X, Medgar Evers, and countless others, Mrs. Shreve suggests that Parker "had many enemies" in the United States: "In light of today's occurrences foul play is a natural assumption" (D. S. Shreve to J. K., N. Buxton, Ontario, Canada, July 16, 1968).

29 Ewell L. Newman, "Death in the Heart of This People," *The Crisis*, vol. 80, no. 2, whole no. 700 (February 1973), pp. 51–56; M. D. Maclean, "The First Bloodshed of the Civil War," *The Crisis*, vol. 2, no. 6 (October 1911), pp. 246–250; Charles Flint Kellogg, *NAACP* (Baltimore, 1967), vol. 1, pp. 212–213.

30 C. S. Slokum to W. U. Hensel, in Lanc. Co. Hist. Soc. A mistake in the original—"the three *letters* Law-Liberty-Peace"—has been corrected.

31 Letter dated New York City, September 7, 1911 (Lanc. Co. Hist. Soc.).

32 Hensel, *Christiana*, pp. 152–159.

33 Unidentified newspaper clipping, Lanc. Co. Hist. Soc. (contains legend "Greater Lancaster Edition," October 24, 1927).

34 Jack Ward Loose, "The Christiana Riot Anniversary Exercises," *Lanc. Co. Hist. Soc. Papers*, vol. 55, no. 7 (1951), pp. 181–185.

35 The title of Dr. Bond's speech is given in the Lancaster *Intelligencer*, September 10, 1951; the first part of Bond's speech is reconstructed from original notes sent to me by Bond, July 28, 1969; the second part of Bond's speech is quoted by Loose, pp. 184–185. On February 25, 1973, an advertisement in *The New York Times* announced that the Pownall family farm, including the site of the Christiana "riot," would be sold at auction on March 10.

Index

351